M000300182

Radical Responsibility:
Celebrating the Thought of
Chief Rabbi Lord Jonathan Sacks

**London School
of Jewish Studies**

MAGGID

Michael Scharf
Publication Trust
Yeshiva University Press

RADICAL
RESPONSIBILITY

Celebrating the Thought
of Chief Rabbi Lord Jonathan Sacks

EDITED BY
Michael J. Harris,
Daniel Rynhold,
and Tamra Wright

London School of Jewish Studies
The Michael Scharf Publication Trust / YU Press
Maggid Books

Radical Responsibility:
Celebrating the Thought of
Chief Rabbi Lord Jonathan Sacks

First Edition, 2012

Maggid Books
An imprint of Koren Publishers Jerusalem Ltd.

Gila Fine, Editor in Chief

POB 8531, New Milford, CT 06776-8531, USA
& POB 4044, Jerusalem 91040, Israel
www.korenpub.com

ISBN 978 1 59264 366 0, *hardcover*

A CIP catalogue record for this title is
available from the British Library.

Printed and bound in the United States

Contents

Editors' Preface   ix

Introduction: Torah and Wisdom in a Secular Age
Michael J. Harris and Daniel Rynhold   *xiii*

Major Works of Jonathan Sacks   *xxix*

List of Abbreviations   *xxxi*

SECTION I:
JEWISH ETHICS AND MORAL PHILOSOPHY

Torah and Moral Philosophy
Alasdair MacIntyre   3

Ego, Love, and Self-Sacrifice:
Altruism in Jewish Thought and Law
David Shatz   17

Collective Responsibility and the Sin of Achan
Joshua Berman   39

Responsibility: Communal and Individual
Binyamin Lau   57

v

SECTION II:
THE PURSUIT OF JUSTICE

Justice, Justice Shalt Thou Pursue
Michael Walzer   79

Addressing the Needs of Others: What Is the Stance of Justice?
Moshe Halbertal   95

Access to Justice in Jewish Financial Law:
The Case of Returning Lost Property
Michael J. Broyde   111

SECTION III:
RELIGION AND CONTEMPORARY SOCIETY

The Space of Exchange
Charles Taylor   127

We Are Not Alone
Menachem Kellner   139

Halakhic Authority in a World of Personal Autonomy
Jacob J. Schacter   155

SECTION IV:
LEADERSHIP

Operating Across Boundaries:
Leading Adaptive Change
Ronald Heifetz   179

Texts, Values, and Historical Change:
Reflections on the Dynamics of Jewish Law
David Berger   201

'From Another Shore': Moses and Korah
Avivah Gottlieb Zornberg   217

Afterword: A New Musar?
Tamra Wright   245

Contributors   259

About Jonathan Sacks   263

Editors' Preface

One appoints as a judge on the Sanhedrin, taught Rabbi Yohanan, only someone familiar with each of the seventy languages of the world, so that the court will not need to rely on an interpreter.[1] There may be a further and deeper reason behind this requirement. A Jewish scholar acquainted with the world's languages is likely also to enjoy some familiarity with global culture and wisdom. Thoroughly rooted in the soil of Torah, his intellectual breadth and proficiency in secular knowledge will immeasurably enrich his guidance of the Jewish community.

In the contemporary Jewish world, it is difficult to think of a leader who better fits this description than Chief Rabbi Lord Jonathan Sacks. His ability to bring the Torah into conversation with Western thought with unmatched grace and lucidity, in both the written and spoken word, has earned him followers and disciples across both national and religious boundaries. During more than two decades as Chief Rabbi of the United Kingdom and the Commonwealth, his intellectual gifts and moral voice have enabled British Jewry to punch far above its weight on both the national British stage and on the global Jewish scene. In

---

1.   BT *San.* 17a, *Men.* 65a.

Jonathan Sacks, British Jewry has had a voice to which the rest of the Jewish world has yearned to listen. Long may that voice continue to articulate its noble and compelling vision of a traditional Judaism that also bears an important message for all of humanity.

This collection of essays, presented to Jonathan Sacks on the occasion of his sixty-fifth birthday and as he prepares to retire from the position of Chief Rabbi, celebrates his magnificent intellectual contribution by following his example and engaging in the deep encounter between Jewish tradition and secular wisdom which he has called *torah vehokhmah* (Torah and wisdom). For all of us involved in the project, work on this Festschrift has been motivated by our gratitude for everything Jonathan Sacks has taught us, through his writings, his teaching, and his personal example.

The editors would also like to thank the Chief Rabbi for the role he has played, directly and indirectly, in our academic careers. He has provided guidance and encouragement for each of us in our intellectual pursuits. On an institutional level, each of us was shaped by Jews' College at an early stage of our development as Jewish studies researchers and teachers, and we are grateful to Lord Sacks for his leadership of, and devotion to, the College. Over three decades, first as Principal and then as President of Jews' College (now the London School of Jewish Studies), Rabbi Sacks has led this venerable Anglo-Jewish institution through periods of turbulence and transition, and enabled it to emerge as a flourishing centre of Modern Orthodox Jewish scholarship and teaching.

Almost as soon as we began work on this project, we realized that Yeshiva University, from which the Chief Rabbi holds an honorary doctorate and received the Norman Lamm Prize, and Koren Publishers, who have recently published several of his books, would be the most suitable partners for this Festschrift. We thank Yeshiva University's President Richard Joel and Vice President Joshua Joseph for their support of the idea to produce this volume, as well as Yeshiva University Press and the Michael Scharf Publication Trust for their involvement, and, in particular, Professor Jeffrey Gurock for his advice and wholehearted endorsement of the project from its very inception. Yeshiva University's vision of a world suffused with *torah umada* (Torah and worldly knowledge) shares many important similarities with the Chief Rabbi's ideal of *torah veḥokhmah. Torah veḥokhmah* both guides LSJS's work and is the organizing theme of this Festschrift.

We are enormously grateful to Matthew Miller of Koren Publishers for his willingness to publish this volume, and to Gila Fine, Editor in Chief of Maggid Books, and her team, for all the hard work and painstaking attention to detail that they have devoted to this project. Special mention should go to the proofreaders Suzanne Libensohn and Shoshana Rotem.

Many people at LSJS have had a hand in this project. We are particularly grateful to the chair of trustees, Professor Anthony Warrens; the Dean, Dr Raphael Zarum; and the Chief Executive, Jason Marantz, for their commitment to the Festschrift and valuable contributions at different stages of its development. Gerry Shaer's administrative support and the professional expertise of librarian Erla Zimmels were enormously helpful and greatly appreciated.

The thirteen scholars who have contributed to this volume – some of them colleagues and friends of long standing, others whom we previously knew only by reputation – have been a joy to work with. The alacrity and enthusiasm with which they accepted the invitation to write in honour of Lord Sacks are in themselves testimony to the esteem in which he is held by some of the world's leading scholars across a range of disciplines. Collaborating with them on this project has been both an honour and a true pleasure.

There are many others to whom we owe a debt of gratitude: Louise Greenberg, Lord Sacks's literary agent, for her invaluable advice and guidance at every stage; Lindsey Taylor-Guthartz, our excellent copyeditor; Sidney and Lorraine Myers and Michael and Morven Heller for their most generous assistance with copy-editing costs; Peter Sheldon of the Chief Rabbinate Trust for his contributions at the early stages of the project and enthusiastic support of it; the staff of the Office of the Chief Rabbi, and especially its Director, Joanna Benarroch, for their friendly assistance; and The Hampstead Synagogue, and particularly its Chairman, Michael Haringman, for their support and encouragement.

Our grateful thanks go to our respective spouses, Judith, Sharon, and Ian, for their love, understanding, and support.

We are grateful for two permissions to reprint. 'Operating Across

Boundaries' by Ronald Heifetz was originally published in *Crossing the Divide: Intergroup Leadership in a World of Difference,* edited by Todd L. Pittinsky (Boston: Harvard Business Press/Center for Public Leadership, 2009), chapter 10. Professor Heifetz's essay in this volume is adapted from that article.

Much of the material in the final section of David Shatz's article is adapted from pp. 30–38 of his 'Concepts of Autonomy in Jewish Medical Ethics', *Jewish Law Annual,* 12 (1997), 3–43. We thank Routledge Publishers for permission to use the material here.

We hope that this Festschrift will bring pleasure to its recipient and advance the great enterprise of *torah veḥokhmah* to which he has made such an outstanding contribution.

Michael J. Harris
Daniel Rynhold
Tamra Wright
Autumn 2012, 5773

Introduction

Torah and Wisdom in a Secular Age

Michael J. Harris

Daniel Rynhold

> *Chokhmah is the truth we discover; Torah is*
> *the truth we inherit. Chokhmah is the universal*
> *language of humankind; Torah is the specific*
> *heritage of Israel. Chokhmah is what we attain by*
> *being in the image of God; Torah is what guides*
> *Jews as the people of God. Chokhmah is acquired*
> *by seeing and reasoning; Torah is received by*
> *listening and responding. Chokhmah tells us what*
> *is; Torah tells us what ought to be.*
>
> – JONATHAN SACKS[1]

Jonathan Sacks's contribution to the intellectual discourse of Jewish thought is not only significant in its own right, but serves as an indicator

---

1. Jonathan Sacks, *Future Tense* (London: Hodder and Stoughton, 2009), 221.

of a future path for Jewish and non-Jewish theology. Yet in the best traditions of Jewish thought, while being forward-looking, this contribution can also be seen as the latest incarnation of a concern that can be traced back to the very origins of Jewish philosophy. A narrative thread that connects the practitioners of Jewish philosophy throughout the ages is the tension that arose out of their relationship as Jews to the wider world about them. In the mediaeval period, Moses Maimonides (1138–1204), in his *Guide of the Perplexed*, spoke of the bewilderment of the educated elite regarding the contradictions between the teachings of Torah and the truths demonstrated by Arabic Aristotelianism. The subject of such 'a state of perplexity and confusion' was left with a dilemma: whether to follow his intellect at the expense of religion, or maintain his religious path and renounce philosophical reason. That the first choice is religiously untenable is clear, but, notably, Maimonides writes that the alternative also brings 'loss to himself and harm to his religion'.[2] Yet, however pressing the need for a solution to this dilemma, or at least one that would avoid impaling him on either of its horns, the problem was primarily an academic one, limited to those with such elevated concerns. 'If you don't have questions, you don't need answers,' as the saying goes. And even for those engaged in this quest, the questions and answers were primarily matters of theory: was the world created *ex nihilo*, or was it eternal? How was one to reconcile the anthropomorphisms of the Tanakh with the more rarefied God of the philosophers? And how could a supernatural phenomenon such as revelation be reconciled with the rational cosmology of the day?

As time and world-views move on, the questions change, but the impetus remains the same. Thus, in the days of Moses Mendelssohn (1729–86) the pressing question was again imposed by tensions between Judaism and the world around it. How was one to maintain the Judaism of old in the face of a hoped-for emancipation that would open the doors of civil society to Jewish communities that had up until then been limited (and yet in a manner also protected) by self-governance? As Mendelssohn's anonymous critic, the 'Searcher for Light and Right'

---

2. Moses Maimonides, *Guide of the Perplexed*, trans. Shlomo Pines, 2 vols. (Chicago: University of Chicago Press, 1963), introduction to Part I, 5–6.

put it,[3] in a society where, at least de facto, adherence to Judaism had become voluntary, what becomes of the obligatory nature of Jewish law?[4] Here, the question was more practical than theoretical. Gone were the more scholastic ruminations on divine attributes and prophecy, and in their place were attempts to deal with the practical philosophical issue of how to maintain an apparently archaic system while participating in the modern world, a question that would continue to exercise thinkers as diverse as Rabbi Samson Raphael Hirsch (1808–88) and Rabbi Mordecai Kaplan (1881–1983) as the nineteenth century turned into the twentieth. The primary focus thus remained on Judaism getting its philosophical and theological house in order so as to survive its encounter with the surrounding culture.

As a modus vivendi (or a number of them) appeared in the public communal sphere, Jewish thinkers in the twentieth century turned to more existential philosophical questions in an attempt to combat the prevailing positivistic intellectual trends. As Rabbi Joseph Soloveitchik (1903–93) asked, how can the man of faith 'living by a doctrine which has no technical potential, by a law which cannot be tested in a laboratory' have anything to say 'to a functional utilitarian society... whose practical reasons of the mind have long ago supplanted the sensitive reasons of the heart'?[5] Nonetheless, the intellectual focus remained very much on how Judaism should understand *itself* in the face of external challenges. In addition, although the thought of twentieth-century Jewish thinkers, such as Martin Buber (1878–1965) and Soloveitchik, was relevant to secular readers as well, their primary focus was on religion itself, on inward-looking attempts to maintain religion's relevance in

---

3. 'Searching for Light and Right in a Letter to Herr Moses Mendelssohn' (Das Forschen nach Licht und Recht in einem schreiben an Herrn MM) was a 47-page pamphlet attacking Mendelssohn's attempt to affirm his Judaism while simultaneously arguing for an end to ecclesiastical power. It was signed 'S*** Vienna, 12 June 1782'. Mendelssohn laboured under the illusion that it was written by the politician Joseph Baron von Sonnenfels, but it was in fact penned by the far less significant August Cranz. *Jerusalem* was Mendelssohn's response.

4. Moses Mendelssohn, *Jerusalem*, trans. Allan Arkush (Hanover, NH: University Press of New England, 1983), 85.

5. Joseph B. Soloveitchik, *The Lonely Man of Faith* (New York: Random House, 2006), 6–7.

the modern world. The relevance of their thought beyond the religious sphere was a side-effect – perhaps not a negligible side-effect, but a side-effect nonetheless.

In the twenty-first century, the chimera of a universal faith has been revealed for the illusion that it always was. The idea of particularism has reasserted itself, and those who pour scorn on others who lead a particular way of life are themselves seen as narrow-minded. Thus, while the internal 'Jewish question' remains that of dealing with the challenges that the external world throws out, and reinterpreting the eternal texts of Judaism in order to deal with them, the notion that those of a particular faith need to justify themselves before the bar of universal reason has become somewhat less pressing. Yet religion remains under interrogation. Particularly in the post-9/11 world, many people assume that religion has become 'the problem' in contemporary society.

The special contribution made by the thought of Chief Rabbi Sacks is that it not only continues the venerable Jewish philosophical tradition of maintaining traditional faith in the face of external intellectual challenges, but also moves beyond this tradition by showing how core Jewish teachings can address the dilemmas of the secular world itself. What makes Lord Sacks's approach so effective is that he is able to do this without any expectation of the wider world taking on Judaism's theological beliefs.

Jonathan Sacks has written works, such as *Crisis and Covenant*, that address the modern equivalent of the theoretical theological questions that concerned his mediaeval forbears. He has written on the classical texts of the Jewish tradition in the *Covenant and Conversation* series and his *Haggadah*. He has written works that address how Judaism is to deal with its own difficulties in the modern world, such as *One People* and *Radical Then, Radical Now* (published as *A Letter in the Scroll* in the USA). But perhaps the most important theme of his work for the world at large, the one that best embodies the message of *torah veḥokhmah*, is that the imperative today is to elucidate what faith means to those within the fold without losing hold of how that internal understanding of faith can affect those outside it. However, this is expressly not to be carried out through a reduction of faith to a form of meaningless universalism. It is to be done in a manner that is proudly particularistic, and yet able to engage the world around it and contribute to its rebuilding in an age when many would have us believe that religious faith is the cause of its destruction.

A critique that has been directed at modern Jewish thinkers such as Buber and Emmanuel Levinas (1906–95), rightly or wrongly, is that their thought cannot be applied beyond the sphere of the individual to that of society. That is not a critique that can be levelled at Jonathan Sacks. From *The Politics of Hope* through *To Heal a Fractured World* and *Future Tense*, through his articles in broadsheet newspapers across the English-speaking world and his television and radio broadcasts, the interest in civil and political society as a specifically religious concern is central to his work, but in a manner that is utterly opposed to the sort of theocracy or fanaticism that currently besmirches religion in the eyes of the world. Lord Sacks is fond of saying that religion is an essential part of the human conversation. His thought therefore suggests to us that in a world in which, paradoxically, the more difference has become accepted, the more difference becomes a cause of strife, the role that religion can play, in each of its legitimate guises, is a matter for immediate and urgent engagement. And it is the attempt to engage that paradox and find a way to neutralize it on which the Chief Rabbi has spoken, to members of all religions and to those with none. It is this combination of the inward-looking and the outward-looking that Jonathan Sacks brings to the forefront of his thought and our minds. In writing of the need for Jews to recover faith, he notes that he searches not for 'simple faith, not naïve optimism, but faith that [we] are not alone in the world'.[6] It is a challenge to faiths to understand themselves on their own terms with an eye on how those terms can nonetheless form part of a global tapestry. It is an understanding of one's own faith on one's own terms, without any recourse to simple reductionism, in a manner that maintains its uniqueness without leaving it isolated, that Lord Sacks endeavours to formulate. His work challenges religious thinkers to chart a new direction for religious thought that works towards a form of universalism in which they can simultaneously remain proud of their particularity. In the spirit of this world-view, this volume is devoted to the overarching framework

---

6. Sacks, *Future Tense*, 2.

within which the Chief Rabbi grapples with the interaction of the universal and the particular – a framework that he calls *torah veḥokhmah*.

Torah, for Jonathan Sacks, represents the particularistic, inherited teachings of Judaism, while *ḥokhmah* (wisdom) refers to the universal realm of the sciences and humanities. Framed in religious terms, 'Chokhmah is where we encounter God through creation; Torah is how we hear God through revelation.'[7]

Although there is much overlap between Lord Sacks's approach and the outlook of some earlier Orthodox thinkers, the Chief Rabbi prefers his formulation both to the Hirschian *torah im derekh erets* and to Norman Lamm's *torah umada*. Referring to his own approach as an 'old-new way' of studying, teaching, and writing Torah, Lord Sacks explains the difference between his approach and previous attempts at delineating a contemporary Orthodox intellectual agenda.

> In nineteenth century Germany the favoured phrase among disciples of Rabbi Samson Raphael Hirsch was *Torah im derekh eretz*, 'Torah and general culture'. In the United States, the preferred principle was *Torah u-Madda*, 'Torah and Science'. Neither of these rubrics is particularly helpful. *Torah im derekh eretz* is a quotation from the teachings of Rabban Gamliel III (third century CE) who used it to mean something else, 'Torah together with a worldly occupation'. *Torah u-Madda* is a modern coinage with no source in tradition. *Chokhmah*, by contrast, is a biblical category. One book, Proverbs, is devoted to it, and several others – notably Job and Ecclesiastes – belong to what is generally known as the 'wisdom literature'. *Chokhmah* is a concept with many shades of meaning, but its primary sense is human wisdom as such: the universals of mankind's intellectual quest.[8]

The essays in this volume focus on Judaism's interaction with 'the universals of mankind's intellectual quest' within the context of areas that have been of particular concern and interest to Jonathan Sacks as

---

7. Sacks, *The Chief Rabbi's Haggadah* (London: HarperCollins, 2003), essays section, 6.
8. Ibid.

both a Jewish scholar and a public intellectual: ethics, justice, the role of religion in contemporary society, and leadership. Each of the four sections of this book begins with a contribution from a prominent thinker in the relevant secular field, followed by essays written by Jewish studies scholars, which combine Torah and *ḥokhmah* in varying degrees. Philosophy is particularly well represented in the essays. Although Lord Sacks reads widely and deeply across an impressive range of academic disciplines and secular literature, philosophy was his 'first love' and the core of his formal academic training.

Section I is entitled 'Jewish Ethics and Moral Philosophy'. The opening contribution is by Alasdair MacIntyre, the author, among many other works, of *After Virtue*, an analysis of the condition of contemporary moral philosophy that remains one of the most influential books in the field. *After Virtue* has been a significant influence on Jonathan Sacks's thinking and he has continued to refer to it frequently in his teaching and writing over many years. MacIntyre's essay, 'Torah and Moral Philosophy', takes an overall look at the mindsets of those committed to Torah and moral philosophy respectively and, most appropriately for this volume, engages closely with some of the writings of the Chief Rabbi, identifying his important contribution to this topic. MacIntyre's article begins by drawing a sharp contrast between the beliefs and attitudes of committed students of Torah, on the one hand, and those of moral philosophers on the other. For a person faithful to Torah, what matters is God's command. For the moral philosopher, every proposition is debatable and provisional. It seems at first glance, then, that there is little common ground between one devoted to Torah and the moral philosopher. But MacIntyre argues that this is not in fact the case. He shows that the practice of moral philosophy itself requires an absolute commitment to certain virtues, including responsibility and compassion. Even more importantly, perhaps, MacIntyre explains how the Chief Rabbi helps to resolve the dilemma of the religiously-committed moral philosopher, who must live by the precepts of his or her religion but, as a philosopher, must remain open to further debate.

David Shatz contributes an essay on the major topic of altruism in Jewish thought and law, which is informed throughout by the author's expertise in moral philosophy as well as Jewish ethics. Shatz demonstrates that although halakhah and Jewish tradition make many and varied demands on us to act altruistically, Judaism recognizes self-interest not only as real but also as legitimate. He goes on to consider the issue of why, in Jewish terms, we should be altruistic, referring to the debate in Jewish thought concerning whether our altruistic acts should be motivated by God's command or rather by sympathy and compassion. Next, Shatz discusses the sources and scope of altruism in Jewish tradition, focusing first on the famous commandment 'Love your neighbour as yourself,'[9] and asking, among other things, whether the Torah truly requires that our love of others match our love of ourselves. Second, in this section of his article, Shatz presents an alternative basis for altruism, the commandment of walking in God's compassionate ways, or *imitatio Dei*, and notes the difficulties involved in this approach. The final part of Shatz's essay deals with the fascinating question of the limits of altruistic self-sacrifice.

Addressing directly the topic of responsibility which has been one of Lord Sacks's major concerns in both his communal leadership and his intellectual endeavours, Joshua Berman discusses the sin of Achan in Joshua 7. This biblical episode raises the issue of collective responsibility, how we can be held liable for the wrongdoing of others – in this instance, a single individual – in our community. Berman offers a detailed and compelling literary reading of the biblical narrative that sheds light on this question. He argues that the key to understanding this episode lies in the report of the spies sent by Joshua to the city of Ai, the location of Israel's defeat in battle following Achan's transgression. The spies' overconfidence and lack of acknowledgement of divine assistance create the attitudinal climate which makes Achan's sin possible. Achan's misdemeanour reflects a communal failing. Berman shows how the 'winnowing' process by which Achan is identified as the perpetrator of the sin reinforces this message. In the concluding and more theoretical section of his essay, Berman fruitfully compares and contrasts the notion of collective responsibility implicit in Joshua 7 with contemporary notions, showing how the biblical concept is in important respects more rigorous.

---

9. Lev. 19:18.

Binyamin Lau's article continues and expands upon the theme of responsibility, nicely complementing Berman's contribution by addressing different dimensions of the topic. Like Berman, Lau acknowledges the Chief Rabbi's book *To Heal a Fractured World: The Ethics of Responsibility* as an important influence on his reflections. Lau emphasizes that in Jewish tradition, the fact that the community takes responsibility for addressing the cries of the needy by no means absolves each individual from his or her duty to assist. The bulk of Lau's essay, however, focuses on individual responsibility in a different sense, namely the responsibility of the needy person to endeavour to help him- or herself as much as possible. Referring to the work of the psychoanalyst and philosopher Erich Fromm (1900–80) and drawing on traditional Jewish sources, Lau stresses the importance of education towards individual independence and self-reliance before analysing Jewish texts that clearly insist on the individual taking a measure of responsibility and not relying solely on others.

The three essays that comprise Section II, 'Justice, Justice Shalt Thou Pursue', focus on a major concern in the writings of Jonathan Sacks. The section opens with an article on distributive justice by Michael Walzer, a political philosopher whose work is much admired and frequently cited by the Chief Rabbi. Walzer argues that regarding the distribution of basic goods, the appropriate principle is 'from each according to his ability, to each according to his need.' He does not see this principle as worthy of endorsement only by Marxists, but as the obviously correct and biblically mandated course of action. Next, Walzer considers social goods which are not basic necessities, including education, political office, and leisure time. He argues, following the position elaborated in his influential work *Spheres of Justice*, that here justice is best served by distributing social goods according to their social meaning, i.e. how they are understood and valued in a given time and place. Walzer discusses several interesting examples of the operation of this principle of distribution, including Jewish education in mediaeval Europe. He contends that one can only appropriately criticize the distribution of social goods in a given society as unjust if one begins by accepting the culture of that society. Walzer then discusses the distinction between holidays and vacations and how discrimination in the context of holidays, which are by nature communal, infringes upon the requirements of justice. At the end of his essay, Walzer reminds us that while justice is crucial, it is not everything. That a society has achieved just distributive arrangements for social goods does not necessarily mean that it has identified the optimum such goods.

Moshe Halbertal's essay returns us to the issue of addressing the needs of others discussed by Binyamin Lau, but from the perspective of justice rather than responsibility. To what extent does Jewish tradition oblige one's charitable giving to satisfy the purely particular, subjective needs of others? Halbertal offers an intriguing analysis of a series of talmudic stories surrounding this issue in Tractate *Ketubot* of the Babylonian Talmud, pointing out the ambiguities that lie beneath the surface. He goes on to focus on mediaeval and later halakhic discussions of the principle of subjective need, addressing, in particular, a dispute between two central figures in the history of halakhah, Maimonides and Rabbi Moses Isserles (1520–72), and penetratingly relates Maimonides' view to the philosophical issue of the stance of the individual as a moral agent. Underpinning Maimonides' ruling that the individual donor must supply the subjective needs of the poor person is the conviction that such a donor should not behave like an impersonal distributor of limited resources, focused solely on ensuring their best overall deployment. The individual giver is a subject confronting the suffering of another subject, and the moral imperative, what justice requires, is to address that subject's needs, for the donor fully to acknowledge the individual pain that he or she now confronts.

Michael Broyde offers a stimulating contribution that differs from the other essays in this volume by providing a detailed halakhic discussion of a specific topic. He focuses on one intriguing area concerning justice within Jewish financial law, that of returning lost property, showing how the issue of reciprocity plays a key role. In the case of lost property, Jewish law does not compel a Jew to return the lost property of a gentile because the gentile is not obliged to observe Jewish law, and is not therefore obliged to return the lost property of a Jew. The exclusion of the gentile is based here on non-reciprocity; the privileges of Jewish law in this area are granted only to those who are fully obliged to observe that law. Broyde deploys a model of four possible societies to demonstrate the fairness of these provisions, and draws attention to the fact that all legal systems practise some form of exclusion based on citizenship. He goes on to point out that a Jew who refuses to observe Jewish law, and might therefore decline to return lost property, is subject to the same exclusion, grounded in the same rationale of non-reciprocity. Broyde goes on to discuss the controversial view of Rabbi Menahem Me'iri (1249–c.1310) in mediaeval Provence (arguably, as Broyde points out, falsely attributed to him), which apparently mandates the return of lost property to monotheistic gentiles. Broyde then discusses the role of the sanctification of God's Name and its desecration in returning lost property, showing that here, too, the notion of reciprocity is significant.

Section III, 'Religion and Contemporary Society', features three essays that consider faith in a larger context. The first essay in this section is by Charles Taylor, author of the influential study *A Secular Age*, which Jonathan Sacks frequently cites. Taylor takes both as his starting-point and his focus the Chief Rabbi's observation in *The Dignity of Difference* that 'those who are confident in their faith are not threatened but enlarged by the different faith of others', and his essay is intended as a commentary and elaboration on this observation. Taylor's first point is that Lord Sacks's statement does not equate to something like: 'Because I believe in my own faith so strongly that in fact I *know* it to be true, I am not troubled by the beliefs of adherents of other religions.' Religious faith, Taylor argues, is not a matter only of belief in certain factual claims, but also of a certain spiritual hope or anticipation for the future. It involves the sense of being on a journey. To make progress on this journey, doubt may be indispensable, as it can help us to move towards deeper religious understanding. Taylor then recommends following Jonathan Sacks's teaching by what he terms 'exchange' with other faiths. This kind of exchange or encounter involves the attempt to understand the faith of another and to appreciate its religious power. Taylor discusses how such an encounter can benefit one's own religious journey, before going on to criticize the attempt made by many over the last century to abandon particular religions entirely in favour of what he terms a 'synthetic super-religion'. In the final part of his article, Taylor emphasizes the need for humility in every religion in acknowledging that not everything may be comprehensible from its standpoint. And while acknowledging the dangers inherent in interfaith encounter, Taylor endorses it as an enlargement – to return to the Chief Rabbi's terminology – of his own religious life.

Menachem Kellner highlights precisely the same statement from *The Dignity of Difference* that serves as the focus of Charles Taylor's essay. Kellner, however, develops his own argument in a different direction, using the Chief Rabbi's remark as a lens through which to view a central debate in mediaeval Jewish thought. For Rabbi Judah Halevi (1075–1141), Kellner explains, Jews are essentially different from and superior to non-Jews, capable of achieving prophecy. This doctrine of the innate ontological superiority of the Jews continued to be advocated by some Jewish thinkers after Halevi and, Kellner suggests, was the product of a psychological defence mechanism in the face of persecution of the Jewish people. Additionally, he surmises, it might have been the outgrowth of the kind of lack of religious self-confidence referred to in Lord Sacks's observation. The opposing position to that of Halevi in the mediaeval philosophical debate was taken, Kellner explains, by Maimonides, a staunch universalist who rejected absolutely the idea of inherent Jewish superiority. Since Maimonides is confident and secure in his own faith, Kellner argues, he does not feel the need to make any claim about the natural advantages of Jews over non-Jews. Moreover, Maimonides' confidence enables him to acknowledge that Christian and Islamic theology are both partially true, insofar as they preserve some of the central teachings of Judaism. Kellner concludes his essay with a plea for theological modesty in which Jews acknowledge that they are not alone in the world and do not reject the spiritual nourishment available from non-Jews who seek God. Having taken a different route inspired by the same teaching of the Chief Rabbi, Kellner thus arrives at a conclusion similar to Taylor's concerning the importance of the encounter between people of different faiths.

Jacob J. Schacter's essay addresses a further dimension of the relationship between Jewish faith and the wider world. Personal autonomy and individual choice are key values in contemporary Western culture. Schacter explores the issue of whether they can be integrated into the life of traditional Jewish observance in which the authority of the halakhah is central. Drawing on the work of leading sociologists, Schacter first documents the pervasiveness of the ideal of individual autonomy and choice in modern American and European society and demonstrates its influence on today's Jewish world. He then notes how a cluster of concepts radically at odds with personal autonomy, including commandment, obligation, submission, and obedience, are central to traditional Judaism. Can anything be done to bridge the gap, to enable the contemporary Jew who cannot but accept the premium placed on autonomy to embrace fully a life of traditional halakhic commitment? Schacter argues that it can, in two major respects. First, the life of halakhah often permits and indeed requires personal expression and autonomy. Crucial here is a distinction between 'religion in manifestation' and 'religion in essence'. 'Religion in manifestation', in a Jewish context, is the outward performance of the mitzvot (commandments). 'Religion in essence', on the other hand, designates the subjective, personal feeling or experience one has while performing the mitzvah. Halakhah insists on the indispensability of both these elements, as emphasized in particular in the thought of Rabbi Joseph B. Soloveitchik. Secondly, as Schacter demonstrates with several examples, even the realm of 'religion in manifestation' with its 'objective' practical requirements leaves room for a significant degree of personal choice.

The final group of essays addresses the theme of 'Leadership'. The section opens with an essay by Ronald Heifetz, a scholar in the burgeoning field of academic leadership studies whom the Chief Rabbi frequently cites. Heifetz probes the nature of the task faced by leaders in dealing with problems across the boundaries of groups or communities in situations of 'adaptive challenge' or 'adaptive change'. An engaging feature of Heifetz's essay is his use of historical examples from, inter alia, both ancient and modern Israel. A prime example of adaptive challenge is the Exodus from Egypt, which required the Israelites to develop a new identity based on new inter-group relationships. Adaptive challengers tend to spark a defensive reaction as people in groups try to minimize the negative impact of change. Leadership in such a situation – and this, Heifetz suggests, was the most difficult task facing Moses in his leadership – involves the ability to counteract these defences in order to keep people engaged. Heifetz discusses in detail three dimensions of the mission of adaptive leadership: coping with the commonality of loss, negotiating the politics of inclusion and exclusion, and addressing the need to renegotiate loyalties.

David Berger deals with rabbinic leadership in a halakhic context, providing an overview of the important and much-discussed topic of how halakhic norms have sometimes adapted in response to external factors. Discussing various halakhic leniencies of mediaeval authorities in response to severe economic difficulties facing the Jewish community, Berger makes the point that when extra-halakhic factors affect a law in a particular context, the ramifications can be wider and can impinge on other areas of halakhah. At the same time, he urges caution in assuming that the rabbis allowed economic pressures to influence their halakhic reasoning in directions that it would not otherwise have taken. Berger goes on to discuss the impact on halakhic rulings of what he calls 'competing religious values', broader concerns which are not present in the textual halakhic discourse on a given topic and which pull in a different direction. One category of such competing religious values is ideological. An example offered by Berger concerns the responses of Orthodox halakhic decisors to the rise of Reform Judaism. Both lenient and stringent responses emerged, based on broad ideological considerations which went beyond the particular halakhic issues at stake. The second kind of 'competing religious value' on which Berger focuses is humanitarian values. He provides many examples of issues of personal status in which halakhic authorities have taken such values into account rather than making decisions based solely on narrow textual analysis. Halakhic decisors, Berger concludes, have certainly and indeed consciously allowed their rulings to be impacted by economic, ideological, and humanitarian considerations. However, Berger insists, that is entirely proper. Halakhic decision-making involves, and has always involved, recognition of the validity of both narrower textual and broader religious considerations.

Avivah Gottlieb Zornberg's essay vividly embodies *torah veḥokhmah*; in the words of Jonathan Sacks, she shows us 'how to combine a reading of Torah with a finely honed literary sensibility'.[10]

---

10. Sacks, *Future Tense*, 230.

Zornberg's focus in this essay is the famous biblical episode of Korah (Numbers 16), in which Korah leads a rebellion against Moses' leadership and is ultimately swallowed up by the earth. She argues that Moses and Korah ultimately differ not only about issues of power, authority, and leadership but also on the very nature of language. In articulating her profound reading of the Moses/Korah controversy, Zornberg presents a series of insights involving Korah's rejection of language; Moses' vulnerabilities, rooted in his earlier life and career, concerning language; and the distrust of language evinced by Korah's supporters Dathan and Aviram. She goes on to explore Korah's intolerance for incompleteness and evocative spaces, his inability to open himself to otherness or to infinity, his attempt to fashion a hermetically sealed self. The essay closes on a more optimistic note, reflecting on a talmudic tradition that Korah's children repented and sang to God.

In this collection, both the editors and the authors have used Jonathan Sacks's work as a catalyst for further reflection. In the Afterword, Tamra Wright draws on the Chief Rabbi's work to suggest further avenues of intellectual exploration for Jewish scholars. The wide-ranging articles described above are witness to Jonathan Sacks's ability not only to produce innovative intellectual work of his own, but also to stimulate other thinkers from a variety of backgrounds in creative ways.

Major Works of Jonathan Sacks

BOOKS

The Great Partnership: God, Science and the Search for Meaning (London: Hodder, 2011; New York: Schocken, 2012)

Covenant and Conversation: Exodus (Jerusalem: Maggid Books, 2010)

Future Tense (London: Hodder, 2009; New York: Schocken, 2010)

Covenant and Conversation: Genesis (Jerusalem: Maggid Books, 2009)

The Home We Build Together (London: Continuum, 2007)

To Heal a Fractured World (London: Continuum, 2005; New York: Schocken, 2005)

From Optimism to Hope (London: Continuum, 2004)

The Chief Rabbi's Haggadah (London: Collins, 2003); published in the USA as *Rabbi Jonathan Sacks's Haggadah* (New York: Continuum, 2003)

The Dignity of Difference: How to Avoid the Clash of Civilizations (London / New York / Toronto: Continuum, 2002; 2nd, revised edition, 2003)

Radical Then, Radical Now (London: HarperCollins, 2001); published in the USA as *A Letter in the Scroll* (New York: The Free Press, 2000)

The Politics of Hope (London: Vintage, 2000)

Celebrating Life (London: Fount, 2000)

Morals and Markets (Occasional Paper 108) (London: Institute of Economic Affairs, 1998)

Community of Faith (London: Peter Halban, 1995)

Faith in the Future (London: Darton, Longman and Todd, 1995)

Will We Have Jewish Grandchildren? (London: Vallentine Mitchell, 1994)

One People? Tradition, Modernity, and Jewish Unity (London: Littman Library of Jewish Civilization, 1993)

Crisis and Covenant (Manchester: Manchester University Press, 1992)

The Persistence of Faith: Religion, Morality and Society in a Secular Age (London: Weidenfeld & Nicolson, 1991)

Arguments for the Sake of Heaven (Northvale, NJ: Jason Aronson, 1991)

Tradition in an Untraditional Age (London: Vallentine Mitchell, 1990)

BOOKS EDITED

Torah Studies (New York: Kehot, 1996)

Orthodoxy Confronts Modernity (New York: KTAV, 1991)

Tradition and Transition (London: Jews' College Publications, 1986)

TRANSLATIONS AND COMMENTARIES

The Koren Sacks Yom Kippur Mahzor (Jerusalem: Koren Publishers, 2012)

The Koren Sacks Rosh HaShana Mahzor (Jerusalem: Koren Publishers, 2011)

The Koren Sacks Siddur (Jerusalem: Koren Publishers, 2009)

The Authorised Daily Prayer Book (London: HarperCollins, 2006)

List of Abbreviations

BT	Babylonian Talmud
JT	Jerusalem Talmud

TRACTATES OF THE MISHNAH/TALMUD

AZ	*Avoda zara*
BB	*Bava batra*
Bek.	*Bekhorot*
Ber.	*Berakhot*
BK	*Bava kama*
BM	*Bava metsia*
Ḥag.	*Ḥagigah*
Hor.	*Horayot*
Ket.	*Ketubot*
Men.	*Menaḥot*
MK	*Mo'ed katan*
Ned.	*Nedarim*
Pes.	*Pesaḥim*
San.	*Sanhedrin*
Shab.	*Shabat*
Ta'an.	*Ta'anit*
Yev.	*Yevamot*

Section I

*Jewish Ethics and
Moral Philosophy*

Chapter 1

Torah and Moral Philosophy

Alasdair MacIntyre

Jonathan Sacks is one of the notable teachers of our time, speaking and writing effectively not only to those Jewish communities for whom, as Chief Rabbi, he has had peculiar responsibility, but also to the wider public of the United Kingdom and the Commonwealth. What he has said and written on a remarkable range of topics deserves careful and attentive listening and reading by both his audiences, by reason of his insights and his analytical powers, both as rabbi and as philosopher; but what has in fact secured such close attention has been his evident integrity, his ability to speak in both roles without compromising his message in either. Indeed it might seem that his extraordinary achievement makes my task of writing about the relationship of Torah and moral philosophy unnecessary. For how could there be a better example of how they are related than that provided by the teaching of Jonathan Sacks? Yet we will not appreciate just how much he has achieved until we understand how difficult it is to bring Torah and moral philosophy together. And my task is to identify that difficulty. I do so by asking first what Torah is and then what moral philosophy is.

I

What is Torah? What does 'Torah' name? It names a set of Hebrew texts, the texts of the Pentateuch. It names the instruction in God's law that those texts provide in a number of genres. And it names the presentation through those texts of God as lawgiver. To be open to what those texts present is to encounter God revealing Himself as lawgiver. So they are not just texts awaiting exegesis by scholars. They are texts that may have to be read with fear and trembling, if we are to learn from them what we need to learn. So what do we learn, if we so read them?

We learn first that the laws of God require immediate and unconditional assent from those to whom they are addressed, whether His people Israel or humankind in general. The precepts that are enjoined are exceptionless. Their authority is not contingent on circumstance. They do not hold for this or that time and place, but for all times and places. And they do so because God is the God of all times and places. This is a law that cannot be detached from its lawgiver without becoming something other than the law that it is. Yet it does not follow that the lawgiver cannot be put to the question, as Abraham put God to the question concerning the requirements of justice. And it does not follow that understanding what God requires is a simple and straightforward task, for one of the tasks to which believers are set by God is that of understanding and interpreting His law. It was as such interpreters that rabbis drew a distinction between those commandments of God for which a reason can be given and those for which no reason can be found, perhaps because there is no reason, perhaps because it is unknowable by human beings. Here I am in the happy position of being able to follow David Novak's account of the relevant rabbinical discussions in his *Natural Law in Judaism*.[1] Novak distinguishes reasons 'based on universal nature' from reasons 'based on specific history'. The former 'pertain to

---

1. (Cambridge: Cambridge University Press, 1998).

humankind per se', the latter 'to the history of a particular community' (p. 70). An example of the latter is the reason given in Exodus 12: 17 for the injunction to observe Passover 'because [*ki*] on this very day I brought your ranks out of Egypt'. Examples of the former are the prohibitions on shedding blood and on theft. These are prohibitions that any human being has good reason to obey, given that the human condition is what it is, independently of knowing anything about God's revelation of His law to Moses at Sinai.

What then is the relationship between this latter kind of reason for obeying divine commandments and the reason that we have for obeying them, that they are divine commandments? It is not the same as the relationship between the similar reasons that we might have for obedience to certain human laws – that they are injunctions that it is reasonable to obey, whether they are duly enacted laws or not – and the reason that we have for obeying them, that they are duly enacted laws. For once we have grasped the reasons that we have for obeying the injunctions of some particular law, whether it has ever been enacted as a law or not, we can always ask if, in the light of those reasons, we might not improve upon that law. If the reason for having a law that forbids driving at more than fifty miles per hour is that by so doing we save lives, then, if by having a law that prohibits driving at more than forty miles an hour, we could save even more lives, we have a good reason for changing the law. But, as Novak emphasizes, this, on the rabbinical view, is not at all the case with divine law. To discern a reason for a divine law never provides a premise for arguing that that law could be improved upon. Someone therefore who was not a believer in divine law, but who hit upon the reason for having a rule that enjoined or prohibited exactly what some divine law enjoined or prohibited, and for that reason adopted that rule as a rule governing his actions, would not in fact be obeying the divine law, even though his actions were, from the standpoint of an external observer, indistinguishable from the actions of an obedient believer.

We should therefore not be surprised that Maimonides declared in the *Mishneh torah* that someone who observes all seven Noahide laws, but only because of his own conclusions, based on reason, and not because God commanded them in the Torah, has no part in the world to come.[2] What matters is not only to act as God commands, but to do so because God commands it in the Torah, rather than because reason enjoins it.[3] And here there becomes evident what is at least a tension – and perhaps a good deal more than that – between what respect for Torah requires and the standards governing argument in moral philosophy. What, then, is moral philosophy?

II

One way to begin is by remarking that it is, nowadays, an academic trade, a profession, a way of earning a living, a career path. For what are moral philosophers paid? For teaching undergraduates and graduate students and for writing and publishing. To be successful in one's professional career is to teach, especially graduate students, in a prestigious department in a prestigious university and to publish in professionally prestigious journals. What is the content of that teaching and writing? The teaching introduces students to – and the writing contributes to and carries further – a number of ongoing debates, some of them continuous with ancient and mediaeval debates, but all of them shaped by the large and continuing disagreements of eighteenth- and nineteenth-century Enlightenment and post-Enlightenment moral philosophy. Those disagreements are of at least three kinds: some arise from rival theoretical accounts of the norms that govern the conduct of rational agents, some have regard to metaethical issues concerning the meaning and use of normative and evaluative expressions, and some are generated in the course of attempts to apply different moral theories in a variety of situations. So utilitarians dispute with Kantians and contractarians, expressivists

---

2. On the Noahide laws, see Appendix 2 in Raymond L. Weiss, *Maimonides' Ethics* (Chicago: University of Chicago Press, 1991), 204–5.
3. Maimonides, *Mishneh torah*, 'Laws of Kings' 8: 11. According to a different and, in the opinion of most scholars, more accurate version of this well-known text, Maimonides is more positive about such a person, considering him 'not one of the righteous of the nations of the world, but one of their wise men'. For a recent discussion of the textual and broader issues arising from this passage, see Eugene Korn, 'Gentiles, the World to Come, and Judaism: The Odyssey of a Rabbinic Text', *Modern Judaism*, 14 (1994), 265–87. (See also n. 30 of Jacob J. Schacter's article in this volume, as well as David Shatz's discussion of motivations for observing the commandments in the section on 'Motivating Altruism' in his contribution [eds.].)

contend with moral realists, and those who believe that the moral requirements of public life are not the same as those of private life are at odds with those who affirm a single universal set of moral principles.

It is important that in all three areas, no end to these debates, no resolution to these disagreements, is in sight, and this not because of any lack of philosophical progress in formulating and reformulating each of the contending positions. As the debates have progressed, new distinctions have been made and new concepts introduced, the structure of each position has been better understood, and arguments have been revised or rejected, so that increasingly sophisticated versions of each position have emerged. And the same has been true in those other areas of contemporary philosophy whose conclusions are relevant to moral theorizing, such as the philosophy of mind and action. Yet in all these disputes, the members of each contending party remain in the end unconvinced by considerations that to their opponents appear compelling. So there remain, for example, both philosophers who affirm that right action is action productive of the best set of consequences, and philosophers who deny this and affirm that right action is action in accordance with the universalizable maxims of the Categorical Imperative; both philosophers who have concluded that the standards determining right action are what they are independently of our feelings and attitudes and philosophers who have concluded that our ascriptions of rightness and wrongness to actions are expressions of our feelings and attitudes; both philosophers who hold that it is permissible for agents of democratic governments to tell certain kinds of lie that are forbidden in other contexts and philosophers who deny this.

Were we to do justice to their continuing disagreements, we would have to rehearse the sequences of detailed argument and counter-argument through which each of these contending parties has arrived at its present position. We would have to take note of the different versions of each position that have been presented and of the different weight that even those who agree in their conclusions give to this or that set of considerations. But, happily for our present purposes, we can dispense with these complexities and attend instead to three notable characteristics of contemporary moral philosophy as a practice. The first is the widely shared tacit agreement that in moral philosophy, as elsewhere in analytic philosophy, we are to assent to any thesis only insofar as there are arguments sufficient to warrant that assent. How seriously some thesis is to be taken is a function of the strength of the arguments that can be advanced for or against it. It follows – and this is a second notable characteristic of moral philosophy as a practice – that it does not matter whose argument it is. Books and articles in moral philosophy are published with the names of their authors, but if such books and articles were to be published anonymously, we would have no more and no less reason than we do now for assenting to or dissenting from the conclusions advanced by their authors. And, thirdly, almost every thesis of any significance is contested and *every* thesis is treated as contestable. The strongest arguments that we are able to adduce in support of our own assertions are never more than the best arguments so far. And it always remains possible that tomorrow some new argument will be advanced that will put in question those theses of which their defenders had been most confident. So to some degree all our conclusions are provisional.

At this point, even a not very acute observer of the philosophical scene, and more especially of the practice of moral philosophers, may demur, pointing out, for example, that in fact some, at least, of the protagonists of various points of view exhibit a confidence in their conclusions that seems disproportionate to the considerations that they are able to adduce in support of them. Moreover, it does on occasion seem to matter whose name is at the head of an article or on the spine of a book. There are prestigious names and names that lack prestige, and sometimes at least what kind of name it is plays a significant part in determining whether or not a book or article is taken seriously. So, it will be said, my portrayal of contemporary moral philosophy is an idealization. To which the reply must be: Yes indeed. What I have portrayed is how contemporary moral philosophy functions when its practitioners are true to the norms and ideals of their practice, as remarkably enough they often are. So we shall not be badly misled if we treat this idealization as a true portrait of contemporary moral philosophy. If we do, we will be struck at once by a sharp contrast with those whose thinking and doing is informed by an acceptance of Torah as God's law.

For moral philosophers, every affirmation is to some degree conditional and provisional, open to modification or even rejection by some compelling argument that is yet to be advanced. For devoted students of Torah, unconditional acceptance of and obedience to its precepts is required. God has spoken and that is enough. For moral philosophers, whether or not we should assent to any thesis depends solely upon the strength of the arguments that can be given for such assent. For devoted students of Torah, because it is God who has commanded obedience to this particular set of precepts, that is sufficient, whether or not there are independent good reasons for obedience to them. For moral philosophers, every thesis is contestable. For devoted students of Torah, divine commands are incontestable. But now someone may object to the way in which I have framed this contrast, pointing out that there are contemporary moral philosophers in good standing who argue in favour of a 'divine command' theory of moral judgement. Moral judgements, they argue, have a claim to our respect because and insofar as they accord with divine commands. Different defenders of this theory have defended different versions of it, but the mere fact that theirs is one of the contending positions within contemporary moral philosophy seems to show that a respect for God's commands is not at all incompatible with the accepted norms governing the practice of moral philosophers. If so, then my attempt to draw the sharpest of contrasts between the attitudes and beliefs of the moral philosopher and the attitudes and beliefs of the devoted student of Torah must be judged to have failed.

This objection fails, however. The philosophers who defend some version of divine command theory may indeed themselves be as obedient to God's commands as any devoted student of Torah. But what they defend in their role as moral philosophers is a *theory* and no more than a theory, held, defended, and criticized in the same way and in the same spirit as all other philosophical theories. Its conclusions are no stronger than the arguments adduced in support of it. It is, qua philosophical theory, affirmed conditionally and provisionally. And it is, as the discussion of it shows, contestable and contested. There is indeed the sharpest of contrasts between the beliefs and attitudes of moral philosophers and the attitudes and beliefs of devoted students of Torah. What then can they have to say to each other? If we are to answer this question, we need to examine a little more closely the characteristics both of the moral philosopher and of the student of Torah. I begin with the former.

III

Socrates thought that there was something very wrong with being paid to engage in philosophy. And about this he was – as so often with Socrates – in a way right. For if we were to ask the questions that moral philosophers ask *only* because we are paid to ask them, there would be something wrong with us as human beings. The questions that moral philosophers initially ask in setting out their systematic and rigorous enquiries are questions that reflective plain people, people innocent of philosophy, pose unsystematically and unrigorously just because they are thoughtful human beings, such questions as 'What is my/our/their good?', 'For what am I/are we/are they responsible?', 'To whom do I owe the truth?'. Plain people pose these questions in terms of the particular circumstances of their everyday lives, while professional moral philosophers frame them at a high level of abstraction. But such philosophers ask them not only because they are by profession moral philosophers, for which they happen to be paid, but also because they are human beings, for which they are not. Ours is, unfortunately, a culture in which many influences discourage or inhibit this kind of thoughtfulness and reflection on the part of plain people and so we are apt to lose sight of this important relationship between the questioning of moral philosophers and the questioning of plain people. But once we call it to mind, it is difficult to resist the thought that what may be important about moral philosophy is the questions that are asked, quite as much as or even more than the rival answers that are advanced by this or that philosopher.

A second and related characteristic of contemporary moral philosophy that we have not yet noticed concerns the disagreements to which I earlier drew attention. Many, even if not all, of those philosophical disagreements mirror moral, social, political, and religious disagreements in our culture, disagreements that arise from a long history of conflict. And perhaps the fact that philosophers have not found a way to resolve their disagreements mirrors the fact that those disagreements remain unresolved in our shared culture. So what plain people should expect from moral philosophers is not a set of answers to, but a clarification of their questions. They should also take note of another obvious, but often unremarked, characteristic of the activities of moral philosophers. Those activities are intelligible only if those engaged in them do in the end care more about truth and about rational justification than they do about the defence of their own particular theoretical stand-point, Kantian, or utilitarian, or contractarian, expressivist or cognitivist, Rawlsian or libertarian or communitarian. By entering into the arenas of debate they open themselves up to correction and even, albeit only on rare occasions, refutation. By so doing they acknowledge truth as a good and a desire in themselves to achieve this good, and they give this good and this desire a place in their lives that is often inconsistent with their own theoretical conclusions. So they make plain the relevance of a question that they themselves too rarely ask: what kind of person would I have to become, if I were to become open to the truth? They rarely ask this question because it is a shared, unspoken, and in fact absurd presupposition of institutionalized moral philosophy that what one needs in order to be open to the truth is a PhD. And it is by the way in which they pose this question that devoted students of Torah put moral philosophy to the question, inviting its practitioners to see themselves and their subject matter in a new light. What light is this?

IV

Twenty years ago, Jonathan Sacks wrote that 'modernity and Jewish tra-dition seem to conflict in their deepest assumptions about the self'.[4] In saying this, he was drawing upon a more general account of the relation-ship between tradition and post-Enlightenment modernity that I had advanced in *After Virtue*.[5] But he made an original and insightful use of that account in finding application for it to the particularities of the his-tory of the encounters of Judaism with that modernity. The transition to modernity is made, so Sacks argued, when *authenticity* becomes the supreme virtue of the self and 'we perceive ethics, or Judaism, as bear-ing the same relationship to the self as a painting to its painter'. And he contrasted the biblical insistence that to do right is to do that which is 'right in the eyes of God' with the post-Kantian view, the view of liberal modernity, that 'Mere obedience is inauthentic…. Moral agency means

---

4. Jonathan Sacks, *One People? Tradition, Modernity, and Jewish Unity* (London and Washington DC: Littman Library of Jewish Civilization, 1993), 157.
5. (London: Duckworth, 1981 and 1984).

to be the author of one's own behavioural code'.[6] But if one is the author of one's own behavioural code, then it is up to one what attitude one takes to Torah, so that even if someone's voluntary and autonomous decision was to live in accordance with the requirements of Torah, this would be only because Torah had been judged morally adequate by one's own standards, whatever these happened to be, Kantian standards, utilitarian standards or whatever. And this of course would not be obedience to Torah.

The history of Liberal Judaism has been the history of a quixotic attempt – the word 'quixotic' is mine, not his – to be at once true to the core of Jewish tradition and true to the standards of liberal modernity. But, as Sacks further argued, this project was incoherent and bound to fail. One consequence was a progressive fragmentation of Jewish thought, so that in its debates a series of disagreements was generated, disagreements that often mirror the apparently irresolvable disagreements of the culture of modernity and of its moral philosophy. So it was important that Sacks did not present himself as just one more contributor to those debates, someone articulating one further set of disagreements, but instead as someone inviting the contemporary participants in those debates to see themselves in a new perspective, to understand how their story might be told in a new way – from the standpoint of Torah. What he offered by so doing was the possibility of a reintegration of Jewish thought, of a renewal that could accommodate the lessons to be learned from the experiences, both Jewish and non-Jewish, of the moral and intellectual adventures of post-Enlightenment modernity within a framework afforded by the tradition of obedience to and study of Torah. He did not present himself as a defender of traditionalism in general, but as someone who wrote and spoke out of his own particular rabbinic tradition. Because of this, he could not escape the task of explaining what he took and takes to be the universal relevance of the particularities of this tradition, of Judaism understood in this particular way. And at this point another dimension of the relationship between Torah and moral philosophy comes into view in Sacks's writings.

'The universality of moral concern is not something we learn by

---

6.   Sacks, *One People?*, 158.

being universal but by being particular.'[7] There are moral philosophers who have said something very much like this, but have then developed this thought in a significantly different way. They agree with Sacks that our initial moral concerns are particular concerns for particular others close to us, family members, neighbours, friends. What we have to learn, according to such philosophers, is that, if our concerns are genuinely moral, they must extend more and more widely, so that they become universal, including all human and indeed all sentient beings. But for them this movement towards universality is a movement away from particularity. I am to be concerned for the moral fate of this or that human individual because and insofar as I am concerned for the moral fate of *any* human individual. With Sacks it is quite otherwise. As we move from concerns for those to whom we are closest to concerns for those outside our immediate circle to concerns for those whom we encounter as alien, as strangers, the objects of our concern remain particular others. 'We learn to love humanity by loving specific human beings', and to speak of universality is to say that there is no one who is excluded by their nature or condition from being an object of our concern. Perhaps most importantly, the strangers whom we encounter are to be peculiar objects of our concern not in spite of, but because of the fact that they are strangers. And Sacks follows rabbinical tradition in noting that 'the Hebrew Bible in one verse, commands "You shall love your neighbour as yourself", but in no fewer than 36 places commands us to "love the stranger."'[8]

Torah speaks to us of the stranger. Recent moral philosophy, especially of the so-called continental persuasion, has spoken instead of otherness, often in this influenced by Levinas, who was at once a moral philosopher and a devoted student of Torah. But what matters about strangers is more and other than their otherness. Strangers, as Sacks remarks, often elicit suspicion and aggression, sometimes, as we may add, justifiably. 'They come from beyond the tribe. They stand outside the network of reciprocity that creates and sustains communities.' But, just as we are to love our family members *as* family members, our

---

7. Jonathan Sacks, *The Dignity of Difference* (London: Continuum, 2002), 58.
8. Ibid., 58.

friends *as* friends, so too we are to love strangers *as* strangers, to love them because and not in spite of their being strangers. And Sacks, by emphasizing this as the injunction of Torah, was able to define a subtle and constructive approach to those great and destructive divisions that constitute so much of our politics, including those divisions that afflict the State of Israel. 'We encounter God in the face of a stranger,'[9] and we therefore have to ask about strangers, even strangers with whom we are bitterly quarrelling, what we have to learn from them. Sacks quotes from the remarkable tribute that he paid to Isaiah Berlin at his funeral, when he retold the story related by Rabbi Shimon of the quarrel between the angels as to whether God should or should not create human beings. What those angels who advised against this creation feared was that human beings would pervert truth into falsehood. God's response was to create a human world in which 'truth on earth cannot be what it is in heaven' and human beings are to 'live by a different standard of truth, one that is human and thus conscious of its limitations. Truth on the ground is multiple, partial.... Each person, culture and language has part of it; none has it all.'[10]

Sacks took it that this rabbinic theological view of truth was the same as that taken by Berlin when he wrote that 'It is a terrible and dangerous arrogance to believe that you alone are right: have a magical eye that sees the truth: and that others cannot be right if they disagree,'[11] and went on to attack the belief 'that there is one and only one true answer to the central questions which have agonized mankind'. But it is important that, had Berlin been pressed to defend his view, his arguments would have been entirely historical and philosophical, not theological. And since truth is not one thing in theology and another in history and philosophy, Sacks's defence of this theological view presupposes that Berlin's philosophical account, or something very like it, could also be sustained as the truth about truth in the arenas of philosophical enquiry and debate. So some of the commitments of Sacks the theologian and rabbinic teacher turn out to be also commitments of a moral philoso-

---

9. Ibid., 59.
10. Ibid., 63–4; the story comes from *Genesis Rabbah* 8:5.
11. Isaiah Berlin, *Liberty* (Oxford: Oxford University Press, 2002), 345.

pher. And they direct our attention to another and crucial dimension of the relationship between Torah and moral philosophy.

If it is right to live as Torah requires, then it is wrong to live as a utilitarian does and wrong to live as a Kantian does. Hence, those who aspire to live as Torah requires presuppose by doing so that the arguments of utilitarians and Kantians fail, and fail as philosophical arguments. Their claim to moral truth is incompatible with the claims of Torah. It follows that educated students of Torah should not be indifferent to the outcomes of the debates of moral philosophers, since they have a large stake in those outcomes. How then are those who acknowledge both the authority of the precepts of Torah and their own inescapable commitments within moral philosophy, with regard to some of the very same precepts, to reconcile their unconditional allegiance to those precepts with their recognition that, as moral philosophers, they have to remain open to the unpredictable outcomes of further argument? This is of course not only a problem for educated and devout Jews. Educated and devout Christians and Muslims confront versions of the same problem. And there are of course well-known proposals for avoiding or resolving it. But it was Sacks's achievement to approach this problem in a new way by asking new questions.

The questions to which Sacks provided answers – and I have in mind here principally, but not only, his essays in *The Dignity of Difference* – are 'What kind of person do I need to become if I am to live and act constructively with these two at first sight incompatible sets of attitudes?', 'What virtues are indispensable?', 'Of what vices should I most beware?'. The catalogue of needed virtues includes responsibility, compassion, and a readiness both to forgive and to ask for forgiveness from others. Only with these virtues will we be able to listen to and speak constructively with those others with whom we are at odds, whether philosophically, theologically, politically, or morally. And only with these same virtues will we be able to sustain the openness to truth required of the moral philosopher. Yet the demands that those virtues make upon us, whatever our standpoint, are categorical and unconditional. Philosophical openness and unconditional commitment have to be understood not as incompatible, but as each requiring the other.

In describing what is involved in the exercise of the relevant virtues, Sacks has identified for us an ethics that is at once not just consistent with the precepts of Torah, but derivable from them, and yet is also an ethics that we contemporary practitioners of moral philosophy need, if our debates are not to be in the end barren. So, after all, there *are* some precepts and virtues to which moral philosophers need to give unconditional allegiance, not as conclusions of their arguments, but as prerequisites for fruitful, rather than sterile, controversy and enquiry.

V

It is because Sacks has recognized this that he has been able to integrate in his speaking and writing both rabbinic fidelity to Torah and an acknowledgement – more often implicit than explicit – of what is philosophically at stake in taking the stands that he does. This is why he has put so many of us in his debt. On a number of substantive issues I remain in serious disagreement with Sacks. But this has not prevented me from learning from him even on those issues, because the conversations that he initiates and sustains are themselves exercises in the practice of the virtues that he praises.

Chapter 2

Ego, Love, and Self-Sacrifice: Altruism in Jewish Thought and Law

David Shatz

One of the salient features of Jewish thought and law, underscored by such recent thinkers as Rabbis Avraham Yitshak Kook, Joseph B. Soloveitchik, Norman Lamm, Aharon Lichtenstein, and Jonathan Sacks, is their embrace of dialectic and balance, their endeavour to accommodate contrasting and conflicting values and ideas, even to the point of paradox. And one of the most complex reflections of this dialectic and balance is Judaism's treatment of the age-old question of egoism versus altruism, self versus other. In what follows we will see this

---

Rabbi Jonathan Sacks's stunning eloquence and insight have captivated diverse audiences. Sensitizing the heart and expanding the mind, his words instil a love for the integration of Torah and world culture that he so vividly embodies. I feel deeply privileged to participate in honouring this extraordinary thinker and leader.

balancing act operating at two levels: the descriptive (Judaism's view of human nature) and the prescriptive (the basis for altruism and the scope of the mandate to be altruistic). Another dialectic will figure in our discussion as well: that between acting altruistically out of obedience to God's laws, and acting altruistically out of emotions like kindness and compassion.

EGOISM: PSYCHOLOGICAL AND ETHICAL

At the beginning of Book 11 of Plato's *Republic*, Plato's brother Glaucon presents a tale that is of vital importance to moral philosophy. The tale is about the ring of Gyges, which, when turned around, renders the wearer invisible and enables him to do as he pleases – steal, kill, rape – with no fear of being caught and punished. The ring-holder can outwardly pretend to be moral and thereby garner the benefits of prestige, reputation, and trust that society confers on people it perceives as ethically upright. Thus does he eat his cake and have it too, reaping both the benefits of seeming moral and those of doing wrong.

Now some people would maintain, Glaucon reports, that no one who came into possession of the ring and understood its power would refuse to use it. For there are those who contend that human beings always indulge their self-interest. Normally, self-interest dictates following conventional morality, but for the ring-holder it dictates flouting that morality. The proffered thesis, that everyone acts so as to satisfy their self-interest, has been called psychological egoism. Essentially, psychological egoism denies the reality of altruism. Not, to be sure, the reality of *acts* that benefit others at a cost to oneself (those acts, to a psychological egoist, arise from the prospect of a net gain), but rather the reality of genuinely altruistic motives – the motive of helping others even with an expected net negative benefit to oneself.

Such challenges to the reality of altruistic motives, or, better put, such attempts to construe altruism as egoism in disguise, are plentiful among philosophers. Thus, in Thomas Hobbes's social contract theory, ethical codes come about because people make a pact out of self-interest, securing protection for themselves by refraining from harming others.[1]

---

1. Glaucon presents this theory as well.

For Hobbes, furthermore, acts that seem altruistically motivated are in actuality products of self-interest; for example, people give charity because it makes them feel superior to their beneficiaries. Friedrich Nietzsche viewed conventional morality, which stresses sympathy, pity, and benevolence, as slave morality, a set of rules developed by the weak in order to protect themselves from the strong. In our times, science, in particular sociobiology, continues the onslaught on altruism. Responding to the famous question of how evolutionary theory can explain altruism given Darwin's stress upon the struggle for survival and survival of the fittest, sociobiology maintains that altruism is a result of animals and humans 'selfishly' seeking to perpetuate their gene pool (kin altruism) or expecting benefits in return (reciprocal altruism).[2] As has often been quipped, such explanations 'take the altruism out of altruism'.[3]

The people whose view Glaucon reports may also endorse, if only by implication, ethical (or normative) egoism – the thesis that one *ought* to do that which is in his self-interest.[4] They believe that the only *rational* thing for one to do when possessing the ring is to use it and pursue one's desires. Now, although psychological egoism and ethical egoism often are espoused as a package, tension exists between them. For 'ought implies can' – to say that someone ought to do x is to imply that, besides being able to do x, that individual can refrain from doing x. But if psychological egoism is true, no one can do otherwise than satisfy his own interests; so, objectors argue, it makes no sense to posit the 'ought'. (Those philosophers who *infer* ethical egoism from psychological egoism face this challenge in an especially acute form.) Egoists struggle with this problem, but we need not solve it to realize that we have in Glaucon's speech central issues for ethical theory.

So we face a battery of questions:

---

2. Edward Wilson and Richard Dawkins are the best known advocates of the 'selfish gene' view. The literature on the origins of altruistic behaviour is now extensive.

3. The phrase was coined by the biologist Robert L. Trivers, 'The Evolution of Reciprocal Altruism', *Quarterly Review of Biology*, 46 (1971), 35–57.

4. The terminology of 'psychological' versus 'ethical' egoism is used by James Rachels and Stuart Rachels, *The Elements of Moral Philosophy*, 7th edn. (New York: McGraw-Hill, 2012), ch. 5.

1. Does altruism really exist?
2. What reasons could there be for being altruistic – i.e. why be moral?
3. If we should be altruists, when, if ever, is acting out of self-interested motives justified? How much must one be willing to sacrifice for others?

My aim here is to explore where Judaism stands on these issues. As is typical, we will find a wide range of views. In addition to discussing Jewish views of altruism, I will also consider the related question of motivation for fulfilling mitzvot, a topic specific to Judaism.[5]

THE REALITY AND LEGITIMACY OF SELF-INTEREST

In Judaism's view, human nature is both egoistic and altruistic. We famously possess two *yetsarim*, or inclinations – one good, one evil, the *yetser hatov* and *yetser hara* (BT *Kidushin* 30b and an immense number of other sources). Some schools of thought stress one, some stress the other; some thinkers of the *musar* movement,[6] for example, view life as a perpetual struggle against wrongful urges.

Although human beings are created in God's image, the Bible certainly is under no illusions as to the human potential for evil. Nor could anyone with a modicum of historical knowledge harbour ignorance of human malevolence. But Rabbi Aharon Lichtenstein plausibly presents the following as the Jewish view: 'Man is not inherently good, but he is capable of great good provided he is trained properly.'[7] Submitting

---

5. For convenience's sake, I will conflate the concepts of altruism and benevolence. Altruism, as I see it, requires the sacrifice of self-interest, of things one cares about, while benevolence does not. (An occasional $1 donation to a *pushka* [charity box] is benevolent but not altruistic; a daily one is, for people of modest means, altruistic.) Again, God is benevolent but not altruistic; when He helps others, even lavishly, He does not sacrifice self-interest. It is in fact unclear what self-interest could mean in God's case. But blurring the distinction between benevolence and altruism in what follows will, I think, be harmless.

6. An ethical and educational movement that arose among Eastern European Jews of the nineteenth century and that stressed striving for the highest levels of religious-ethical conduct through a programme of self-discipline.

7. R. Aharon Lichtenstein, '"Is Anything New under the Sun?" Reflections on the First

to divine discipline curbs the ego.[8] Indeed, as Eliezer Berkovits argues, 'The law is a sign of God's confidence in man.'[9] This is not to ignore, of course, the fact that the *yetser hara* at times exercises one-upmanship, preventing people from adhering to that very discipline.

Considering the power of the *yetser hara*, it is striking how much Judaism's commandments demand from the *yetser hatov*. Charity (*tsedakah*) and the duty of rescue ('Do not stand idly over the blood of your neighbour' [Leviticus 19:16]) are the most obvious examples of mandated interpersonal responsibility. There are positive duties to visit the sick, comfort mourners, assist with funeral matters, and rejoice with a bride and groom and provide a meal for them, all of which Maimonides subsumes under 'Love your neighbour', as rabbinic applications of the biblical law. Hospitality, too, is a duty. Moreover, as Maimonides notes,[10] some benevolent behaviour commanded by the Torah seems extreme – and decidedly not behaviour that philosophers would consider a duty. For example: if a farmer forgets some crop after gathering the harvest, upon remembering, he must not turn back; instead, he must leave the produce in the field for strangers, orphans, and widows (Deuteronomy 24:19).

Gemilut ḥasadim (performing acts of *ḥesed*, or lovingkindness),[11] is said to be one of three pillars on which the world stands (Mishnah *Avot* 1:2). The Psalmist declares, 'The world will be built by *ḥesed*' (Psalm 89:3). *Gemilut ḥasadim* 'has no *shiur* [lit.: measure]' (Mishnah *Pe'ah* 1:1) – plausibly taken to mean that it has no upper limit. Duties to others include responsibility for their *spiritual* welfare: 'All of Israel are

---

Anniversary of the Attack on the Twin Towers', in Michael Broyde (ed.), *Confronting Catastrophe: 9/11 in Jewish Tradition* (New York: K'hal Publishing and the Beth Din of America, 2011), 189–96.

8. See Eliezer Berkovits, *Essential Essays on Judaism*, ed. David Hazony (Jerusalem: Shalem Press, 2002), 3–39.

9. Eliezer Berkovits, *Judaism: Fossil or Ferment?* (New York: Philosophical Library, 1956), 61.

10. In the fourth chapter of his *Eight Chapters* (introduction to his commentary on Mishnah *Avot*), part of his commentary on the Mishnah.

11. See BT *Sukah* 49b for differences between *tsedakah* and *gemilut ḥasadim*.

responsible for one another' (BT *Shevuot* 39a).[12] We form one body or one soul, say the kabbalists.[13] A host of writers understand the commandment to 'walk in His ways' (Deuteronomy 30:16) – the imperative of *imitatio Dei* – as dictating a broad emulation of God's attributes, including graciousness, lovingkindness, and compassion, as opposed to doing only what technical rules require. And, of course, no biblical precept is better known than 'Love your neighbour as yourself' (Leviticus 19:18). Finally, in areas not governed by specific regulations, one must always do 'the straight and the good'.[14] In short: notwithstanding the strength of the *yetser hara*, the altruistic demands of Judaism are varied and challenging.

In the face of these imperatives, is it ever legitimate to have self-interested motives and to act in a self-interested, non-altruistic way? As a matter of logic, it must be legitimate. If everyone who receives some good feels disposed to give that good to another, or simply to refuse the offer, altruism isn't possible. We'll have givers but no receivers, and no meaningful mitzvot *bein adam laḥavero* (commandments governing interpersonal relations). That is especially clear when the recipient of benevolence has received physical assistance, which he can't pass on to others. So mandating altruism entails legitimizing self-interest.

Beyond this logical argument for legitimizing self-interest, there are specifically Jewish bases for doing so. Consider the question of motivation for doing mitzvot. Many of us, influenced by Maimonides, probably denigrate the performance of commandments from self-interested (or ulterior) reasons, *lo lishmah* (not for its own sake). Thus does Antigonus of Sokho teach: 'Do not be like servants who serve the master to receive reward, but, rather, like servants who serve the master not to receive reward'.[15] Maimonides vigorously endorses Antigonus' position and considers acting without ulterior motives to constitute service of

---

12. Whether one must sin to benefit another's spiritual welfare is discussed at BT *Shab. 4a*, *Pes. 59a*, and *Ḥag. 2a–b*.
13. For selections that illustrate this and other kabbalistic bases for concern for the other, see Norman Lamm (ed.), *The Religious Thought of Hasidism* (New York: Michael Scharf Publication Trust of Yeshiva University Press, 1999), 415–39.
14. See Nahmanides, commentary on Deut. 6:18.
15. Mishnah *Avot* 1:3.

God out of love. He explains that the rabbis criticize Antigonus only for *announcing* this, since the masses will not be able to live up to the ideal. At the same time, though, Maimonides recognizes that the rabbis state that performing mitzvot not for their own sake will lead to doing them for their own sake. This legitimizes doing mitzvot out of ulterior motives, even though that orientation is not ideal.[16]

There is a deeper reason to approve of self-interest. Isaac Abarbanel (1437–1508) argues that acting out of a desire for reward serves to express our belief in divine providence.[17] The Talmud declares, furthermore, as Abarbanel notes, that if someone gives *tsedakah* in order that he merit the world to come or that his son be cured, this is (depending on the textual variants) 'complete *tsedakah*' or 'he is a complete *tsadik* [righteous person]'.[18] And questions remain, rooted in that same text, as to whether doing mitzvot solely to attain the world to come is proper; even Maimonides, in one place, bids his readers to consider the spiritual delights, the bliss, of the world to come.[19]

Judaism's legitimizing of self-interested actions that fulfil halakhah's behavioural requirements may be grounded in the utilitarian value of encouraging people to do them. Similarly, Kant encouraged praise of beneficial actions even when they are ulteriorly motivated and for that reason are, in his opinion, devoid of moral worth. We want people to be helped; dictating intentions is subordinated to that goal.[20] The rabbis show appreciation of the social utility of self-interest when they observe that, if not for the *yetser hara*, people would not build

---

16. See Maimonides' introduction to *Perek ḥelek* (Maimonides' commentary on Mishnah *Sanhedrin* 10: 1).

17. Isaac Abarbanel, *Naḥalot avot*, on Mishnah *Avot* 1:3. Abarbanel seeks to reconcile his view with the fact that the rabbis present performing mitzvot for their own sake as ideal.

18. BT *Pes.* 8a.

19. Introduction to *Perek ḥelek*. Cf., however, *Mishneh torah*, 'Laws of Repentance', 10: 1, where Maimonides states that a person should not serve God to attain any benefit, even the world to come. For additional sources and analysis, see Yitzchak Blau, 'Purity of Motivation and Desiring the World to Come', *Torah u-Madda Journal*, 14 (2005–6), 137–56; on the BT *Pes.* passage, see 144–5.

20. See also Jonathan Sacks, *To Heal a Fractured World* (New York: Schocken Books, 2005), 104–06.

houses, marry, procreate, or engage in commerce.[21] And alongside 'duties between human beings and God' and 'duties between people' lie what have sometimes been called 'duties between a person and himself', such as caring for one's health. It would seem also that 'Love your neighbour *as yourself*' implies a duty of self-love, though it is difficult to be sure. Additionally, as we shall see, halakhah at times allows prioritizing oneself and those close to oneself.

Rabbi Meir states the following:

> He who eulogizes the deceased will be eulogized at his death; he who buries the dead will be buried when he passes on; he who carries the coffin will be carried by others [when his body is ready for burial]; he who mourns for others will be mourned by others.[22]

The context suggests that Rabbi Meir is not merely describing the ways of the world; he is not merely noting that people who do *ḥesed* have *ḥesed* done for them. Rather, Rabbi Meir supplies a self-interested utilitarian *reason* for altruistic acts: do unto others *so that* they will do unto you. He urges 'reciprocal altruism' – altruistic behaviour that is predicated on an expectation of reciprocity and hence on self-interest.

Clearly, then, Judaism gives substantial legitimacy to self-interested motives, even if acting on such motives is not the ideal level of mitzvah-performance. Judaism understands human limitations – the difficulty of overcoming self-interest – and appreciates even acts that are ulteriorly motivated.

MOTIVATING ALTRUISM:
DIVINE COMMANDS VS. NATURAL FEELING

Is there a non-self-interested rationale for altruism?

One answer simply says: 'Yes – God commands us to be altruistic.'

---

21. *Bereshit raba* 9.
22. BT *MK* 28b. For discussion of this and some other sources on altruism, see R. Joseph B. Soloveitchik, 'Kibbud u-Mora: The Honor and Fear of Parents', in id., *Family Redeemed: Essays on Family Relationships*, ed. David Shatz and Joel B. Wolowelsky (New York: Toras HoRav Foundation, 2000), 126–57.

According to a 'divine command theory' of ethics, right and wrong are defined by God's will; there is no logical grounding for ethical action besides divine imperatives. Advocates of this view will deny that God must have a reason for commanding altruism. *We*, by contrast, have a reason to be altruistic: God commands us to be.

Divine command theories are often rejected because, inter alia, they make God's commands arbitrary.[23] Suppose, therefore, by contrast, that there *is* a standard of ethics independent of God's will, and that God forms His commands in accordance with that standard. Given that supposition, we have available an independent reason for being altruistic – and, plausibly, it is for that reason that God commands us to be altruistic. Note, however, that the question 'Why does God command us to do x?' is distinct from the question 'Why should we do x?'. A commander may have a reason for commanding, but expects the commanded individuals to act out of obedience to the command, and not for the independent reason that generated the command. Thus, even if we deny a divine command theory of ethics, that does not entail that *our* motivation for benevolent acts must be, say, sympathy for the suffering of others, or commitment to a Kantian universalizability principle. God may want the motivation for altruism to be obedience to His command, even if He has reasons for commanding it.

If this is so, it carries significant consequences. Kant, notoriously, regarded a charitable act motivated by sympathetic feeling as having 'no moral worth'.[24] In parallel though substantively different fashion, some Jewish thinkers maintain that altruistic acts must be motivated by wanting to fulfil divine commands and not by feelings of compassion and kindness. Some rabbinic sources suggest precisely this: 'Whoever is greater than his fellow has a stronger *yetser*';[25] and a well-known *midrash*

23. For a closely-reasoned treatment of this topic, encompassing both philosophical arguments and close readings of rabbinic texts, see Michael J. Harris, *Divine Command Ethics: Jewish and Christian Perspectives* (London and New York: RoutledgeCurzon, 2003).

24. Kant, *Groundwork of the Metaphysic of Morals*, first section. Some interpreters of Kant suggest that an act done both from duty and from sympathy has moral worth, for him, if duty would dominate were the person *un*sympathetic.

25. BT *Sukah* 52b.

states that a person should not say 'I don't want to do x [where God prohibited x]' but rather 'I want to do x, but what can I do? My Father in Heaven has decreed otherwise.'[26]

Maimonides, however, limited the application of such texts. He applied them only to cases of – putting it somewhat imprecisely – ritual acts. With regard to interpersonal actions, he maintained, one who is by nature benevolent (or has made his nature benevolent by repeated acts of benevolence) and who thus acts out of sympathy, kindness, and so on, is greater than one who conquers urges to act unkindly.[27] Rabbi Jacob Emden (1697–1776) differed with Maimonides here, but Maimonides' view has dominated.[28]

In fact, some thinkers take the idea of virtuous character so far as to say that when I give charity I must *not* incorporate divine rules into my motivation. After all, suppose I visit a friend in the hospital. When I begin to leave, my friend thanks me. I reply, 'Visiting the sick [*bikur ḥolim*] is a mitzvah.' That hardly seems like the right attitude! We might therefore hold that someone who is not thinking of what acts and traits God commands has a more proper motivation than one who is – because he acts out of pure kindness.[29] At the same time, some may argue that even if altruistic acts must be motivated by emotions, the positive evaluation of the emotions, along with the desire to develop them, derives only from divine commands and rules.[30] This fact, that even though ideally actions should issue from certain emotions, the emotions are themselves commanded, shows the difficulty of removing the dialectic between rules and sympathy.

---

26. *Sifra*, on Lev. 20:26. See also Mishnah *Avot* 5:23 – struggle increases reward (a theme often applied to our topic).

27. See Maimonides, *Eight Chapters*, ch. 6. (Note that there is an explicit command not to give charity begrudgingly [Deut. 15:10].)

28. R. Jacob Emden, *Hagahot yavets, ad. loc.*, printed in the Vilna Talmud under Maimonides' commentary on the Mishnah. For additional sources on the issue, see Yitzchak Blau, 'The Implications of a Jewish Virtue Ethic', *Torah u-Madda Journal*, 9 (2000), 30.

29. For further discussion, see Blau, 'The Implications of a Jewish Virtue Ethic', 31–3.

30. See R. Judah Loeb ben Bezalel (Maharal, *c.*1529–1609), *Tiferet yisra'el*, ch. 6.

THE BASIS AND SCOPE OF ALTRUISM

How altruistic must I be? And what does altruism demand?

A good starting point is the commandment 'Love your neighbour as yourself'. One may note (facetiously) that there are merely three things that are unclear in the commandment: the meaning of 'love', the meaning of 'your neighbour', and the meaning of 'as yourself'. Is the commanded 'love' affective (a command to have certain emotions) or behavioural (a command to act in certain ways), or both? Is the commandment positive (do unto others as you would have them do unto you) or negative (do not do unto others as you would not want them to do unto you)?[31] Who is your neighbour – all people? All Jews? All observant Jews? All Jews who believe the basic principles of Judaism? These are delicate questions in a society that champions equality and freedom of thought, and in which, as Rabbi Norman Lamm notes, attachment to the Jewish people is no longer a matter of believing certain principles or performing certain actions, but rather consists of certain sorts of identification.[32]

I confine myself to one comment on one of these questions. Some argue that the affective interpretation of love is untenable on the grounds that emotions cannot be commanded. But this last argument would call into question not only affective understandings of love of neighbour, but also of love of God, love of the stranger, respect and fear of parents, festival rejoicing, and mourning (a rabbinic commandment). Lest it be retorted that these commandments, too, are purely behavioural, the commandment 'Do not hate your brother in your heart' (Leviticus 19:17), along with the commandments to 'not desire' others' possessions (Deuteronomy 5:18),[33] not to give charity begrudgingly

---

31. As per Hillel's formulation (BT *Shab.* 31*a*). Maimonides uses both affective and behavioural language; see his *Book of Commandments*, positive commandment 206, and *Mishneh torah*, 'Laws of Character Traits' ('Hilkhot de'ot') 6: 3. See the valuable references and analyses in Daniel Z. Feldman, *The Right and the Good: Halakhah and Human Relations*, expanded edn. (New York: Yashar Books, 2005), 169–83.

32. Norman Lamm, 'Loving and Hating Jews as Halakhic Categories', *Tradition*, 24/2 (1989), 98–122. R. Avraham Yeshayahu Karelitz, the Hazon Ish (1878–1953), called for love of secular Jews because of certain changes in social realities. R. Avraham Yitshak Kook (1865–1935) famously advocated love of all people and of all creation.

33. This should be differentiated from 'not coveting', since many authorities believe the latter entails some sort of action.

(Deuteronomy 15:10), and not to pity one who seduces others to idolatry (Deuteronomy 13:9), should suffice to show that Judaism does command emotions. Rabbi Joseph Soloveitchik writes forcefully: 'The Halakhah is firmly convinced that man is free and that he is master not only of his deeds but of his emotions as well.'[34] Although one cannot produce an emotion at the snap of a finger, we are able, through reflective and critical introspection, to become aware of negative emotions and take steps to correct them. Hence 'Love your neighbour' entails both acts (and refraining from acts) and emotions.

The most difficult question is how much 'as yourself' demands. Must my other-love really *match* my self-love in its quantity and quality, both affective and behavioural? Must I treat others' interests utterly equally with my own? Nahmanides (in his commentary on Leviticus 19:18) says no, on two grounds. First, it is psychologically impossible for someone to love another as he does himself. Second, Rabbi Akiva states 'your life versus the life of your comrade – your life takes precedence.'[35] Nahmanides therefore calls the phrase 'as yourself' a hyperbole (*haflagah*). No one, he states, can love another as he loves himself, and the law does not demand it.[36]

Psychological impossibility aside, there is a deeper problem with 'as yourself', brought out in a *midrash*. The text appears in several variants, but the reconstruction below, not found in standard printings, seems most compelling:

> Rabbi Akiva says: 'Love your neighbour as yourself' is a great principle of the Torah. Ben Azzai says: '[God] created man in His likeness' [Genesis 5:1] is a greater principle than this. So that you should not say 'Since I have been humiliated, my friend

---

34. R. Joseph Soloveitchik, *Out of the Whirlwind*, ed. David Shatz, Joel B. Wolowelsky, and Reuven Ziegler (New York: Toras HoRav Foundation, 2003), 3; see also 10.

35. BT *BM* 62*a*.

36. The rest of Nahmanides' comment is difficult to reconcile with this, since he explains that the mitzvah requires equality of concern – desire for your fellow all that you desire for yourself – and he instances David and Jonathan as people who loved each other as they loved themselves. There is a popular misconception that Nahmanides construes the commandment as behavioural.

should be as well' or 'Since I have been cursed, he should be as well.' Rabbi Tanhuma says: If you have done so, know whom you have abused: 'He created him in His *demut* [likeness].'[37]

Ben Azzai's objection to the encomium Rabbi Akiva bestows on 'Love your neighbour' seems mistaken. He assumes that 'as yourself' should be read as: 'Do unto others as they *have done* unto you.' Obviously if *this* is the imperative, then, as Ben Azzai says, I can justify hurting those who have hurt me; 'as yourself' then amounts to 'Two wrongs make a right', which Ben Azzai rightly rejects. But 'as yourself' could be read rather differently, as 'Do unto others as you *would like them* to do unto you.' Unfortunately, even though this reading escapes Ben Azzai's objection, it invites similar problems of its own. Specifically, (1) a person who wants nothing from others would have no obligation to them either. Thus a person who is thick-skinned, unaffected by insult, gains permission to insult others; (2) an 'independence fanatic', someone who thinks people ought to be totally self-sufficient and adheres to his belief even when it affects him adversely, would, counterintuitively, be exempted from aiding others; and (3) if a person wants extravagant things from others, he is obligated to provide others with those things. Thus, the attempt to define a person's duties to others by reference to what that person cares about – to let my self-interests define what I do for others – runs into a variety of problems, and it is probably best to take *kamokha* (as yourself) somewhat loosely rather than as setting a measure.[38]

In Ben Azzai's and Rabbi Tanhuma's words lies another proposal for grounding altruism: you should not abuse or harm or curse human

---

37. *Bereshit raba*, 24:7. On the textual variants, see the edition of J. Theodor and Chanoch Albeck (Jerusalem: Shalem Books, 1996), 237.

38. Nehama Leibowitz, building upon a comment by Moses Mendelssohn, raises the interesting suggestion that *kamokha* be understood as it can be in a law concerning the stranger (*ger*): 'you should love him *kamokha* for you were strangers in the land of Egypt' (Lev. 19:34). *Kamokha*, she proposes, is the *reason* for the love of the stranger – he is *kamokha*, he is like you, since both of you know the experience of being a stranger. See N. Leibowitz, *Studies in Vayikra*, trans. Aryeh Newman (Jerusalem: World Zionist Organization, 1980), 195–7.

beings because they are created in the divine likeness (*demut*),[39] and such actions strike against their dignity.

A different and popular approach is that loving, compassionate behaviour emulates God and therefore fulfils the commandment of *imitatio Dei* (to walk in His ways).[40] One might say that if we truly love God, we will love what He loves and want to act as He acts.[41] In this view, the divine image in the human being constrains behaviour not because of the *other*'s divine image, but because *I* am created in the image of God, and I must imitate Him. Rabbi Norman Lamm combines these two ways of using 'the image of God' idea by distinguishing *tselem Elokim* (the image of God) and *demut Elokim* (the likeness of God). *Tselem* is a natural endowment; *demut* is something a person creates in himself or herself through ethical action. When I act altruistically towards you, I at once respect your *tselem* and develop my *demut*.[42] Judaism will not condemn an act that is not motivated this way, but acting out of the specified mandate is the ideal. Some halakhists classify *imitatio Dei* as a duty *bein adam laMakom* (between man and God) rather than *bein adam laḥavero* (between man and others).

Many interpreters regard the Torah's mandated altruism as carrying two aspects, love of neighbour and *imitatio Dei*; they note, too,

---

39. 'Divine likeness' is the usual translation; *tselem Elokim* is usually rendered as 'divine image'.

40. Deut. 8:6, 11:22, 13:5, 28:9; see also BT *Sotah* 14a, Maimonides, *Mishneh torah*, 'Laws of Character Traits' 1:5–6. BT *Sotah* 14a mentions only actions, while other sources seem to refer to character traits (BT *Shab.* 133b; *Sifrei* on Deut. 11:22). In *Guide of the Perplexed* i. 54, Maimonides objects to assigning emotions to God and explains *imitatio Dei* by reference to *actions* by a leader that resemble God's – and that, like God's, are performed without emotion. Instead these actions are performed out of recognition of what others (especially wrongdoers) deserve. By contrast, in another, earlier text (*Mishneh torah*, 'Laws of Character Traits' 1:5), Maimonides apparently regards certain emotions and states of mind as fulfilling *imitatio Dei*. The formulation in the *Guide* enables Maimonides to include harsh attributes within *imitatio Dei*. See my discussion of harsh attributes later in this essay.

41. See Robert Merrihew Adams's notion of 'theonomy' in his 'Autonomy and Theological Ethics', in id., *The Virtue of Faith and Other Essays in Philosophical Theology* (Oxford: Oxford University Press, 1987), 126–7.

42. Norman Lamm, 'Some Notes on the Concept of *Imitatio Dei*', in Leo Landman (ed.), *Rabbi Joseph H. Lookstein Memorial Volume* (Hoboken, NJ: KTAV, 1980), 217–29.

that helping others benefits both the recipient and the benefactor, for the latter grows in character.[43] These two paths to altruism diverge in certain cases. Suppose someone does not try to help himself, e.g. by getting a job. Are others obligated to help him? Rabbi Aharon Lichtenstein, among others, argues that 'Based on "Love your neighbor as yourself," it is unreasonable to obligate a person to do for his neighbor that which he would not make the effort to do for himself.' However, since our sages tell us that God (contrary to the expression, 'God helps those who help themselves') is gracious even to those who do not deserve it,[44] 'the obligation to imitate God does not depend upon any other factor, for God's kindness is unconditional.'[45]

> Not with calculated and planned steps, and not out of considerations of reciprocity and mutuality, agreement and parallelism, does man walk in the footsteps of the Creator, but precisely with acts of kindness that breach the dams of balance and reckoning.[46]

Rabbi Lichtenstein goes on to limit the role of *imitatio Dei* in the case at hand, but clearly *imitatio Dei* expands the scope of our obligations.[47]

Indeed, Rabbi Yitzchak Blau shows how *imitatio Dei* and the concomitant nurturing of kind and compassionate emotions mandates treating animals, wicked people, slaves, and gentiles in a kinder way than technical rules require. In addition, Maimonides maintains that it is better to give one coin to each of one thousand paupers than to give a thousand coins to one person – for the repetitive acts will

---

43. I will not here take into account differences between love, ḥesed, and tsedakah as distinct modes of altruism.

44. BT *Ber. 7a*.

45. R. Aharon Lichtenstein, 'The Responsibilities of the Recipient of Charity' (trans. David Strauss), *Alei Etzion*, 16 (Iyar 5769), 18.

46. Ibid., 19.

47. R. J. David Bleich argues, however, that one fulfils *imitatio Dei* with a particular act only if the character trait is already entrenched in him. See Bleich, 'The Commandment "Love Your Neighbour" and the Commandment "Walk in His Ways"' (Heb.), in id., *Binetivot hahalakhah* (New York: Michael Scharf Publication Trust of Yeshiva University Press, 1998), 266–74.

improve character.[48] Furthermore, in some situations a person might have to refrain from a permissible act because of the possible harmful effects on character (though, to be clear, one could not, say, escape the military draft this way). Lastly, whereas a failed or unneeded attempt at benevolence counts as fulfilment of *imitatio Dei* (the virtue having been exercised), it does not count as a fulfilment of 'Love your neighbour'.[49]

Despite its popularity, the use of *imitatio Dei* as a genuine principle of ethics confronts difficulties. Most important, there are attributes of God that specifically should not be imitated. God is an avenging and zealous deity, but human beings, as a *midrash* notes,[50] should not imitate that attribute, or others which this *midrash* enumerates. In fact, imposing *nekamah* (revenge) is specifically prohibited (Leviticus 19:18). Given that, the command of *imitatio Dei* becomes 'Emulate God in those attributes that should be emulated.' That hardly seems to be a helpful principle. Consequently, one might maintain that *imitatio Dei* is a way of categorizing or thinking about certain things we must do, but is not truly a principle for *deriving* obligations. It embellishes our understanding of ethics but is not a generator of ethical conduct in a rigorous sense.[51] Yet the fact that *imitatio Dei* is difficult to apply rigorously and across the board does not preclude its generating duties in many cases. Perhaps human beings are not capable of emulating 'harsh' traits that God possesses, and attempting to do so would have a negative effect.[52] Moral

---

48. Maimonides, commentary on the Mishnah, *Avot* 3:18. R. Jacob Emden disagrees with Maimonides, noting, for one thing, that any improvements in the donor's character that result from his performing many acts of charity must be weighed against the fact that each poor person would receive a meagre benefit if we were to follow Maimonides' proposal. See R. Emden's comment on the *mishnah* in *Avot*, in *Leḥem shamayim* (Jerusalem: Kolel u-Mekhon Pere Shabat, 1977). I thank R. Yitzchak Blau for this reference.

49. See BT *BK* 16b together with Daniel Feldman, *Divine Footsteps: Chesed and the Jewish Soul* (New York: Yeshiva University Press, 2008), 9–16, esp. 9–11.

50. *Midrash hagadol* on Gen. 37:1.

51. See also Leon Roth, 'Imitatio Dei and the Idea of Holiness', in id., *Is There a Jewish Philosophy?: Rethinking Fundamentals* (London: Littman Library of Jewish Civilization, 1999), 22–3.

52. My thanks to R. Yitzchak Blau for this formulation.

principles can legitimately be used to derive courses of action in many cases even if they don't apply in all.

A second problem in *imitatio Dei* is a problem in virtue ethics generally. In virtue ethics, you strive to be altruistic because you want to have a certain sort of character. Formulated this way, with its *purposes* in mind, virtue ethics seems self-centred and egoistic, which is paradoxical since it demands altruism.[53]

THE LIMITS OF ALTRUISTIC SELF-SACRIFICE

Samuel Scheffler and other philosophers have objected to the notion, common in classical utilitarianism (and indeed in deontological theories as well), that in ethical decisions people must treat their interests equally with others' interests, in other words, impartially. People enjoy, instead, says Scheffler, 'agent-centred prerogatives', the prerogatives to weight their interests more than the interests of others.[54]

What does Judaism say? May a person assign more weight to his or her interests and thereby draw a limit to benevolence? How much more? With respect to charity, no more than one-fifth of one's assets should be donated, lest people impoverish themselves and become dependent on others' assistance.[55] ('If I am not for myself, who will be?' suggests that prioritization of self has some validity, but the statement is not a halakhic ruling.[56])

Self-concern, however, is sometimes used to ground concern for others, using an expanding circle model. A person distributing charity prioritizes relatives, and 'The poor of your city take precedence over the

---

53. If we construe *imitatio Dei* as demanding certain acts rather than virtues (see n. 40 above), the problem is resolved. William Kolbrener raises a similar problem; see his 'Don't Take Away My Mitzvah', in id., *Open-Minded Torah: Of Irony, Fundamentalism, and Love* (London: Continuum, 2011), 104–06.

54. See Samuel Scheffler, *The Rejection of Consequentialism* (New York: Oxford University Press, 1994).

55. BT *Ket.* 50a.

56. Mishnah *Avot* 1:14. With respect to *ḥesed*, as distinct from *tsedakah*, financial loss and other factors may exempt a person, but ideally one should not use the exemptions. See Feldman, *Divine Footsteps*, 25–37. Another issue related to how much self-sacrifice Judaism requires is how much must one expend to ensure that another person performs a mitzvah or avoids a transgression.

poor of another city',[57] at least in cases of equal need. As Rabbi Daniel Feldman puts it, *ḥesed* 'is expressed as an outgrowth of the concern one has for oneself, expanding in a direct path outward, strongest in the points that are closest.... The notion of kindness to others develops from a core of self-concern... it is only logical that the closest will get the highest priority.'[58] Such priorities also appear in laws of *pidyon shevuyim* (redeeming captives). One should distinguish between using one's own funds (where personal relationships may have weight) and using communal funds.

The most difficult – and sometimes tragic and heart-wrenching – questions about weighing one's interests against those of others have to do with sacrificing or risking one's life for the sake of others.[59] These arise most forcefully in medical ethics: organ transplants, experimentation on consenting human subjects, and medical management of infectious diseases that threaten the lives of health-care personnel. Let us review some of the sources and issues.[60]

The Bible puts forth a duty of rescue: 'Do not stand idly over the blood of your neighbour' (Leviticus 19:16). The Talmud requires significant effort and expenditure to rescue others when there is little risk to oneself.[61] Because it is not clear whether the mitzvah is positive or negative, some maintain that one must not expend more than one-fifth of his assets (as with charity), while others require *kol mamono* – all one's assets must be expended to perform a rescue. However, in contrast

57. *Shulḥan arukh*, 'Yoreh de'ah' 251:3; see BT *Ned.* 80b.

58. Feldman, *Divine Footsteps*, 224–5. We might explain the laws in other ways: greater physical and emotional proximity increases responsibility (R. Yitzchak Blau's suggestion); or society functions best when communities are to a degree self-reliant.

59. Much of the material in this section is adapted from pp. 30–38 of my 'Concepts of Autonomy in Jewish Medical Ethics', *Jewish Law Annual*, 12 (1997), 3–43. Because of space limitations, I have limited my citation of sources and instead refer interested readers to the article. I thank Routledge Publishers for permission to use the material here. Page references to the article are to the version in my *Jewish Thought in Dialogue: Essays on Thinkers, Theologies, and Moral Theories* (Boston, MA: Academic Studies Press, 2009), 355–84.

60. The Holocaust generated challenging and tragic questions about risky missions. See, for example, R. Ephraim Oshry, *She'elot uteshuvot mima'amakim* 11. 1.

61. BT *San.* 73a.

to non-Jewish systems of ethics, both Christian and secular, Judaism does not unequivocally laud a person's giving up his life to save another, nor even risking one's life to save another. Quite the contrary: in some situations halakhists sometimes classify such acts as akin to suicide. A famous Christian teaching maintains: 'Greater love hath no man than to give his life for his friends' (John 15:13). Judaism sets limits to that love.

For example, consider rescue missions that pose risks to the rescuer. A widespread view among rabbinic decisors is that there are three tiers. The tiers are minimal risk, which must be undertaken; moderate risk, which may be undertaken as an act of special piety (*hasidut*); and significant risk, which should not be undertaken, on pain of being regarded as a 'pious fool.'[62] At the middle level, we find a type of autonomy: one must not be forced into an act of altruism that carries this moderate degree of risk, but one may volunteer to undertake it. Note the striking polarity: mandated altruism on one end, *prohibited* altruism on the other. (Organ donations by the living are usually assimilated to 'rescue' cases.)

Next consider 'resource' cases. Person x is in danger but possesses a resource – water or medicine – that he can use to survive. Person y also needs the resource, and will die if x does not turn it over.[63]

Two people are travelling on a road, and one of them has [*beyad eḥad mehem*] a flask of water. If both drink, both will die; if one drinks, he will arrive at civilization [or: a town]. Ben Petura expounded: Better that both drink and die, and one of them not witness the death of his comrade. Until Rabbi Akiva came and taught: 'And your brother shall live with you' [Leviticus 25:36] –

---

62. For references, see my 'Concepts of Autonomy'.

63. 'Rescue' missions might seem more problematic than 'resource' cases in that an altruistic rescue mission involves *creating* a risk where one did not exist previously, whereas in the classic resource cases, the possessor of the resource is in danger already. However, most writers explain that the *resource* cases are more problematic: here one will *certainly* die if he saves the other, whereas in rescue cases one will be merely *risking* one's life to save another.

your life [*ḥayekha*] takes precedence over the life of your comrade.[64]

Let us assume that the halakhah accords with Rabbi Akiva.[65] He did not say whether you are *obligated* to keep the water, in which case transfer of the flask would be prohibited, or whether you are merely permitted to, in which case transfer to the other would be permissible and possibly even supererogatory. Three positions about this question appear in halakhic sources.

(1) It is prohibited for the possessor of the flask to give the water to his comrade.[66]

(2) The possessor is permitted to give the flask. To do so, moreover, is to exemplify a *midat ḥasidut* (pious trait).[67]

(3) The possessor is permitted to give the flask, and to do so is to exemplify a *midat ḥasidut*, but only when the other's life ranks higher in terms of the halakhah's own priorities for a third party who must choose whom to save. So, for instance, the Mishnah implies that a scholar is to be saved before an *am ha'aretz* (ignoramus).[68] An ignoramus could transfer his flask to a scholar, but not the other way around. Also, an individual could surrender himself for the *rabim* (collective).[69]

---

64. BT BM 62b; see also *Sifra* on Lev. 25:36.

65. Although not codified by Maimonides or R. Joseph Karo, R. Akiva's *ḥayekha* principle has become critical in rabbinic decision-making.

66. See R. Moshe Feinstein, *Iggerot mosheh* (New York, 1973), 'Yoreh de'ah' 2:174:4, pp. 292–3. (As mentioned above, a fuller citation of sources is given in my 'Concepts of Autonomy'. See also the references in my '"As Thyself": The Limits of Altruism in Jewish Ethics', repr. in Shatz, *Jewish Thought in Dialogue*, 326–54.

67. R. Yehiel Ya'akov Weinberg, *She'elot uteshuvot seridei esh* (Jerusalem, 1977), i. 314–15.

68. Mishnah *Hor.* 3: 7–8. Contemporary rabbinic authorities severely limit the application of these criteria.

69. R. Avraham Yitshak Kook, *Mishpat kohen* (Jerusalem, 1966), no. 143, at pp. 310–12 and no. 144 sections 15–16, pp. 339–40. (He offers the account tentatively.) See also *Sefer ḥasidim*, ed. J. Wistinetski (Frankfurt, 1924), no. 252, as well as nos. 162, 165; in the Margulies edn. (Jerusalem, 5733), nos. 698, 674, and 677. See also R. Eliezer Waldenberg, *Tsits eli'ezer* (Jerusalem, 1984), 10:5:7; cf. 9:45.

We might characterize these positions by means of a distinction between blind altruistic self-sacrifice and calculated altruistic self-sacrifice. The former is allowed (indeed, encouraged) by position (2), but prohibited by positions (1) and (3). The latter (calculated altruism) is permitted by position (3) and position (2).

Position (1) suggests something very important about Rabbi Akiva's ruling, namely the fact that the owner keeps the flask is *not* grounded in partiality towards the self. Rather, it is grounded in an impartial moral principle, what might be called the 'least change' principle. According to that principle, dire choices about whom to save are decided in accordance with the course of action that will introduce the least change into the *status quo*. That x owns the flask is part of the *status quo*; therefore, x should not transfer the flask. For advocates of position (1), considerations of autonomy or a quest for a 'higher ethic' by which one prioritizes the other cannot override this least-change principle. In short, the assignment of priority to the flask's owner does not reflect an inegalitarian, egoistic priority of self over other, but rather an impartial principle that cannot be overridden by the owner's generous wishes and emotions. Least-change principles enable us to reconcile Rabbi Akiva's ruling with the ruling that one must not actively kill another person in order to save oneself;[70] for when active killing would be demanded, the 'least change' is to submit to being killed.[71]

While legions of cases have been omitted from our discussion, we may sum up by saying that Judaism places limits on self-sacrifice, but the precise limits are a matter for debate.

CONCLUSION

Judaism is full of antinomy, dialectic, balance, and paradox. It is both realistic and aspirational. It recognizes the reality of self-interest, but affirms the capacity of human beings to escape its grip. It understands that self-interested actions can promote the good of others, but it looks as well at inner intentions and emotions. It sees ethics as emanating from God,

---

70. BT *San.* 74a, *Pes.* 25b.
71. In '"As Thyself"', I have proposed a detailed explanation of the striking contrast between position (1) and secular and Christian ethical systems.

but creates bulwarks against the potential ill effects of strict legalism. It values right action but also desires good character. Its norms incorporate both equalities and inequalities, impartiality and partiality. It adjudicates moral dilemmas with a blend of rigour, sensitivity, and spiritual depth.

Our discussion has, I hope, brought this stunning dialectic to the fore. But let us not lose sight of the ultimate impact of Jewish ethics, which is clear and unequivocal. Lord Sacks, as always, puts it so well: 'By making extraordinary demands, it inspires ordinary people to live extraordinary lives.'[72]

---

72. *To Heal a Fractured World*, 10.

I thank the editors of this volume, along with R. Yitzchak Blau, for their comments on an earlier draft. Thanks, too, to R. Daniel Z. Feldman for valuable discussions, and to Uriel Gellman, Yehuda Gellman, Michael Morgan, and Marc Shapiro for their gracious responses to queries.

Chapter 3

Collective Responsibility and the Sin of Achan

Joshua Berman

I

It is a great privilege to contribute to this volume in honour of my mentor and friend Chief Rabbi Jonathan Sacks. I have had the privilege of having great teachers who taught me how to think and others who taught me how to feel with spiritual passion. Within Orthodoxy today, however, the spiritual climate is often such that one soars with either the intellect or the spirit, but not both. Born in the United States and living in Israel, I have no direct connection to Anglo-Jewry. Yet on every trip that I have made to London in the last twenty years, the Chief Rabbi has generously opened his doors to me and I have discovered a mentor who has taught me how to think critically and boldly, yet with a passion for the Almighty, His Torah, and His people Israel that is the passion of a true hasid. May the Jewish world and the wider society enjoy his leadership for many years to come.

The social thought of the Chief Rabbi strikes a distinct chord among the many voices of contemporary theorists. Where most speak about the importance of the individual, the Chief Rabbi reminds us of the importance of the collective. Where others speak about rights, the Chief Rabbi emphasizes responsibilities. It is no surprise, then, that the topic of *collective responsibility* is one that the Chief Rabbi has revisited in many of his writings. Like others, he speaks of our collective responsibility to those less fortunate than we are. But in bold fashion he extends the notion of collective responsibility to mean *collective liability* – that we are responsible as a collective for the misdeeds of others around us. This idea is most fully developed in his *To Heal a Fractured World: The Ethics of Responsibility*, where he concludes: 'We bear responsibility for whatever we could have prevented but did not' (p. 123). Many, however, bristle at this notion. Are we not each responsible for our own actions? How may I be held liable in any way for an act I did not commit?

To get to a deeper understanding of why we may be held responsible for acts we did not commit, I'd like to turn to what surely must be one of the most misunderstood and under-appreciated stories in the Hebrew Bible, the story of the sin of Achan in Joshua 7. The story has posed a theological challenge to commentators, mediaeval and modern alike. In the battle for Jericho described in Joshua 6, Joshua commands his troops that no goods be taken from Jericho as booty. Specifically, he commands that all gold and silver are to be set aside as *ḥerem* (devoted goods), and consecrated for use in the Tabernacle (6:17–19). Defying the ban, Achan son of Carmi, of the tribe of Judah, steals several items from the proscribed goods (7:1). Although Scripture is quite clear that Achan acted alone, it describes his sin as a breach by the entire people of Israel (7:1). Because of the presence of the devoted goods within the camp of Israel, the ensuing campaign against the city of Ai fails. Israel is routed and in the course of fleeing suffers thirty-six casualties (7:2–5). Explaining the turn of events to Joshua, God blames the entire polity of Israel for the infraction in the harshest terms: 'Israel has sinned! And they have violated the covenant that I have commanded them! And they have taken from the devoted goods! And they have stolen! And they have denied it! And they have hidden it away in their possessions!' (7:11). Israel is doomed to fail in all subsequent battles as well, God says, unless the lone perpetrator is identified, and the devoted goods purged from within the camp of Israel (7:12–16).

The quandary is baffling. If God Himself recognizes that only a lone individual committed the offence, why is the entire polity held responsible? As the nineteenth-century rabbinic exegete Rabbi Meir Leibush Weiser (Malbim) wrote, quoting the plea of Moses and Aaron to God in the wake of the Korah rebellion, 'Can it be that one man sins, and Your fury will be upon the entire people?' (Numbers 16:22). The Cambridge biblicist R.E. Clements sums up what is a barely concealed sentiment that runs throughout modern scholarship when he writes that 'the story projects a portrait of a deity who is cruel, petty and vengeful',[1] concluding, 'It is difficult to find within the story of Achan's sin any residual merit or moral lesson... [it exhibits] painful savagery.'[2]

Traditional rabbinic commentators struggled to resolve the quandary. Malbim, whom I quoted earlier, states that all of Israel is one corporate entity; just as a diseased organ can bring illness to the entire body, so too, the entire body of Israel is held accountable for the misdeeds of any one of its members. But, surely, Malbim's ethics here are out of step with Jewish tradition. Jews were called a surety for one another to perform the commandments. And, indeed, we postulate that on the High Holidays of Rosh Hashana and Yom Kippur we are judged as a collective, and that righteous individuals may suffer if the collective is found guilty. Malbim's formulation, however, is drastic. Nowhere else in the tradition do we find the notion that the whole of Israel is held accountable for the sin of a lone individual committed in secrecy.

The eighteenth-century commentator Rabbi David Altshuler, author of the commentary *Metsudat david*, suggests, 'Because they did not watch over one another, it is as if they all stole from the devoted goods.' Yet the narrative makes it clear that Achan acted alone, and that with the possible exception of his own family, no one even knew that he had taken the goods. How many people even knew this nondescript character? How many people could have possibly watched over him?

---

1. R.E. Clements, 'Achan's Sin: Warfare and Holiness', in David Penchansky and Paul L. Redditt (eds.), *Shall Not the Judge of the Earth Do What is Right: Studies on the Nature of God in Tribute to James L. Crenshaw* (Winona Lake, IN: Eisenbrauns, 2000), 114.
2. Clements, 'Achan's Sin', 125.

I would suggest that the collective guilt ascribed in the story of the sin of Achan may best be understood by engaging in a close literary reading of the story, one that is informed by the behavioural sciences and social theory.

II

The starting point towards a new assessment of the story of Achan begins with an appreciation of a biblical convention. Formally speaking, the story of the sin of Achan is a battle report. Following the report of Achan's infraction in verse 1, Scripture cuts to a different scene altogether: the campaign to take the city of Ai. Joshua sends spies (vv. 2–4), and the battle that ensues ends in a rout (vv. 5–6). Joshua's pleas to God (vv. 6–9) and God's prescription concerning the steps that must be taken before Israel will once again triumph on the battlefield represent the aftermath of the battle and its results (vv. 10–18). Battle reports are among the most common forms of narrative in the Hebrew Bible, with some seventy such stories of a length of more than a few verses. The battle report has no set form or pattern, but rather will contain typical elements: spiritual preparations for battle; physical preparations for battle; pre-battle instruction from the leader to his troops; enumeration of the various stages of a battle; summary reports of casualties, prisoners, booty, and the geographic parameters of the battle; and collective responses to the victory or to the defeat. It is unsurprising to find in our story, for example, that Scripture focuses mainly on the aftermath of the battle: Joshua's response to the rout. Within our narrative, however, one aspect of the battle does seem to have drawn disproportionate attention: the report of the spies, in verses 2–3. Seemingly, had the author omitted this element, the story could have flowed on without any loss. What seems to be of import in the battle story is the rout itself, as reported in verses 4–5, and this, it seems, could well have been reported without the detail of what the spies had reported to Joshua. It is precisely the superfluous nature of the spies' report that should call our attention to it. Indeed, it is there that we will discover the key to the entire episode and the core of the explanation of why collective guilt is ascribed to the entire polity for the misdeed of a single individual.

Upon their return from Ai, the spies report to Joshua (7:3):

> Do not send up the entire nation; some two thousand, or, some three thousand men will go up and smite Ai. Do not trouble the entire people there, for they are few in number.

The spies are short on information, and long on prescriptions. In fact, the only information that they bring is contained in the last statement they make, that the residents of Ai are few in number. The greater part of their 'report', in fact, is comprised of a prescription, that, it must be said, is fraught with confidence. It is extremely rare in the Bible's report of direct speech to include the highly vernacular 'or': 'Some two thousand, *or*, some three thousand men will go up and smite Ai.' The type of hemming and hawing that are the regular fare of daily speech is normally completely removed in the concise style of biblical prose. Indeed, what difference could it possibly make to the audience to know that the spies wavered concerning the size of the troop deployment? The significance of the detail rests not in the particular numbers but in the sense and tone that they convey: having proposed only two thousand, the spies seem to backtrack, lest they appear too lackadaisical, and increase the suggested figure to three thousand. The sense conveyed, however, is one of great confidence.

That confidence, it would seem, was well-justified, coming on the heels of the victory over the impregnable Jericho (cf. 6:1). Yet there is something disturbing about the source of their confidence. They are sure of victory – and with only a partial deployment – because 'they [i.e. Ai] are few in number'. Yet, surely, from the perspective of Scripture, victory is assured not because the residents of Ai are few in number, but because God has promised victory to Israel in their conquest of the land. Conspicuously absent from their report is any mention of God at all. Had they said, 'We will take Ai for the Lord is with us' (cf. the words of Joshua and Caleb to this effect, Numbers 14:8–9), their confidence would have been rooted in a proper source. Indeed, in the second battle for Ai (Joshua 8), following the extirpation of the devoted goods, Joshua stresses that the forthcoming victory will be a grant of the Lord (8:7). Moreover, we discover that Joshua sent up 30,000 troops – ten times the number that the spies had originally specified, suggesting that they had been overconfident in their assessment of the enemy's strength.

How could the spies have failed to ascribe the anticipated victory to God, and this so soon following the defeat of Jericho? A close reading of that battle narrative is revealing. In Joshua 6, we find that the battle for Jericho was carefully choreographed by God Himself. God dictates that following the circumambulations of the city and the shofar-blowing, at the moment of attack, the people were to raise a great shout, and then 'the wall will fall to its foundation, and the people are to go up, and fight face-to-face' (6:5). This is, in fact, what unfolded (6:20): 'The people gave a great shout, the wall fell to its foundation, and the people charged forward, face-to-face, and they vanquished the city.' Put differently, the popular conception – that the walls of Jericho simply 'came a-tumblin' down' – is only part of the story. God brought down the city's defences, opening the door, as it were, to allow the Israelite troops the opportunity to engage in real 'face-to-face' combat (*ish negdo*, vv. 5, 20). As noted, this is not merely what happened (v. 20), but was by divine design (v. 5).

We may speculate as to why God designed the battle in this fashion. On the one hand, He desired to show His might, so that the people would not become drunk with their own power, or, in the language of Deuteronomy, that they should not declare 'my own power, and the might of my own hand has granted me this great victory' (Deuteronomy 8:17). At the same time, God wanted to begin to prepare Israel for the battlefield testing they would endure in the ensuing battles for the land. Thus Jericho was not simply swallowed up into the earth. Rather, God opened the door – in an unambiguous manner, by felling the walls – and then the people were meant to get their first taste of real warfare by engaging – and winning – in hand-to-hand combat.

From the spies' report, however, it would appear that the message got lost. Perhaps inebriated by their first experience of power, the spies seem to place the emphasis on Israel's capacities in relation to such a small foe as Ai, rather than upon the greatness of the Lord and His commitment to Israel.

The spies' report seems to be entirely unrelated to the sin of Achan – indeed, one can hardly assume that the spies knew Achan, let alone of his transgression – yet it is the key to understanding the entire Achan episode. The moral philosopher Larry May offers an account of collective responsibility that is illuminating. For May, people share in the production of an attitudinal climate.[3] While individuals may maintain their own attitudes, individual behaviour is at all times deeply influenced by the climate of opinion within a person's community. Common experiences, shared identification, and solidarity produce actions and attitudes within individuals.

When the anonymous spies express supreme confidence, yet make no reference to God, they give expression to a prevailing feeling within the people as a whole: we won at Jericho on our own fighting merits. The names of the spies are not offered. Their anonymity gives us licence to see them as representative members of the people. When they speak, they give expression to feelings that are held throughout the entire polity.

What the spies said and the people implicitly thought, Achan took a step further, translating attitude into action. Note the language of his confession in verse 21: 'I saw amongst the *spoils* a goodly Babylonian cloak, 200 shekels of silver, and a talent of gold.' Throughout chapters 6 and 7, Scripture refers to the items taken at Jericho as *ḥerem*, goods that were expressly off-limits to the Israelite warriors (6:17–19, 21; 7:1, 11–15). Yet, in recounting his transgression, Achan refers to the items as belonging to the 'spoils' (*shalal*). Achan saw the pile of booty as the legitimate spoils of war and thus rightfully available for the taking. Achan merely translated into action what was in the minds and hearts of the rest of Israel: the notion that victory at Jericho had been theirs.

This explanation resonates with midrashic material found in the commentary of Rashi on Joshua 7:21. Seeking to understand what drew Achan to a Babylonian cloak (cited first in his list of stolen items), Rashi suggests: 'No king of yore would be satisfied with his kingship unless he had a holding in the land of Israel. The king of Babylon had his holding in Jericho, and when he would visit Jericho, he would don this cloak.' This gloss clearly departs from the simple meaning of our passage. However, it is clear that Rashi wishes to cast Achan as one who saw himself as the rightful victor over Jericho, as one who now considers himself to bear the right to don the mantle of kingship over the city.

---

3.   Larry May, *Sharing Responsibility* (Chicago, IL: University of Chicago Press, 1992), 47.

When God says that the *Israelites* transgressed his covenant and that *they* took from the devoted goods, stole, lied, and so on (v. 11), He is offering a taxonomy of the sin. This was not the sin of a wayward individual, a proverbial 'bad apple'. Achan's sin was born out of a social milieu and collective frame of mind.

Many facets of the story become much more intelligible when we read the story in light of this understanding. The depiction of the battle is rendered in verses 4–5:

> And some three thousand men went up from there, and they fled before the men of Ai. And the men of Ai smote from them – some 36 men – and pursued them from the gate until Shevarim, and they smote them on the decline, and the heart of the people melted and became like water.

Notice how the battle unfolds: Scripture does not say that a battle ensued, that the fighting was tough, and that the men of Ai got the upper hand. Rather, it seems that the Israelites approached the gate of Ai, and as soon as they reached the city, they simply began to flee, as the enemy showed its face. We may understand that, inebriated with their own success at Jericho, the troops arrived mentally ill-prepared for a real battle in which the enemy would not be intimidated, as it had been when the walls of Jericho fell. The flight then turns into a rout. One need not explain that God 'punished' the Israelites at this juncture. God is not mentioned at all in the verses depicting the battle. Rather, social and behavioural forces did their own work. God didn't 'defeat' the Israelites; arriving mentally unprepared at the battlefield against a determined foe, the Israelites defeated themselves.

Even more telling is the language of Joshua in his plea in verses 6–9. At first, we are drawn to sympathize with Joshua. At this juncture in the story, he still has no inkling that the devoted goods have been stolen. In light of God's promise to him that the land would be open before him to conquer (1:2–6), Joshua, it would seem, had every right to be bewildered by God's seeming betrayal. Yet, as some commentators have pointed out, Joshua's litany against God resonates – uncomfortably so – with the litany of the ungrateful Israelites wandering in the desert. Compare the following:

> Joshua 7:7: 'O Lord, why have you brought us across the Jordan simply to give us into the hand of the Amorites to destroy us? If only we had been content to remain on the other side of the Jordan!'
>
> Numbers 14:3: 'Why has the Lord brought us to this land to fall by the sword, that our wives and children should fall spoil? It is better that we should return to Egypt!'[4]

Put differently, by framing Joshua's plea not in terms reminiscent of the pleas of Moses on behalf of the people, but in terms of the ingrates of a previous generation, Scripture signals to us that we are to view Joshua here critically – even though he had no knowledge of Achan's infraction. This can be understood if we accept the notion that the issue here is greater than Achan himself; that Achan is simply an aggravated symptom of a larger phenomenon. Joshua is at fault on many levels. Having heard the spies speak with bloated confidence, and without even mentioning God at all in their assertion of victory assured at Ai, Joshua should have taken them to task for this oversight. Once the rout had transpired, moreover, we could have expected a different tack from Joshua. His questions are almost rhetorical, and accusatory in tone. Joshua might have concluded, figuratively speaking, that where there is smoke, there is fire; that where there is something that looks like a punishment, there must have been a misdeed. Apparently Joshua, too, was certain that victory would be his, and never entertained the possibility that misdeeds could affect the outcome.

That we are to judge Joshua's lament critically is further seen in God's highly impatient response: 'And God said to Joshua, "Get up! What is this – falling on your face?"' God's impatience is comprehensible if Joshua failed to sense the unhealthy winds prevailing within the camp

---

4. Cf. also Exod. 16:3, 17:3; Num. 20:3–5.

of Israel, and to realize that the defeat was itself a sign that something had gone very wrong on a large scale.

Yet the part of the story that is illuminated the most when we view Achan's misdeed as a manifestation of a larger spiritual malaise among the people is not the *content* of God's revelation to Joshua, but its *timing*. God does not reveal to Joshua that the devoted goods had been stolen at the moment of the transgression, but only after the debacle at Ai. Compare this to another biblical episode, one which likewise elicits God's anger: the story of the Golden Calf. Exodus 32:7 reports that at the very moment that the people began to worship the idol, God immediately told Moses to descend the mount and attend to the crisis. One might well have expected the same here: that with an infraction of the magnitude of Achan's deed, God would immediately inform Joshua of what had happened. And yet it is only in the wake of the debacle of Ai, and Joshua's entreaty (vv. 6–9), that God informs him of what had happened.

This chronology is clear if we assume that Achan's crime was merely an aggravated expression of what the people as a whole were feeling. Had God informed Joshua immediately at the moment of transgression, Joshua would have mistakenly assumed that Achan was an unrepresentative 'bad apple' and that his action was the deed of a lone, wayward individual. By standing back, as it were, leaving Joshua and Israel to their own devices, with the disastrous results to show, God could now reveal to Joshua what had happened and the lesson would be clear: it was not Achan alone who had failed. The people collectively had failed.

Seeing Achan and his misdeed as the product of his environment may shed light on a final aspect of the story. We note that God's instructions to Joshua on the manner in which he is to identify the perpetrator are quite specific: first the tribe in whose midst he resides is to be identified, then his clan, his sub-clan, then his family, and finally the guilty individual himself (7:13–15).[5] Why such a process?

One can well imagine that when all of Israel is brought for judgement in verse 16, tension pervades the camp: *whodunit?* No one can be sure that the guilty party is not a near relative of his. Now, as the winnowing process proceeds, more and more people are relieved of this

---

5. Note also the full patrilineal genealogy listed for Achan in v. 1.

tension. Yet at each stage, all those who remain implicated suffer ever greater and greater angst, as the walls of indictment close in on them. To be sure, at the end of the day, it is only Achan who is directly accused. Along the way to identifying him as the guilty party, however, a great many people are put through the emotional wringer – and in direct proportion to how closely related they are to him. Distant cousins may have already been exonerated in the second or third round. But the members of Achan's immediate branch of the family are left to sweat, as it were, right down until the final cuts. More than the process seems laborious, it seems unfair.

Scripture does not see identity as something freely constructed by autonomous, unconnected individuals. Rather, identity is something that is supplied by social and genealogical networks. By insisting that Achan be identified in this manner, however, Scripture may be taking the lessons we have drawn one step further. Achan, we have said, acted upon impulses that were present throughout the polity of Israel. By identifying the perpetrator through this winnowing process, with the attendant stress that it produces for all those who surround Achan, Scripture may be implicitly suggesting that Achan – like any Israelite – is a product of the circles of influence from which he stems. These circles are not equal in their influence. The closer the relation, the greater the influence, and, hence, the greater the responsibility. Put differently, we may say that the winnowing process – with its various degrees of implication and ascription of guilt – reveals a view of individual behaviour that reflects a pyramid of responsibility:

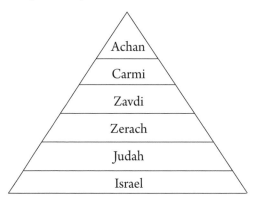

Achan
Carmi
Zavdi
Zerach
Judah
Israel

This graphic most completely answers the question of who is guilty in this story. At the apex of the pyramid is Achan. He is the most culpable. He is the only one who took from the devoted goods, and he is the only one who will be sentenced to death.[6] At the base of the pyramid stands all of Israel. They, too, are implicated, for hubris infected the whole of Israel in the wake of the victory at Jericho. It was the whole of Israel that created the climate in which Achan could commit his sin. However, there are levels of implication between the individual at the apex and the entire polity at the bottom. Achan comes from somewhere. He is most proximately a product of the family of Carmi, and hence all Carmites are made to suffer the angst of inclusion with the guilty until the very last round of winnowing. At the same time he is also the product of other, concentric spheres of influence, and each is apportioned blame for the creation of this perpetrator, according to proximity.[7]

It is telling that we find such a process of winnowing elsewhere, but with connotations that are wholly positive: the story of the election of Saul as king (1 Samuel 10:20–1). Using the same language present in our narrative, Samuel gathers all Israel, identifies the tribe in whose midst the new king resides, and from there, the elected clan, family, and sub-family. The implication is that a worthy king comes from somewhere. His virtues are not to his credit alone; those virtues come from somewhere. He is the product, on the broadest level, of a national culture, but then more narrowly, and more intensively, of a tribe, a clan, a family, and a sub-family. There is an African folk saying that it takes an entire village to raise a child. In the Bible's terms, that is expanded and deepened. A person – for better or for worse – is a product of his or her *multiple* environments, to a greater or lesser extent, depending on intimacy. It is critical to note that not all infractions reflect this dynamic, and indeed, I have already described some instances of individual wayward

---

6. Though it would seem from v. 25 that his children may have also perished, perhaps for having been privy to his act and complicit in the act of concealment in their own tent (vv. 21–2).

7. Note that in v. 22 Joshua sends messengers to retrieve the devoted goods, and that these messengers 'run' to the tent. Rashi comments that the messengers ran out of concern that members of the implicated tribe, the tribe of Judah, would themselves rush to tamper with the evidence and thereby clear the name of the tribe.

behaviour that were not viewed by Scripture as representative of wider phenomena. But at times, the actions of individuals are but expressions of widely-held opinions and attitudes.

In conclusion, we may appreciate anew the remarks cited earlier by the author of the commentary *Metsudat david*. Explaining why the whole of Israel was implicated for Achan's infraction, he wrote, 'Because *they did not watch over one another* [*lo shamru zeh et zeh*], it is as if they all stole from the devoted goods.' 'Watching over' may not necessarily imply that there were too few sentries standing watch over the devoted goods. The failure to 'watch over one another' was the failure of each individual to create an environment of proper reverence for the Almighty and appreciation of His role in the conquest of Jericho.

III

When unpacked in this fashion, the story of the sin of Achan reveals a theory of collective responsibility that may be fruitfully examined in light of contemporary theories of collective responsibility.

The notion of collective responsibility laid out here stresses that the more interwoven a community is, the more its members share in the responsibility for each other's actions. The winnowing process of judgement in verses 7–17 identifies not only the perpetrator. It lays bare the multilayered fabric of the society from which Achan stemmed, assigning blame in proportion to proximity to him.

I would like to proceed by identifying several facets of the theory of collective responsibility that emerge from Joshua 7, and then to sharpen these conclusions in light of the contemporary debate on the subject. The first observation to be made is that a distinction is made between the perpetrator, Achan, and the collective that somehow shares the blame, Israel. It is only Achan, who directly caused the harm, who is tried, and it is only Achan who is directly punished.[8] The interesting question, of course, is how we are to construe the role and blame ascribed to the rest of the people. Verse 11 may be seen both to intensify the question, and, perhaps, also provide the key to the answer: 'Israel has sinned!

---

8. As noted earlier, it may be that Achan's family was also put to death for their complicity in hiding the devoted goods.

And they have violated the covenant that I have commanded them! And they have taken from the devoted goods! And they have stolen! And they have denied it! And they have hidden it away in their possessions!' What is most striking about this verse is that it suggests not only that all of Israel shares in Achan's guilt, but that each person is viewed as having done each of the actions that Achan did. *They* have taken from the devoted goods. *They* have stolen. *They* have hidden it away in *their* possessions. Yet, surely, this was not the case!

The apportionment of blame in this way may be well understood in light of common-law distinctions between perpetrators and inciters, or accomplices, to a crime. An inciter is defined as 'one who…aids, counsels, commands, procures or…encourages another to commit a crime or, supplies him with the weapons, tools, or information needed for his criminal purpose'.[9] The judgement of the accomplice will always be a function of the final act of the perpetrator. If the perpetrator commits a murder, then the accomplice will be an accomplice to murder; if the perpetrator commits a fraud, then the accomplice will be an accomplice to a fraud. If the perpetrator never carries through with his act at all, the accomplice may go scot-free as well.

The same dynamic is also at play here. Israel created the attitudinal climate that allowed Achan to view the 'devoted things', as he says in verse 21, as 'spoils'. They 'aided' and 'encouraged' the crime. Had Achan never done anything, Israel would not have been at all implicated. But once Achan became a perpetrator of the theft and the hiding of devoted things, Israel became accomplices to that crime. They are not as culpable as the perpetrator himself, and, hence, they are not tried like Achan, nor punished like him. At the same time, they are accomplices, and are therefore morally blameworthy. They are accomplices to theft, accomplices to hiding the devoted things in their possessions.

While the notion of collective responsibility involved here bears affinity to some existing notions within contemporary discourse on the subject, it also stands distinct in three ways.

The first concerns the issue of intention. One of the main contentions raised by those who oppose the notion of collective responsibility

---

9. R.M. Perkins, *Criminal Law* (Brooklyn, NY: Foundation Press, 1957), 558.

is that in order to hold someone responsible for an action, there must be intention to perform that action, and that intention can only be fully determined with regard to the mindset of discrete individuals. We run the risk, they maintain, of blaming members of the collective who may not have intended to inflict the harm. To ascribe responsibility to groups for wrongs committed by only a few of its members is by definition unjust. To be sure, those who uphold notions of collective responsibility uniformly agree that intention is critical in order to assign blameworthiness, but they adduce various strategies to demonstrate that even among collectives it is possible to determine intention to commit a wrong. Thus, Margaret Gilbert maintains that we may have evidence of intention in groups when 'they are jointly committed to intending as a body' to perform the act in question.[10]

Joshua 7 bucks the question of intention entirely. Within its theory of collective responsibility, intention by the group to commit the infraction is not required. Achan, we recall, hid the stolen devoted goods and apparently was afraid to show off his spoils. Presumably, he knew that his act would not be favourably received. Indeed, we may even go so far as to say that the vast majority of Israelites would have opposed the taking of devoted goods, and might even have been horrified had they learned of Achan's infraction. Yet they are still held accountable, because the attitudinal climate that they produced as a collective enabled Achan to commit his crime. Persons are responsible not only for their own actions, but for their attitudes. Herein lies the great contribution of our story to the theory of responsibility generally: *persons are responsible as accomplices, if their baneful attitudes, in turn, spur others to harmful action, even if as accomplices they themselves would not have condoned those acts.*

The idea that we may ascribe responsibility to persons even in the absence of intent may seem radical to some. In fact, however, there is one area of law where we do precisely that, namely, in the area of negligence.

---

10. Margaret Gilbert, *On Social Facts* (New York: Routledge, 1989); ead., *Sociality and Responsibility* (Lanham, MD: Rowman and Littlefield, 2000), 22; Michael Bratman, 'Shared Cooperative Activity', *Philosophical Review*, 101/1 (1992), 327–42; id., 'Shared Intention', *Ethics*, 104 (1993), 97–103; Larry May, *The Morality of Groups* (Notre Dame, IN: University of Notre Dame Press, 1987), 65.

Negligence is ascribed precisely in the absence of intention, or of *mens rea*. The standard set for negligence is that of the reasonable person:

> If a reasonable man would have recognized the risk of a conse-
> quence occurring or a circumstance existing in the situation in
> which the accused acted (or omitted to act), the accused will be
> liable whether or not he gave any thought to the possibility of
> there being a risk involved in his conduct.[11]

It should be emphasized that the standard is not what the *aver-age* person would have done, but the *reasonable* person. For Scripture in Joshua 7, members of the Israelite polity had a responsibility to inter-nalize the lessons of the conquest of Jericho, and to hold the Lord in awe and fear. That was the standard set for the reasonable person. They were meant to view the devoted things as His realm entirely, and were to recoil at the thought that anyone would fail to understand that. It was a collective responsibility for all to ensure that this was the spirit that pervaded the people. No one intended for Achan to take from the devoted things. At the same time, they displayed negligence by allowing an attitudinal climate to develop that would enable Achan to perform his sin. Because the *sine qua non* of modern theories of responsibility is the ascription of intention, contemporary legal and moral theorists who work in the area of collective responsibility have not yet explored the issue from the vantage point of theories of negligence. The account of Joshua 7 may have a contribution to make in this regard, and open future avenues of exploration: groups may be held accountable in the absence of intention, even in the absence of commission, due to col-lective negligence.

The second area where the theory of collective responsibility in Joshua 7 stands distinct concerns the criteria that are required to establish that we have a bona fide group acting in concert, collectively. Many theo-rists limit collective responsibility to nations and corporations – groups that have organized procedures for making decisions. Such bodies have

---

11. Michael Allen, *Textbook on Criminal Law* (7th edn.; New York: Oxford University Press, 2003), 96.

the advantage, it is said, of possessing an identifiable moral agent, such as an authoritative body that effectively oversees the execution of the group action. Only such defining organization allows us to say that the group has expressed its intention as a group.[12]

In Joshua 7, collective responsibility is in no way a function of organized, decision-making bodies. Rather, the collective responsibility is born out of collective experience, solidarity, and common sentiment. The people's first battle experience in the land of Israel was, no doubt, a formative and forging experience for the people as a collective. Its responses to that experience, therefore, are considered to be collective in nature, even without the declaration of a representative body.

Finally, the theory implicit in Joshua 7 offers a new perspective concerning the issue of the proportion of the populace involved in the infraction relative to the proportion of the populace who remain passive. In some regards, the theory inherent in Joshua 7 bears great affinity to that propounded by Karl Jaspers in his meditation on the moral culpability of ordinary Germans during World War II in his famous treatise, *The Question of German Guilt*. In a passage cited by the Chief Rabbi in *To Heal a Fractured World* (p. 123), Jaspers maintains that '[t]here exists a solidarity among men as human beings that makes each as responsible for every wrong and every injustice in the world, especially for crimes committed in his presence or with his knowledge. If I fail to do whatever I can do to prevent them, I too am guilty.'[13] Yet Joshua 7 goes much farther than does Jaspers. Jaspers considered the moral status of Germans who were passive in the face of many wrongs committed by many members of their own community. The implication is that the sheer scale of the wrongdoing, in itself, heightens the moral culpability of those who did not act. In the case of Joshua 7, the argument is

12. Cf. Peter French, *Collective and Corporate Responsibility* (New York: Columbia University Press, 1984). More recently, other theorists have experimented with notions of the responsibility of citizens in a global framework where collective responsibility is ascribed even in the absence of defining organizational structures. See Iris Marion Young, 'Responsibility and Global Justice: A Social-Connection Model', *Social Policy and Philosophy*, 23 (2006), 102–30.

13. Karl Jaspers, *The Question of German Guilt* (trans. E.B. Ashton; New York: Capricorn Books, 1961), 36.

taken to its full conclusion. If even only a single individual commits an infraction that is informed by a collective attitudinal climate, should the whole that created that climate be held accountable? Joshua 7 answers in the affirmative.

In an age in which many believe that our actions stem from autonomous decisions that we take on our own, the social ethics of Joshua 7 remind us that we are social beings, that at all times our attitudes radiate outwards towards those around us, and that we are influenced in myriad ways by those around us as well. A cognizance of this reality can only make us more responsible members of the circles within which we function: as members of a family, of a community, of the wider Jewish world, and as citizens in the global community.

Chapter 4

Responsibility: Communal and Individual

Binyamin Lau

INTRODUCTION

The fundamental question 'Am I my brother's keeper?' accompanies man from the day of his creation. It casts doubt on the initial presumption in favour of collective responsibility in the social context. The alternative to mutual responsibility is the protection of the rights of the individual in an ordered framework and emphasis on respect for the individual and his freedom.

The liberal character of contemporary Western society radically endorses concepts of human rights, and in general emphasizes their exclusivity, which makes it possible for the individual to ignore the other. The social framework is instrumental and designed for the furtherance of personal interest. If there is no advantage for the individual within the social framework, he will endeavour to ignore it.

Translated by Michael J. Harris. Thanks are due to Ariel Weiss for many helpful comments on an earlier draft of the translation.

It is almost unnecessary to note that traditional Jewish thought from the Torah onwards opposes such alienation and attempts to make the individual encounter the face of the other.[1] Alongside this social obligation, the Torah aims at the empowerment of the individual and his or her individual responsibility. Jewish thought thus strikes a balance between the extremes of patronizing assumption of systematic responsibility for society and individual autonomy that isolates the individual from his surroundings. In this article I will explore how Jewish thought attempts to achieve this balance.

The article is directly influenced by Chief Rabbi Sacks's book *To Heal a Fractured World*. In this work, Rabbi Sacks leads us in a Jewish conception which follows faithfully in the footsteps of Abraham and illuminates our world by emphasizing the importance of social responsibility.[2] I am proud to dedicate this article in honour of Chief Rabbi Jonathan Sacks, and pray that we will continue to enjoy his Torah for many years to come.

I. COMMUNAL RESPONSIBILITY

The cry of the poor

Embedded in Jewish consciousness is the great cry which arose from the hearts of Israel enslaved in Egypt: 'And it was in those many days that the

---

1. Editors' note: The philosophy of Emmanuel Levinas (1906–95) is devoted to this encounter. According to Levinas's quasi-phenomenological account of ethics, developed in *Totality and Infinity* (1961) and subsequent works, to encounter another person is to become aware of one's infinite and inescapable responsibility for him or her. In his occasional writings on Judaism and commentaries on the Talmud, Levinas put forward an understanding of Judaism as primarily ethical teaching. See 'To Love the Torah More than God', 'An Adult Religion', and other essays in his collection *Difficult Freedom*, trans. Seán Hand (London: Athlone, 1990), as well as the talmudic commentaries in *Nine Talmudic Readings*, trans. Annette Aaronowicz (Bloomington, IN: Indiana University Press, 1990). For a short, accessible introduction to Levinas's philosophy and his Jewish thought, see Seán Hand, *Emmanuel Levinas* (London and New York: Routledge, 2009). A more comprehensive discussion of Levinas's writings and key debates in the secondary literature can be found in Michael Morgan, *Discovering Levinas* (Cambridge: Cambridge University Press, 2007).
2. See my introduction to the Hebrew edition of R. Sacks's book.

king of Egypt died, and the children of Israel sighed from their work and they cried, and their cry arose to God from the servitude' (Exodus 2:23). The people cry out because the situation has become desperate. The death of Pharaoh has changed nothing in the situation of the slaves. That drains hope. The cry comes forth but it lacks an address. God hears the cry of the rootless slaves, even if it is not directed to Him.

The cry, the opening stage of the redemption from Egypt, is also mentioned in the continuation of the biblical story, at the burning bush, when God charges Moses to take Israel out of slavery: 'And God said: I have surely seen the affliction of my people who are in Egypt, and I have heard their cry because of their oppressors, for I know their pain' (Exodus 3:7). God's description is formulated precisely. Israel's cry was not directed to Him. It was a cry which arose from a broken heart. It did not reflect the spiritual condition of the people but rather the depth of their pain. However, when succeeding generations arrive in the land of Israel and bring an offering of first fruits from the produce of their land, they tell the story of the cry in a religious vein: 'And the Egyptians enslaved us and they afflicted us and they put hard labour upon us, and *we cried out to the Lord God* of our fathers; and God heard our voice and saw our affliction and our toil and our oppression' (Deuteronomy 26:6–7).

We cried out to God, and in response to our cry, God answered us. This is a religious interpretation that revises our national biography and connects us, while yet in Egypt, to the God of Israel. However, there is value in the original account, according to which the cry was heard by God even though it was not explicitly directed to Him. For there is no connection between the religious status of the person who cries out and God's listening. On the verse in Exodus (22:26) 'And I will hear for I am compassionate', which describes the cry of the oppressed person, Nahmanides (1194–1270) explains:

> '[I am] compassionate and accept the supplication of every person, even if he is not righteous'.… This teaches that one should not say: 'I will not take as a pledge the garment of a righteous person, but I will take the garment of an unrighteous person, and I will not return it because God will not hear his cry.' Therefore

the Torah says: 'For I am compassionate – I hear the cry of all who entreat me.'

The Torah commands us to preserve the memory of the cry in our national consciousness: 'And you shall not oppress the stranger and not persecute him, for you were strangers in the land of Egypt. You shall not oppress any widow or orphan. If you do oppress him, when he cries to Me I will surely hear his cry, and My anger will be kindled' (Exodus 22:20–3). Because of that memory, Jewish society is supposed to understand the law for the protection of the minority which lives in our midst: 'for you were strangers in the land of Egypt'.

Whose responsibility is it to respond to the cry?

Social organization is liable to excuse the individual from hearing the cry of the oppressed. As the number of official agencies responsible for the care of the oppressed and for responding to their needs increases, the obligations of the individual to listen and act are reduced. The strengthening of the welfare state in the twentieth century spawned frameworks which attempt to take cradle-to-grave responsibility for every citizen of the state. Such collective responsibility creates a sense of freeing the individual from the cry of the oppressed. This dilemma did not originate with the establishment of the welfare state but was already well recognized in ancient times, during the period in which communities began to arise in Israel.

In third-century Babylon, the rule of the exilarch became powerful and a model for the organization of communities for centuries to come. The following story illustrates the moral dilemma of one of the greatest sages of the Talmud, the *amora* (talmudic sage) Shmuel, in the face of the cry of the poor:

> Rabbi Yehudah was sitting in front of Shmuel. A woman entered and cried out before him, but he paid no attention to her. Rabbi Yehudah said to Shmuel: 'Does the master not agree with the verse [Proverbs 21:13] "He who closes his ear to the cry of the poor will himself cry out and not be answered"?' He replied: 'Clever

one! Your head is in cold water, and the head of your head is in boiling water. Mar Ukva is the head of the court. As it is written [Jeremiah 21:12]: "House of David, thus says the Lord: Judge in order to visit justice and save the oppressed from the hand of the oppressor."[3]

Shmuel is the head of the yeshiva in Nehardea, the greatest and most important of the yeshivas of Babylon in the first generations of the talmudic rabbis, the *amora'im* (first half of the third century CE). Rabbi Yehudah is a disciple who grew up in the academy of Sura, and after the passing of his teacher, Rav, moved to Nehardea in order to study Torah with Shmuel. The Sassanian regime in Persia developed autonomous Jewish government, a community within a state, and placed the exilarch at its head. The authority of the exilarch included judicial power and the collection of taxes. He was also in charge of granting exemptions from taxes and regulating economic gaps within Jewish society.

We have here an extreme example of a wise man, an outstanding teacher, rabbi, and leader, who closes his ears to the cry of an oppressed woman because the ability to address her complaint is beyond his reach. In his reaction, he directs the responsibility, in the best bureaucratic tradition, to the local ruler, who fills the shoes of the House of David (the royal house). The biblical verse which supports Shmuel's position is taken from a letter of severe rebuke by the prophet Jeremiah, protesting the king's turning away from the cries of the oppressed in his kingdom.

Prima facie, the last word in the story is that of the teacher, who points out to the disciple that he is fortunate, in that the disciple's head has entered lukewarm water which causes no harm (i.e. his temperate and moderate teacher is not insulted by criticism). By contrast, the teacher is likely to pay for every word of criticism that he utters concerning the exilarch's house. Those in the exilarch's house do not respond forgivingly to social criticism and are known for their violence.

Despite this, later tradition sharply criticised Shmuel. In another source (BT *Bava batra* 10b) and in another place (Tiberias, beginning

---

3. BT *Shab.* 55a.

of the third century CE), Yosef the son of Rabbi Yehoshua, one of the leaders of Jewry in the land of Israel, became ill. Apparently, the son underwent a kind of clinical death, and when he returned to consciousness, his father asked him: 'What did you see?' The son answered: 'I saw a world turned upside down: those above beneath, and those beneath above.' The mediaeval sages who studied this text after the talmudic period (the *ge'onim*) explained it in the following way:

> They received a tradition, handed down from each master to his disciple, that the meaning of 'a world turned upside down' is that he saw Shmuel sitting before Rabbi Yehudah, his disciple [as a student], because he rebuked Shmuel.[4]

According to this tradition, Shmuel lost his seniority to his disciple Rabbi Yehudah, who had protested against his silence and indifference to the cry of the oppressed woman. This is a later reading than the talmudic reading that accepts the helplessness of the teacher vis-à-vis the authorities. This tradition suggests that even if there are official frameworks which bear responsibility, this does not excuse the individual (and certainly not the rabbi, a person of spiritual and moral stature) from protesting injustice in the community.

II. INDIVIDUAL RESPONSIBILITY

It is appropriate to divide the discussion of individual responsibility into two parts: first, education towards responsibility and independence; and second, the placing of responsibility for changing a person's circumstances on him- or herself.

Educating towards responsibility

The contemporary religious educational system often fosters an attitude of obedience to the *gedolei hatorah*, the sages of the generation. The search for great figures who will guide us through a world of doubts and uncertainties fosters division of the community into small, well-defined subgroups. This reality gives rise to profound concern. We find

---

4. Tosafot on BT *BB* 10*b*.

ourselves in an environment of education towards obedience and the acceptance of authority rather than to empowerment and responsibility. Yet Jewish sources – from the sages to the writings of contemporary rabbis – emphasize the importance of fostering independence and educating towards individual responsibility. In the introduction to his commentary on the Passover Hagadah, Rav Avraham Yitshak Kook writes:

> The difference between the slave and the free person is not just a difference of status, such that by chance this person is enslaved to another but the other is not enslaved.
>
> We can encounter an intelligent slave whose spirit is full of freedom, and conversely, a free person whose spirit is the spirit of a slave.
>
> [F]reedom consists in that elevated spirit... faithful to its inner individuality... of the image of God which is in its midst; and with this characteristic it can experience its life as a life with purpose which is worthwhile.
>
> In contrast to this is the person who possesses a spirit of slavery, the content of whose life and whose feelings are never illuminated by the characteristics of his own soul, only by what is good and pleasant in the eyes of the other who rules over him in some way... by what the other person considers to be pleasant and good.

With these words, Rav Kook attempts to base the entire festival of Passover, whose theme is the exodus from slavery to freedom, on the self-consciousness of the individual (and the people). The self-consciousness of the free person, created in the divine image, consists in faithfulness to a personal spirit. But the free person is not born like this. It is necessary to prepare people, through a long and demanding educational process both in the home and at school, to carry the yoke of independence in which responsibility and authority become part of their essential make-up. The natural tendency of a child (childhood here is not necessarily dependent on age) is to seek dependence on some external address that can make decisions on its behalf. In the early stages of life, this tendency is decisive.

Rav Kook's demand to bring the human being to freedom parallels to a large extent the widespread approach among scholars who discuss man's dependence and his flight from freedom. Thus, Erich Fromm entitled his book *Escape from Freedom*, and identifies the fundamental basis of the struggle between freedom and subjugation as the problem of dependence. Fromm argues that the main approach that opposes freedom is authoritarianism, education in blind obedience, and automatic submission towards external entities such as 'establishments', ideas, and people. The common models in practice are totalitarian governments and religious 'establishments', both of which demand the sacrifice of individual freedom and the restriction of self-expression. Obedience, which in itself lacks significance and value, is transformed by these institutions into a supreme value and virtue, while disobedience is considered a serious infringement leading to severe punishment.

A further obstacle to human freedom is described by Viktor Frankl, namely, conformism, which expresses itself in adaptability, proceeding in a furrow, and accepting authority and norms in an automatic and uncritical way. We believe that we live in a liberal Western society of freedom and choice, but everybody accepts that the forces that operate in forming public opinion and in marketing are very effective in creating a society of uncritical people lacking the spirit of freedom. People imitate others. They think, want, feel, and even act according to what society and conventional thinking demand of them, and thus deny the individuality that would make them separate, and intensify their fear of standing alone in the face of the terror of existence.

Let us now address the issues of education towards freedom and the escape from freedom in the language of the Torah and its sages.

Obedience as a value: 'Make a rabbi for yourself
and remove yourself from doubt'
The key source supporting education towards almost blind obedience and listening to the sages without deploying one's critical faculties is a dictum of Rabban Gamliel. It appears in a complex and interesting formulation in the early mediaeval work *Avot derabi natan*:

Rabban Gamliel says: Make a rabbi for yourself, and acquire a friend, and remove yourself from cases of doubt, and do not frequently tithe in an approximate way.[5]

In order to feel the full power of Rabban Gamliel's words, let us cite Rabbi Moses Hayim Luzzatto (1707–46) in *Mesilat yesharim*:

> To what can this be compared? To a garden maze, which is a garden planted for pleasure, as is common among the aristocracy. The trees are planted in walls, and between them are many perplexing and entangled paths which all look alike. The object is to reach the porch in the middle. Now some of these paths are straight and really lead to the porch, but some are misleading and take one away from it. Now the person walking on the paths cannot tell at all whether he is on a true or a false path, for they all look the same to the eye, unless one already knows the way well from having previously been on the paths and reaching the porch. But someone who is already standing on the porch can see all the paths and distinguish between the true and false ones, and he is able to warn those who walk on them and to say: 'Take this path!' Whoever chooses to believe him will reach the goal. But whoever chooses not to believe him and to follow his own eyes will certainly remain lost and will not reach the goal.[6]

Rabbi Luzzatto's metaphor is based on the approach of 'Make yourself a rabbi and remove yourself from doubt.' Most books of guidance for the contemporary religious community take the same line. There are great men who have already reached the porch, and they know the way. Instead of wandering around on the dusty paths, we should rely on them. The approach of Rabban Gamliel and the author of *Mesilat yesharim* requires one simply to submit to the guides who know the way and can show us how to progress on it without perplexity.

---

5. *Avot derabi natan* (A), ch. 22.
6. *Mesilat yesharim*, ch. 3, 'Explanation of the Trait of Caution'.

Argument as a value: 'Make your ear like a grain-receiver'
An opposite approach to that of Rabban Gamliel can be found in the
teaching of Rabbi Eleazar ben Azariah, who replaced Rabban Gamliel
as the head of the court in Yavneh:

> And he also took up the text and expounded: 'The words of the
> wise are as goads, and as nails well planted are the words of mas-
> ters of assemblies, which are given from one shepherd' [Eccle-
> siastes 12:11]....
> 'The masters of assemblies': these are the disciples of the
> wise, who sit in manifold assemblies and occupy themselves
> with the Torah, some pronouncing unclean and others pro-
> nouncing clean, some prohibiting and others permitting, some
> disqualifying and others declaring fit. Should a man say: 'How in
> these circumstances shall I learn Torah?' Therefore the text says:
> 'All of them are given from one shepherd.' One God gave them;
> one leader [Moses] uttered them from the mouth of the Lord
> of all creation, blessed be He; for it is written: 'And God spoke
> all these words'.[7] Also make thine ear like the grain-receiver and
> get thee a perceptive heart to understand the words of those
> who pronounce unclean and the words of those who pronounce
> clean, the words of those who prohibit and the words of those
> who permit, the words of those who disqualify and the words
> of those who declare fit.[8]

Rabbi Eleazar interprets the expression 'masters of assemblies' not
in agricultural terms (as the plain meaning of the biblical text would suggest) but as a colourful description of the world of the new *beit midrash*
(house of study). In this *beit midrash*, scholars of Torah, in their hun-
dreds and thousands, enter the world of Torah study without suspicion
of differences of opinion and without prior adjudication between the
different views. They 'sit in manifold assemblies and occupy themselves
with the Torah, some pronouncing unclean and others pronouncing

---

7. Exod. 20:1.
8. BT Ḥag. 3b. Trans. from the Soncino Talmud, ed. I. Epstein, slightly amended.

clean, some prohibiting and others permitting, some disqualifying and others declaring fit.' This is the glorious picture of the *beit midrash* in the eyes of Rabbi Eleazar.

But here a crucial question arises: 'Should a man say: "How in these circumstances shall I learn Torah?"' A person who enters this open world of study, with its many students, many opinions, and multiple possibilities, can easily lose his way. How might it be possible to guide a person wandering around in a world of multiplicity? There are two possible responses.

One response emerges from the *beit midrash* of Rabban Gamliel: 'Make a rabbi for yourself and remove yourself from cases of doubt.'[9] In a world of doubt, one should search not for a path but for a guide. The rabbi, the guide, will relieve one from doubt. It is a waste of precious time to search for oneself. If there are many opinions – make a rabbi for yourself.

But Rabbi Eleazar presents an alternative to Rabban Gamliel's teaching. Rabbi Eleazar seeks to make the individual responsible for forging a path through the labyrinth of doubt. Instead of 'Make a rabbi for yourself', Rabbi Eleazar offers us the teaching 'Make your ear like a grain-receiver.' The origin of the word *afarkeset* (grain-receiver) is Greek, and it refers to a utensil made like a funnel, wide at one end and narrow at the other. The purpose of the wide section is to absorb the sounds in the atmosphere. These sounds are 'poured' into the funnel, go into the tube, and come out of the narrow opening. A person's ear is designed like an *afarkeset*: voices penetrate the external ear, and continue to the person's consciousness. Rabbi Eleazar tells us to make our ear like an *afarkeset*, to open it to absorb all external voices. The *afarkeset* does not classify or censor. Entry to the world of the *beit midrash* overwhelms the ears with noise. Instead of seeking out a guide who will restore calm, Rabbi Eleazar demands that one create one's own calm. All the voices participating in the dispute of the *beit midrash* have their source at Mount Sinai: 'And the Lord spoke all these words' (Exodus 20:1). Only out of comprehensive listening to all the words can the search for a path begin.

---

9. Mishnah *Avot* 1:16; cf. above, n. 5.

Strengthening education towards independent thinking:
The story of the 'four sons'
The importance of developing a child's or a student's independent personality can be learned from the story of the Four Sons from the Hagadah. The story demonstrates the importance the rabbis attached to the obligation of strengthening every child's ability to express him- or herself: 'The father must teach the child according to the child's understanding.' A child who is unable to express his or her thoughts will risk losing his or her independent personality. The preparation for freedom is based on the recognition that each person is a unique creation, and just as each person's face is different, so is his or her mind. One cannot educate towards adulthood through simple obedience and authority.

In this section of the essay I try to argue the case for education towards freedom, individual responsibility, and release from dependence. Contemporary Jewish religious society is in constant fear of the overwhelming and bewildering outside world. This missing sense of security inevitably spawns a search for defences and reliance upon outstanding figures who can show the way and save us from doubt. The knowledge that no one, however wise or great, is a 'Torah scroll', or 'holy', or our master, is certain to assist every parent and teacher in freeing children from overbearing authority and in forging a path for them which recognizes and develops their potential. Of course, *derekh erets* (civility) is essential to social infrastructure: there are rules for how to conduct a difference of opinion.

The real problem therefore is 'the son who does not know how to ask', who perhaps thinks that it is forbidden to ask, or is used to being told this. The Hagadah tells us 'You open up discussion with him' – or in words attributed to Rabbi Solomon Alkabets (one of the mystics of sixteenth-century Safed): 'You give him confidence.'[10] He lacks self-confidence because his environment shapes and limits him. Because you

---

10. The standard Hebrew version of the Hagadah text is *at petaḥ lo*, 'you open up [discussion] with him'. R. Alkabets is reported to have altered the single Hebrew letter *peh* at the beginning of *petaḥ* to the letter *bet*, yielding *at betaḥ lo* – 'You give him confidence.'

believe in the human being and his potential, 'give him confidence' and show him how his light can shine outwards. Rav Kook put it as follows:

> The upright person should believe in his life, in other words believe that his own life and feelings proceed on an upright path from the foundation of his soul, that they are good and upright and lead on an upright path.[11]

This is a crucial message. One should not be afraid, but rather believe and trust. Many decisions can be made without consulting a rabbi or rebbe. They are matters for an individual, couple, or family to determine. External bodies cannot and should not influence the normal course of an individual's life.

Nehama Leibowitz explains what turns a wise child into a wicked one:

> The wise son 'will *ask* of thee' but the wicked sons 'shall *say* to you'. So long as the son asks, however provocative his questions are, it is a sign that he expects an answer, a solution to his difficulties. He is far from being malicious, but is merely a student thirsty for knowledge. The wicked one, on the other hand, does not ask and desires no reply. 'Then when your children say to you' – their attitude is already fixed and pre-determined. They do not want to hear a reply. They are therefore called wicked. The same idea is expressed in *Akedat yitshak*:[12] 'The text here does not refer to constructive questionings but rather to destructive ones, and they are legion.'[13]

This is an exhaustive and accurate definition. The parent's role is to create an opening for dialogue, for questioning, for clarification, and for the

---

11. R. Avraham Yitshak Kook, *Orot hatorah* (Jerusalem: Ḥoshen Publishers, 5733), ch. 11.

12. Commentary on the Torah by R. Yitshak Arama (Spain, 1420–94).

13. Nehama Leibowitz, *Studies in Shemot (Exodus)*, trans. Aryeh Newman (Jerusalem: World Zionist Organization, 1981), 207–8.

deepening of understanding. The home cannot be founded on defiance. The wicked son of the Hagadah is not interested in conducting an argument; his intention is to defy, to mock, to pour scorn. In the language of the Hagadah, he 'has removed himself from the community', which is 'denial of God'.

The obligation of individual responsibility in overcoming crisis

Up to this point we have focused on the need to educate towards individual responsibility. We must now clarify the second issue – individual responsibility in overcoming crisis. In the first section of this article, I dealt with the obligation of the community to hear the cry of the poor. I now seek to show that the person who cries out is obliged to take an active part in releasing him- or herself from crisis.

My first example comes from the Bible, in its description of Israel at the Exodus. We noted earlier the cry of the slaves at a moment of extreme stress. Their cry was directed not to God or to anybody in particular, but to the universe in general. Just before the Exodus itself, God tells Moses to say to the Children of Israel: 'Take [*mishkhu*] or buy [*kehu*] for yourselves from the flock for your families, and slaughter the Passover offering' (Exodus 12:21). The rabbinic exegesis of this verse is: 'Withdraw [*mishkhu*] your hands from idolatry, and put your hands [*kehu*] to fulfilling God's command.' This interpretation focuses on the two successive verbs in the biblical verse, *mishkhu* and *kehu*. It reads *mishkhu* as denoting releasing from one's grasp, and *kehu* as meaning gathering in to oneself. In relation to our theme, we might suggest that the first step on the journey from slavery to freedom is to let go of illusory possessions and to adopt an authentic and stable set of values. The 'idolatry' that the Israelites were commanded to abandon when they left Egypt was Egyptian culture, which had overwhelmed them. Now, Moses commands the people to offload its alien baggage and to foster self-identity.

Reading the story of the Exodus as related in the book of Ezekiel reveals that the slave nation had to be forced to leave. Despite the positive tone which informs the Torah's account, Ezekiel reveals that the slaves were very reluctant to abandon their servitude. As the Torah puts it elsewhere: 'I love my master...I will not go out to freedom' (Exodus 21:5). In chapter 20, Ezekiel describes the coercive nature of the Exodus. In contrast to the uplifting song 'When Israel went out of Egypt' (Psalm 114), which depicts Israel leaving with song and upraised arm, Ezekiel portrays an Israel who refuses to desist from idol-worship and refuses to commit itself to the service of God. Yet God brings the Israelites out of Egypt, because the moment of redemption has arrived. In the same spirit, Ezekiel makes clear to the exiles of Babylon, who are tempted to assimilate, that this simply 'shall not be at all'. He will force independence upon them:

> That which comes into your mind shall not be at all; in that you say: we will be as the nations, as the families of the countries, to serve wood and stone. As I live, says the Lord God, surely with a mighty hand, and with an outstretched arm, and with fury poured out will I be king over you. And I will bring you out from the peoples, and I will gather you from the countries in which you are scattered, with a mighty hand, and with an outstretched arm, and with fury poured out.[14]

I shall now cite two examples from halakhah that oblige a person to take an active role in going out from slavery to freedom: the redeeming of captives and the commandment 'You shall surely assist him'.

The limited obligation of the community
to redeem a habitual captive

The Torah's opposition to a life of servitude based on a person's (apparent) free will finds expression in an interesting halakhic discussion in the Talmud. As is well known, there is a commandment to redeem captives, which is considered a 'great mitzvah' (commandment).[15] However, the Talmud limits a person's right to redemption from captivity in cases where falling into captivity becomes a regular event. Maimonides summarizes this law:

---

14. Ezek. 20:32–4; 1917 JPS trans., amended.
15. BT *BB* 8*b*.

> If a person sells himself and his children to a non-Jew, or borrows [money] from them, and they take them captive or imprison him because of the loan, it is a mitzvah to redeem them the first and second time. On the third occasion we do not redeem them, although we do redeem the children after the death of their father. If they intend to kill him, we redeem him even after [he has become a captive] several times.[16]

The restriction here is very clear. Someone who chooses to live in conditions of servitude in a systematic and compulsive manner cannot expect the community to bail him out. After the second time he is treated differently, and the community is released from its responsibility for him (though it remains obligated to his children).

'You shall surely assist him': The obligation to participate in one's own recovery

The Torah describes the situation of a person who becomes stuck on the road with an animal which has collapsed under the weight of its load: 'If you see your enemy's donkey collapsed under its load, shall you refrain from assisting him? You shall surely assist him' (Exodus 23:5).

As early as a tannaitic *midrash*, the words 'You shall surely assist' are explained as referring to the responsibility placed upon the recipient of assistance:

> 'You shall surely assist him [lit.: you shall surely assist *with* him]': if he [the recipient of assistance] went and sat down, saying: 'Since the commandment is yours to fulfil, if you want to reload [the animal] do so, otherwise do not' – he [the one obliged to give assistance] is exempt.[17]

The obligation to assist is not in question at all, only the scope of the assistance. The above *midrash* is incorporated as an obligation in the Mishnah:

---

16. Maimonides, *Mishneh torah*, 'Hilkhot matenot aniyim' 8:13.
17. *Mekhilta derabi shimon*, ch. 23.

If the load came off and he had to reload even four or five times, he is still obliged to do this, as it says 'You shall surely assist'.[18] But if he [the recipient of assistance] went and sat down, saying: 'Since the commandment is yours to fulfil, if you want to reload [the animal] do so', he [the one obliged to give assistance] is exempt, since it says '*with* him'.[19]

It is possible that one can extrapolate from this law to all other cases of assistance and charity. If the person in need of assistance does not do what he is capable of, others do not have to do more than he. If this is correct, a person who chooses not to work is not entitled to charity since he is not fulfilling his obligation, and he cannot obligate others to do more than he is doing himself. This is, in fact, the view of Rabbi Solomon Ephraim of Luntshitz (1550–1609), the author of the Torah commentary *Keli yakar*. There is no obligation to give charity to poor people who refuse to work or to make any attempt to earn a living through their own efforts:

> Only when he is prepared to work alongside you and pick his animal up with you, then you are obliged to assist him, but if he sits down and says 'Since the obligation is yours, you will have to pick the animal up on your own'…it is permitted for you to refrain from assisting him … and this provides a retort to some of the poor of our people who rely on the community for support and are not willing to work even though they are capable of some kind of work or of doing something to feed their families, and they complain of injustice if they are not provided with all their needs; but God did not command us to do this, only 'you shall surely assist *with* him', 'you shall surely raise [his fallen animal] up *with* him' [Deuteronomy 22:4]. For the poor person must do whatever is in his power, and if he cannot manage despite this, then every other Jew is obliged to help him and strengthen him

---

18. The Hebrew, *azov ta'azov*, repeats the same root, suggesting repeated assistance.
19. Mishnah BM 2:10.

and give him whatever he lacks, and to 'surely assist him' even up to a hundred times.

This approach, which requires every person to assume an active role in getting out of difficult situations of 'slavery', can and must serve as a general model for conducting life in an affluent society. It is halakhically forbidden not only to force people into slavery but also to choose a life of slavery. Even if the Western world has shaken off the classical modes of slavery, nobody can change human nature. The 'escape from freedom' exists in all societies and in many real life situations. Those who work in the Prison Service are very familiar with the great fear felt by prisoners concerning their release from jail. The prospect of standing on the other side of the prison walls is a threatening one. Books have been written about the choice made by prisoners to remain within the walls, which guarantee structure to the day and freedom from responsibility.

CONCLUDING REMARKS

Rabbi Yehudah Aryeh Leib Alter (1847–1905), one of the leaders of the Ger hasidic dynasty and the author of *Sefat emet*, addresses this issue in a daring homily. He takes the words of the Torah in which God says to Jacob (in the dream of the ladder): 'I will be with you' (Genesis 28:15), and the words of God to Moses at the burning bush: 'for I will be with you' (Exodus 3:12), and compares them with the verse 'You shall surely assist him':

> God said to him [i.e. Jacob] 'Behold, I will be with you', and similarly he said to our master Moses 'I will be with you'. From these utterances alone they realized that they would need much help from Heaven, as it is written [Psalms 91:15] 'I am with him in his trouble'. It is similar to the verse 'You shall surely assist him', concerning which the rabbis expounded: 'If he says: "It is your obligation; you unload the animal", one is not obliged to help him.' For the obligation is [only] to help him [with his own efforts]. And so it is with the divine attribute on high.[20]

---

20. R. Judah Aryeh Leib Alter, *Sefat emet*, 'Vayishlaḥ'.

This is the correct general approach for the person who seeks to be connected to the Torah of the patriarchs and the Torah of Moses. One relies on nobody else, not even on God, without doing something oneself. With His help and through our efforts, we will go out from slavery to freedom.

The Torah requires a life of responsibility: the social responsibility of each individual towards every other individual, and individual responsibility in which each person relies on his or her own abilities and takes his destiny into his or her own hands. There is no contradiction between the two. Communal responsibility is the crucial precondition of the right of the Jewish people to live as 'a treasured people in its land'. Without this kind of responsibility, we are not worthy of God's blessing or of the inheritance of the land. Social alienation that fosters the isolation of one person from another serves as a barrier separating Israel from its Father in Heaven. The walls of separation must be removed. This is the first principle. But it does not conflict with the demand that must be made of parents and teachers, welfare and educational systems alike, to rear children who realize their potential and who take responsibility for their future. The full and proper underpinning of a society that is faithful to Jewish tradition consists of individual responsibility together with social responsibility.

Section 11
The Pursuit of Justice

Chapter 5

Justice, Justice Shalt Thou Pursue

Michael Walzer

I believe that the justice we are asked to pursue in the famous biblical line that I've taken as my title is, first of all, the justice of retribution, reparation, and deterrence. It's the justice done in courts, and its only distributive requirement is that it be delivered equally, without prejudice, to rich and poor alike, and to widows, orphans, and strangers. It is equal justice, though obviously its results are not and should not be equal: rich and poor are treated alike, but not the innocent and the guilty. Equality of treatment but not equality of result is what this kind of justice requires. But behind this idea of justice-in-judicial-proceedings there has to be a more substantive idea. And this substantive idea is very close to what we call social justice: it is focused on the most vulnerable members of Israelite society. Without it, we would not be able to understand what the prophets tell us about the cruelty, callousness, and oppression that the judges had to deal with – and often dealt with badly. In practice, every day, we are all bound to pursue social justice as well as judicial fairness. So, what is social justice?

In this paper, I want to make an argument of my own about social justice, revisiting the argument that I made in *Spheres of Justice*[1] and elucidating the principle that social goods should be distributed in accordance with their meaning to the people who make and use them. Then I want to show, with several examples, how the pluralism that follows from this principle accommodates the Jews – and others too. But before doing these things, I need to consider the substantive biblical idea of social justice, which is antecedent to my own argument and which isn't pluralist. Indeed, it is singular in its form and universal in its reach. Only after describing the singularity of justice will I turn to its plural iterations and the differences among them – and then, finally, to the limits of justice.

I

This is the singular, basic, and universal moral rule: that every community must look after its most vulnerable members and undertake whatever redistributions of wealth or other resources this requires. The biblical texts demand this of us – and the demand is widely recognized, though only infrequently met. Whether humanity as a whole is one of those distributive communities is a critical issue, but it's an issue for another occasion; for now, I will focus on particular political communities and religious groups, which is where questions about justice are commonly addressed and decided.

Let's begin with the non-biblical, ancient world: the kings of Assyria and Babylonia claimed in the prefaces to their law codes to protect widows and orphans, supposedly the most vulnerable people in their societies.[2] Insofar as that protection cost money, we can think of it as redistributive in character – since the money presumably couldn't come from the widows and orphans. Egypt's pharaohs made similar claims, though the protection they offered apparently didn't extend, as

---

1. (New York: Basic Books, 1983).
2. For an overview, see Moshe Weinfeld, *Social Justice in Ancient Israel and in the Ancient Near East* (Jerusalem: Magnes Press, 1995).

the ancient Israelites had reason to know, to their slaves. I doubt that it was very effective for anyone, but it is worth noting what kings and pharaohs thought they had to say about their governments. One of the key tasks of any government, from the earliest times, was to take care of the weakest members of society.

In the biblical texts, this is what the writers have to say about God as a supreme ruler and king – that He protects the most vulnerable members of His people. So we are told in Psalm 146:

> The Lord sets prisoners free
> The Lord restores sight to the blind
> The Lord makes those who are bent stand straight
> ... The Lord watches over the stranger
> He gives courage to the widow and orphan.

I suppose that Israelite kings also claimed to do these things – though their claims are no more plausible than those of Egyptian and Mesopotamian kings. But what is distinctive about the Bible is that ordinary Israelites have, after God, the major responsibility for protecting the vulnerable: 'You shall not subvert the rights of the stranger or the fatherless; you shall not take a widow's garment in pawn. Remember that you were a slave in Egypt' (Deuteronomy 24:17–18). 'You' here means you and me; the reference is collective and inclusive. There are many biblical laws designed to protect widows, orphans, strangers, the poor, day labourers, even the perpetrators of accidental homicides, and the responsibility to help these people is widely dispersed. The laws are indeed redistributive in character, but the king and the state (such as it was) don't seem to be engaged in regulating and enforcing the redistributions. As Jon Levenson has written, these are religious commandments addressed to everybody, not matters of state policy.[3]

So we don't know how effective the biblical laws were. We hope that the intended beneficiaries benefited, but it's probably true that they didn't always benefit or benefit much. Think of the corners of the field,

---

3. Jon D. Levenson, 'Poverty and the State in Biblical Thought', *Judaism*, 25/2 (1976), 235.

which must be left unharvested by the landowner so that the poor can collect the yield for themselves (Leviticus 19:9). But how big a corner it should be isn't specified in the Bible (the rabbis later provided the specifications). There is no general definition of a corner, so if some corners were very stingy, the poor had no recourse. We have no record of any royal intervention in these matters. Still, the idea of the biblical writers is clear: Israel should be a society of everyday redistributions.

The mediaeval *kahal* (Jewish community) had a much more developed system, again focused on the most vulnerable people, beginning with Jewish captives held for ransom. Women were ransomed before men, because of the fear of rape (though I suspect that rabbis were often ransomed before anyone else). Orphans were also looked after by the *kahal* – boys needed an education, girls needed dowries – and so were the poor, and the sick, and wandering Jews in need of shelter. Funds were collected for all these purposes, partly as taxes, partly as *tsedakah* – the word is usually translated as 'charity', though that translation can't be right or not exactly right. Working on texts for volume three of *The Jewish Political Tradition*, which is focused on the *kahal* and its institutions, my co-editors and I have had difficulty distinguishing taxes and *tsedakah*.[4] Maimonides, following talmudic precedents, says that you can force people to give *tsedakah* – which doesn't sound like our idea of charity as a freely-given gift.[5] I think that it was crucial to the safety and well-being of the *kahal* that the resources of its members were available to the community, and could be conscripted by the community in times of crisis and, perhaps more generally but not arbitrarily, available and not totally available: the rabbis were concerned to preserve familial wealth – partly for the family's next generation, partly as a future resource for the community. So there was a limit on giving and, I assume, on taking: no more than 20 per cent of income.[6] But the *kahal's* commitment to its

---

4. Michael Walzer, Menachem Lorberbaum, and Noam Zohar (eds.), *The Jewish Political Tradition, 3: Community* (New Haven, CT: Yale University Press, forthcoming), chs. 20 and 21.
5. Maimonides, *Mishneh torah*, 'Laws of Gifts to the Poor' 7:10.
6. BT *Ket.* 50a.

most vulnerable members was very strong – reinforced, perhaps, by the sense that even wealthy Jews were potentially vulnerable.

Let me give a more recent example of that same commitment, which will help us get at the deeper principle that is involved here. I take the example from my own memory, from a moment in my life that had a great influence on me. I celebrated my thirteenth birthday and my bar mitzvah in 1948 in Johnstown, Pennsylvania. That year, my parents brought me with them, as a new member of the community, to the annual United Jewish Appeal banquet – the main fundraising event in the Johnstown Jewish calendar. Nineteen hundred and forty-eight was a critical year, every Jew in town was there, you had to come, no one really had a choice. There was a speaker from New York, who spoke with great emotion about the founding of Israel, the war that was then going on, and the desperate needs of the refugees waiting in Europe. Pledge cards were passed out, and filled out at the table, then put in an envelope and passed to the head of the table. There sat Sam Shapiro (not his real name), who owned one of the biggest stores in town and who knew everyone's business: he knew who was doing well and who wasn't, who was paying college tuition for one or several children, who had a sick mother, and who had money to spare. Sam opened each envelope, looked at the pledge, and if he thought that it wasn't enough, he tore the card in half and passed it back down the table. That's how the Jews of Johnstown raised money, without a state of our own, without, or supposedly without, coercive power. Was that *tsedakah*, or was it the functional equivalent of taxation?

But I want to ask a more important question: what principle was Sam Shapiro applying? I doubt that he could have answered that question. But it seems obvious to me that the principle was 'from each according to his ability, to each according to his need'.[7] Sam was not a Marxist, far from it; he was one of the town's leading businessmen and probably a member of the local Chamber of Commerce. But he was a good Jew, and so there he was, at the UJA banquet, grinding the faces of the rich. He made sure that the wealthier members of the community gave a decent amount of their money, as he understood a decent amount,

---

7. The line comes from Karl Marx, *Critique of the Gotha Programme* (1875).

to the UJA – not to the utmost of their ability, perhaps, but definitely in proportion to their ability (which is what 'from each according to' probably means). And of course we all assumed that the UJA would then distribute the money to the people most in need, which in 1948 meant the refugees who would soon be arriving in the new, and still embattled, State of Israel.

'From each…to each' never afterwards seemed to me a radical principle. It was, it is, the obvious principle that guides the way we should deal with the goods that people really need – to survive, to have a minimally decent life. The prophet Isaiah (58:7) provides the strongest biblical indication of what is required:

> to share your bread with the hungry,
> and to take the wretched poor into your home;
> when you see the naked, to clothe him,
> and not to ignore your own kin.

II

But my interest in *Spheres of Justice* was chiefly in what comes after the provision of these necessities. How are all the other social goods distributed – not only money, which is the first thing that people think of, but education, leisure time, political office, honour, and recognition? And here the fundamental principle that I defended was that social goods should be distributed according to their meanings in a particular time and place – that is, according to how they are understood and how they are valued by the people who actually invent them, make them, distribute them, and use or enjoy them. Once we get past the things that everybody needs to survive – on the other side of necessity, so to speak – there is no singular and universal principle of the sort that philosophers have long searched for. Or, better, there is only this principle, social goods according to their social meanings, which validates many different distributive criteria and authorizes many different distributive agents. My argument here has been called relativist, but it is meant to accord a generalized respect to all the communities and cultures within which men and women have produced and distributed the things they consider good. By contrast, the construction of a singular and systematic theory of justice, and the insistence that it should be realized everywhere, represents, it seems to me, a refusal to respect the (highly diverse) opinions of humankind.[8]

Ordinary medical care provides an easy example of what this understanding of justice requires (emergency care follows the rule I have already described). The care of the sick should go to the sick in accordance with the kind and degree of their sickness. A strong negative injunction follows: not in accordance with their wealth, or their political influence, or their aristocratic birth. None of these should bring special treatment in its train. Preventative care, regular visits to a doctor, all the available tests – these have to be distributed without any form of favouritism.

But this distributive criterion may not always and everywhere be the right one. My own favourite example from *Spheres of Justice* has to do again with medical care – with the cure of bodies but also with the cure of souls.[9] In the Middle Ages, in Christendom, the cure of souls was thought to produce salvation and eternal life, and these were considered very important (as they obviously are). They were also believed to be readily available. If souls were properly looked after, the men and women whose souls they were would enjoy eternal life. So the cure of souls was socialized: tithes were collected, parish churches established, priests recruited, church attendance and regular communion were made compulsory. At the same time, since the cure of bodies was valued much less, and, in any case, was radically uncertain, it was privatized. Men and women got the physical cures they paid for; spiritual cures were free.

Then, very slowly, attitudes changed; medical science improved, religious faith declined, and longevity came to replace eternity as a key (perhaps the key) social good. And so the cure of bodies was gradually socialized, and the cure of souls was privatized. First public health, and then individual health care, was paid for out of the public treasury, while salvation was increasingly sought by each individual on his own or through voluntary associations.

---

8. For a sharp critique of this argument, see Ronald Dworkin, *A Matter of Principle* (Cambridge, MA: Harvard University Press, 1986), ch. 10.
9. Walzer, *Spheres of Justice*, 86–7.

Neither of these arrangements seems to me unjust. So long as salvation goes to the pious and the faithful and not to the rich or the wellborn; so long as medical care goes to the sick and not to the well-connected; so long as each one is distributed in accordance with its social meaning, I see no reason for criticism. Of course, the transition, from the socialized cure of souls to the socialized cure of bodies, will be contentious, and each cure will have its advocates. If we had been around at that time, we would have had to join the argument. But I don't think that philosophy can tell us which side to take – or, better, secular philosophy will support the cure of bodies (as Descartes famously does in his *Discourse on Method* – an early sign of the coming triumph of longevity over eternity[10]) and Christian theology will support the cure of souls, and ordinary men and women will have to choose one or the other.

Consider another example (for my argument works through casuistry, by looking at actual distributive decisions): the Greek decision to subsidize theatrical performances and the Jewish decision to subsidize education.[11] Neither choice, obviously, was ever defended against the other. Nonetheless, they are interestingly different. For the Greeks, theatrical performances had both a religious and a civic character; it was thought to be very important for all Athenian citizens to be there, and to make that possible, citizens were paid the day's wages that they lost by attending. Every working citizen was paid, because of his citizenship, and without regard to any other fact about him. On the other hand, it was thought that most people did not need a formal education. Academies like those of Plato and Aristotle were attended by the children of the rich, and were paid for by their parents. Aristotle himself had another view, one that we might think represented a better reading of the entailments of citizenship. He believed that citizenship in the *polis* gave rise to a right (he wouldn't have called it that) to go to school – and if a right, then a right equally held by all citizens. 'The system of education in a state', he wrote in his *Politics*, 'must ... be one and the same for all, and the provision of this system must be a matter of

---

10. Rene Descartes, *Discourse on Method*, trans. Arthur Wollaston (Harmondsworth: Penguin, 1960), 82.
11. Walzer, *Spheres of Justice*, 68–74.

public action.'[12] But that wasn't the practice of his own city, not because most Athenians didn't accept the principle of 'one and the same for all', but rather because they didn't assign the same weight to education that Aristotle apparently did.

By contrast, the Jews did not pay for theatrical performances, but they did pay for schools, and they did this as 'a matter of public action'. So far as I know, no plays were performed in the *kehilot* of mediaeval Europe (except perhaps for a Purim *spiel* once a year). There were no drama festivals paid for by the *kahal*; there was no Jewish Sophocles or Aristophanes. And this fact, while we might think it sad (it is sad), is certainly not unjust. But the Jews believed that schooling was a religious necessity – at least, for boys – and so the communities collected money to pay for it. And once you recognize the necessity, you are pushed towards an egalitarian system of provision. Thus the Valladolid Synod of 1432 established (or at least promulgated) a full-scale system of public education for Spanish Jewry, and decreed that the richer school districts should help fund the poorer ones.[13] That transfer of funds from rich to poor districts is still an issue in the United States today; I think that the Spanish rabbis and their lay colleagues got it right.

According to the Jews, every Jewish boy needed an education, but this was only a basic education. The distributive principle for higher education was different (as it is for us). And that's the point of the famous story of Hillel on the roof: as a poor student who couldn't afford the fees, he lay on the roof of the schoolhouse trying to listen to the lessons. He was discovered one cold day, and brought into the school – and his fees were waived.[14] Desire has to play a part in the distribution of higher education, and so does ability. But those two are not relevant earlier on in the life of children – I mean male children, and I will come to that restriction in a minute. If education is critical to the life of a Jewish man, then it has to be available, and equally available, to all Jewish boys.

But my larger claim is that we don't have to choose, at least not

12. Aristotle, *The Politics*, 1337a.

13. Louis Finkelstein, *Jewish Self-Government in the Middle Ages* (New York: Jewish Theological Seminary, 1924), 350–5.

14. Walzer, *Spheres of Justice*, 201–2; the Hillel story comes from BT *Yoma* 35b.

as a matter of justice, between Greek theatres and Jewish schools. That choice is shaped by history and culture, and we shouldn't try to climb some mountain, look down from what's called a 'critical distance', rank the public subsidies of the Greeks and the Jews, and insist that one is more just than the other. We can judge whether the plays of Sophocles and Aristophanes were indeed equally available to all Greek citizens, rich and poor alike; we can judge whether all Jewish boys really had the same opportunity to study Torah. We should probably be sceptical about affirmative answers to either of these questions – and so we should be ready to be critical of both these societies. But this has to be a criticism from within the culture of the people whose societies they were, not from the mountain top.

Should we be critical of the fact that the ancient Greeks did not pay women to attend the theatrical performances, or that mediaeval Jews did not pay for the education of girls? And if we are critical, how can this be criticism from within? The most interesting attacks on my argument in *Spheres of Justice* have come from feminists, asking questions like these.[15] They are hard questions – but only so long as we believe that Greek and Jewish women accepted an account of social goods like theatres and schools that excluded them. But what if they didn't accept it? What if some Jewish women in Spain in the fifteenth century (it only has to be some) resented their exclusion from the schools and thought that if a Torah education was necessary for a good Jew, then it was necessary for them? In that case, it isn't clear what the social meaning of education really was with regard to gender: the meaning was in dispute, even if the women were in no position to make the dispute public. And if that's the case, then we can join the dispute, drawing on other aspects of Jewish thought and history… and criticize the prevailing practice.

Critics claim that the principle I have defended – social goods according to their social meanings – can be used, has been used, to argue against a critique of this sort and to defend conventional ideas. But we have to recognize the truth of the leftist claim that conventional ideas, the ruling ideas of an epoch, are the ideas of the rulers – and it isn't

---

15. See Susan Moller Okin, *Justice, Gender, and the Family* (New York: Basic Books, 1989), ch. 6.

only the rulers who have ideas. Subordinate groups also think about the meaning of social goods, and their minds are often not ruled by their rulers. My own inclination is not to accept the idea of some historians (though others disagree) that women acquiesced in their own exclusion from key social goods and in their general subordination. I think that there was a secret resistance to exclusion and subordination (of which we occasionally get glimpses) and that we have to take this resistance into account when we think about social meanings. (For one example of a woman's resentment and anger, see the story of Reyna Batya, wife of Naftali Tsevi Judah Berlin, head of the Volozhin Yeshiva in the nineteenth century, reprinted in volume 2 of *The Jewish Political Tradition*.[16])

It is also possible to look at another country or another culture and decide that they do things, some things, better than we do. Many historians believe that Rabbenu Gershom's ban on polygamy in Ashkenaz, sometime around 1000 CE, derived from a sense that the Christians were behaving in a more civilized way, treating their women better than 'we' treated 'ours'.[17] And so we had to imitate their practice and establish the new distributive principle of one man/one woman. (Perhaps there was also some pressure – I hope so – from the rabbi's female relatives.) Many important arguments for political and social reform start from comparisons. They start from someone on the inside looking out and asking: what's going on over there? – as Rabbenu Gershom apparently did. But I am sure that if he defended his ban (we have no words of his own on that issue), he would have found halakhic precedents, and he would have referred himself to the meaning of marriage in the Rhineland Jewish communities of his time – and perhaps also to the biblical story of Adam and Eve, who were told to cleave to one another and, so far as we know, to no one else. He would have naturalized the Christian practice into the Jewish tradition.

For another example of a distributive practice that was widely imitated, consider the Jewish sabbath. Thinking about the sabbath led

16. Michael Walzer, Menachem Lorberbaum, and Noam Zohar (eds.), *The Jewish Political Tradition, 2: Membership* (New Haven, CT: Yale University Press, 2006), 187–90.

17. Robert Gordis, *The Dynamics of Judaism: A Study of Jewish Law* (Bloomington, IN: Indiana University Press, 1980), 143.

me to make the distinction that's central to the chapter on the distribution of leisure time in *Spheres of Justice* – between holidays and vacations.[18] The sabbath definitely isn't a vacation: it isn't an empty or a vacant day, which is the idea that lies at the root of our understanding of vacations. It isn't a time to go away; it isn't a day when we can do what we please, with whomever we please. Vacations are a feature of a liberal and highly individualistic society; they are free time in the strongest sense – not only free from work (as the sabbath is), but open to the free choices of every individual person or of every family. Vacations are very different from one another. Some people take fancy vacations; some people save money, go hiking, live rough. Some people prefer a shorter vacation and a higher wage, while others will sacrifice income for leisure or for time with friends and family. Vacations are small-scale exercises in self-determination: everyone ought to have them, but each one will turn out differently.

Since we live in a liberal and individualistic society, it is hard to imagine life without vacations. Deprived of an annual vacation, we would feel oppressed, and indeed, the deprivation would be unjust. But in, say, the *kehilot* of mediaeval Europe or in mediaeval Christendom, nobody had a vacation, and nobody felt oppressed by the absence of that particular kind of free time. They had, of course, more holidays than we do today.

The distribution of sabbath rest is more universal than any other distribution commanded in the Bible – since it extends to every man and woman living in the land, Israelites and strangers, masters and servants, and to all the livestock too. But rest is a relative term, and the protocol for sabbath rest, as it was developed by the rabbis, has many requirements. Most important, I suppose, are the required omissions, the things, so many things, that you can't do. But there are also things that you should do, like go to synagogue, and pray, and read and discuss the *parashah* (weekly Torah portion), and eat especially fine meals – the preparation of which makes Friday a hard day for the women of the family, who don't get all that much rest on the sabbath either. Hence the joke

---

18. Walzer, *Spheres of Justice*, 190–2.

about the Jewish couple in seventeenth-century Poland, who worked for the local Polish nobleman, the Pan. Once, in a drunken stupor, the Pan told the couple that if they didn't instantly convert to Christianity, he would banish them from his lands. Faced with destitution, the couple converted. The next day, the Pan came to their home, sober and apologetic, and told them that he was ashamed of himself and that they could immediately return to Judaism. Said the wife: 'Couldn't he have waited until Sunday?' She was looking forward to (what she had never had before) a restful sabbath.

In that joke, there lurks a protest against God's justice – or the justice of the rabbis. But that's a protest from within; it's an insider's joke. Sabbath rest belongs to everybody, and so it should be enjoyed by everybody. But this is rest with a programme, with a liturgy, and it is very important on the sabbath that you rest together with other people. If vacations are individualist, holidays are communal. They are features of a common life, and so we can criticize any restriction of the commonality.

We have holidays like that in the United States. Think of Memorial Day, which used to fall every year on 30 May, but now falls on the nearest Monday. Once again, I remember how the holiday was observed in the years after World War II in Johnstown, Pennsylvania. All the people in the town made their way to the cemetery. Children marched there from every school, carrying flags. And at the cemetery, the mayor spoke briefly, and then we heard from a minister, a priest, and a rabbi – because, as Moshe Halbertal once remarked, 'the religion of America is religion', and religion had to be represented in all its forms. Exclusion would have been unjust. Had someone told me that I couldn't go to the ceremony, or that there wouldn't be a rabbi there, I would have felt wronged – I would have been wronged.

But it's not wrong that the holiday isn't observed these days with the same emotion and with the same level of participation as it was in the late 1940s. I think that moving Memorial Day to the nearest Monday represents a loss, as it were, of communal observance. A long weekend is more like a short vacation than it is like a holiday; people go away; the cemeteries are empty. But long weekends are not unjust.

The argument about whether to have more holidays or more

vacation days on the calendar isn't an argument about justice. But the argument about who participates in the holiday celebrations and who gets an annual vacation (and is it two weeks or three) – those are justice issues. The six-day and then the five-day week, the eight-hour day, vacations with pay: these are actually important justice issues, even if they aren't featured in the standard philosophical theories of justice. Sabbatarian laws (blue laws), which prevent people from working on a particular day or restrict travel and commercial entertainment – these are also justice issues, and not easy ones. Holidays may require some degree of coercion if they are to survive alongside vacations, but coercion is only justified within a community of like-minded people. In a modern state, comprising multiple communities, with different calendars, holidays depend on voluntary compliance, which is always, and perhaps increasingly, precarious.

III

The advantage of a theory of justice focused on particular social goods is that it opens up a whole series of distributive arguments – and it recognizes that these will turn out differently in different times and places. Think of our society, of any society, as a distributive commonwealth, where many different social goods are imagined, produced, circulated, exchanged, divided, allocated, used, and enjoyed. The commonwealth is just if each of these processes is autonomous or relatively autonomous, if each good is had or not had by these men and women for reasons that fit its meaning in their common life. It is the story that I began with: medical care isn't given to the rich but to the sick. Basic education is for everyone, higher education is for people like Hillel, who are committed to the work and capable of doing it – not for the wellborn or for those whose parents endow the college buildings. Societies are unjust when the possession of one good, like political power or great wealth, brings all the others in its train.

But my anthropological account of justice has another feature: it invites us to recognize that the pursuit of justice isn't the whole story. Contemporary moral philosophy tends to be an imperialist enterprise, making everything a matter of rights and duties, giving justice too large a part in human life. Bernard Williams has made this point with great persuasiveness in a series of essays.[19] And I have already repeated it, in arguing that the choice between the cure of souls and bodies, or between theatres and schools, or between holidays and vacations is not what we usually think of as a moral choice. It has to do with what is good or beautiful or meaningful to a particular group of people – but not with what is right or just. We have to act rightly, of course, and since we so often don't, that is an issue of overwhelming importance. But there is another issue, another question: is the particular world of social goods within which we act rightly or wrongly – is that the world we really want to live in? Is it the best of all our possible worlds?

History and culture shape our distributive arrangements, and we need to be sensitive to their intimations of meaning. But we are also historical agents; we participate in the evolution of our cultural traditions; we think and we argue about the good as well as about the right. So, for example, we might want to preserve the Jewish commitment to education but also to open some room for the appreciation and enjoyment of Greek and Elizabethan and modern drama. We might want to preserve the communal celebration of our holidays but, still, take a vacation now and then, even a vacation from the community. These are easy examples, but one can imagine harder ones, where we will disagree as fiercely about what is good as we do about what is just and right.

So we participate in three arguments: first, about how to pursue justice at the most basic level, how to make 'from each…to each' an effective principle; second, about how to distribute social goods more generally, in accordance with what they mean in our culture, religion, and way of life; and third, about how to develop and enhance and sometimes revise our way of life. And for all these, we should be guided by this (adapted) maxim from Mishnah *Avot*: you don't have to win any of these arguments or end them, but you can't walk away from them.

---

19. Bernard Williams, *Ethics and the Limits of Philosophy* (Cambridge, MA: Harvard University Press, 1985), esp. ch. 10.

Chapter 6

Addressing the Needs of Others: What Is the Stance of Justice?

Moshe Halbertal

In an attempt to define the scope of the needs of the poor, the Talmud introduced a bold conception of subjective needs. This conception was presented as a reading of the verse in Deuteronomy that obligates the provision for the poor: 'but thou shalt surely open thy hand unto him, and shalt surely lend him sufficient for his need in that which he wanteth' (15:8).

> Our Rabbis taught: 'Sufficient for his need' [implies] you are commanded to maintain him, but you are not commanded to make him rich; 'in that which he wanteth' [includes] even a horse to ride upon and a slave to run before him. It was related about Hillel the Elder that he bought for a certain poor man who was

of a good family a horse to ride upon and a slave to run before him. On one occasion he could not find a slave to run before him, so he himself ran before him for three miles.[1]

Poverty ought not to be solely defined by a certain impersonal objective threshold; a provider of charity (*tsedakah*) must take into account the particular past habits and status of the poor and his present sense of deprivation. The ruling is reinforced with a precedent from Hillel, who provided an impoverished aristocrat with his former luxurious means of a servant and a horse. The sensibility to individual context, and the realization that a generalized objective measure might blur particular pain and deprivation, is suggestive and promising. And yet such an attitude evokes a whole set of problems which were raised in the talmudic discussion that followed this ruling.[2] The discussion exhibits a rather complex ambivalence towards this definition of need, an ambivalence which was expressed in a set of intriguing stories.

The first story follows another precedent that is brought in support of addressing subjective needs: 'Our rabbis taught: It once happened that the people of Upper Galilee bought for a poor member of a good family of Sepphoris a pound of meat every day' (BT *Ketubot 67b*). The story challenges such a practice of maintaining expensive dietary habits by raising the suggestion that the impoverished person should adjust to his present means, rather than become a burden on his fellow human beings. This is so especially when the one who has to address these needs is willing to share with him whatever he has, even if this falls short of the poor person's former luxurious menu:

A certain man once applied to Rabbi Nehemiah [for maintenance]. 'What do your meals consist of?' [the rabbi] asked him. 'Of fat meat and old wine', the other replied. 'Will you

---

1. BT *Ket. 67b* (Soncino translation); cf. Tosefta, *Pe'ah* 4:10–11. In the Tosefta's version, Hillel only provided funds and there is no mention of Hillel himself running before the impoverished aristocrat. See also *Sifrei devarim*, 116.
2. For a contemporary philosophical discussion of subjective needs, see T. Scanlon, 'Preference and Urgency', *Journal of Philosophy*, 72/19 (1975), 655–69.

consent [the rabbi asked him] to live with me on lentils?' [The other consented,] lived with him on lentils and died. 'Alas', [the rabbi] said, 'for this man whom Nehemiah has killed'. On the contrary, he should [have said] 'Alas for Nehemiah who killed this man'! – [The fact], however, [is that the man himself was to blame, for] he should not have cultivated his luxurious habits to such an extent.[3]

Sometimes, as the story demonstrates, providing the poor man with the diet he was accustomed to is not a mere luxury. The feeding of the poor man with Nehemiah's own modest diet caused his death. And yet it was the poor man who was to be blamed for continuing to cultivate an expensive taste, rather than adjusting his consumption to something affordable.

In the next talmudic story, the ambivalence towards the subjective definition of need is reinforced by questioning the obligation of addressing such expensive tastes altogether, given the scarcity of communal resources that are needed for more acute deprivation and needs:

A man once applied to Raba [for maintenance]. 'What do your meals consist of?' he asked him. 'Of fat chicken and old wine', the other replied. 'Did you not consider', [the rabbi] asked him, 'the burden of the community?' 'Do I', the other replied, 'eat of theirs? I eat [the food] of the All-Merciful; for we learned: "The eyes of all wait for Thee, and Thou givest them their food in due season" [Psalm 145:15] – since it is not said, "in their season" but "in his season" [*be'ito*], this teaches that the Holy One, blessed be He, provides food for every individual in accordance with his own habits.' Meanwhile there arrived Raba's sister, who had not seen him for thirteen years, and brought him a fat chicken and old wine. 'What a remarkable incident!' [Raba] exclaimed; [and then] he said to him, 'I apologize to you, come and eat.'[4]

---

3. BT *Ket.* 67b (Soncino translation).
4. Ibid.

Raba objected to the demand of the poor man for an expensive meal, describing it as an expression of narcissism, oblivious to the limited resources of the community and its urgent, true needs. The poor man didn't yield to the reproach, providing learned support for his demands and claiming that it was Raba who had been presumptuous, since he had assumed that provisions for the poor are supplied by the community's limited resources, which are susceptible to a zero-sum game in which the more one person receives, the less there is for everyone else. But it is God who provides for each of His creatures, and God is not constrained by limited resources. The end of the story settles the matter by means of the surprise arrival of Raba's sister with a lavish meal. Raba's invitation to the poor man to join the meal seems to reaffirm the idea that the luxurious expectation of the poor will be met with God's provision. And yet, the reader is left with an open question. Should we learn from this story that reckless giving is recommended, since in matters of charity there is no set limit?[5] Is it the case that in encountering a need, whatever it costs, we should not hide behind the pressure of limited resources, but rather address the need with the full faith that resources will be provided? Or maybe such extravagant giving ought to be practised only when an immediate, miraculous supply is provided, but caution should be the rule in the daily and common experience of shortage?

To make the matter even more ambiguous, the Talmud relates the following story concerning Mar Ukba and his son:

> Mar Ukba had a poor man in his neighbourhood to whom he regularly sent four hundred *zuz* [coins] on the eve of every Day of Atonement. On one occasion he sent them through his son, who came back and said to him, 'He does not need [your help].' 'What have you seen?' [his father] asked. 'I saw' [the son replied] 'that they were spraying old wine before him.' 'Is he so delicate?' [the father] said, and, doubling the amount, he sent it back to him.[6]

---

5. Raba's story was interpreted as an unambiguous precedent for giving to the poor whatever he subjectively needs in *Sefer maharil* (Minhagim), 'Hilkhot rosh hashanah' 3. See as well R. Shlomoh ben Adret (Rashba), *Responsa*, vol. 3, no. 380.

6. BT *Ket.* 67b (Soncino translation).

Ukba manifested sensitivity to subjective need to its limit. Upon hearing from his son that the poor man was actually accustomed to great luxury, he doubled the amount that he had sent to him. His response lacks the reservations expressed in the preceding stories concerning such a standard of giving. And yet, though Ukba serves as a role model, one wonders whether his behaviour ought to be generalized, since it was prompted by his particular reaction and relation to his son. The son was presumably sent with provisions to the poor in order to educate him in the tradition of giving, and rather than fulfilling what he was sent to do, he found an excuse not to perform his mission. The inquisitorial stance of the son towards the poor, questioning the authenticity of their need, might have been motivated by the fact that he wanted to keep that money within the family, since he was a potential beneficiary of that large sum. Ukba's reaction, therefore, perhaps should not serve as a source of recommended general practice. It was directed to the stingy son, who should have given to the poor generously without any inquiry or hesitation, and instead tried to find a way to avoid spending the family's wealth. The son was taught a lesson by being sent with a doubled sum, and Ukba used his son's precise reason for not giving in order to double the initial sum.

As in many such talmudic discussions, the issue is left unsettled.[7] The Talmud does not provide a fixed point of view on the matter, but rather offers a spectrum of reactions that aims to exhibit the plethora of considerations relevant to assessing such practice.[8] I think the ambiguity that emerges from this talmudic discussion as a whole is foreshadowed

---

7. The stories that appear here in the Babylonian Talmud have their parallels in the Jerusalem Talmud, which also reflects an ambiguous attitude to the spoiled poor. See JT *Pe'ah* 8:9, 21b.

8. The last story in our talmudic discussion represents a refusal to help the spoiled poor:

> R. Hanina had a poor man to whom he regularly sent four *zuz* on the eve of every sabbath. One day he sent that sum through his wife, who came back and told him [that the man was in] no need of it. 'What' [R. Hanina asked her] 'did you see?' [She replied:] 'I heard that he was asked, "On what will you dine; on the silver [coloured] cloths or on the gold [coloured] ones?"' 'It is in view of such cases' [R. Hanina] remarked, 'that R. Eleazar said: Come let us be grateful to the rogues, for were it not for them, we would have been sinning every day,

in its starting point – the original source that legislated the sensibility to subjective needs. In the source that initiated the discussion, as we saw above, the ruling was reinforced by a short narrative in which Hillel provided money for the impoverished aristocrat to buy a horse and a servant to run before him; once, when Hillel could not find a servant, he himself ran before the poor man, functioning as his servant. Although we might think that the function of this story is simply to emphasize or illustrate the ruling, another interpretation is possible. Perhaps Hillel was trying to achieve two goals. The first, and obvious one, was to provide the poor man with his subjective need for a servant. The second goal, a more subtle and subversive one, was to teach the aristocrat that such a need was artificial and wrong. If Hillel the Great did not mind shedding his status symbols and appearing as a servant by running before the man, how much more so was the impoverished aristocrat expected not to be preoccupied with retaining his lost status. The outer signs of class status that were ostensibly being provided by Hillel himself were at the same time subverted through the act of provision. The subtle critique of the provision of subjective needs as a way of affirming and maintaining class structure is therefore woven into the first step of this ruling.

I became aware of this aspect of Hillel's action and the critical role that the narrative plays in juxtaposition to the ruling when I heard the following story about one of the outstanding talmudic scholars of our generation in Jerusalem: a couple came to seek the scholar's advice about a contested matter. The wife claimed that her husband devoted himself to Torah studies but neglected his domestic duties. The rabbi ruled that the husband was acting properly and that he should be relieved

---

for it is said in Scripture [Deut. 15:9], "And he [the poor person] cry unto to the Lord against thee [for failing to assist him], and it be sin unto thee.'" (BT *Ket.* 67b–68a [Soncino translation])

The mediaeval interpreters were troubled by the difference between Mar Ukba's practice and that of R. Hanina. Two possible distinctions were suggested. The first was that the poor in R. Hanina's case were not the poor who were previously accustomed to a lavish life and became impoverished, but rather their luxurious habits were developed while they were poor. The second distinction was that the poor in R. Hanina's case pretended to be poor, yet their lifestyle testified that they had plenty of resources of their own. See Tosafot BT *Ket.* 68a s.v. *betalei kesef* and Menahem Me'iri, *Beit habehirah*, on *Ket.* 68a, s.v. *af al pi*, and below, n. 10.

from such duties in order to devote himself to the study of Torah. On the Friday after the ruling was issued, the husband came back from the study hall to his home right before the sabbath, and to his surprise the great scholar was at his home helping to take the garbage out. He wondered what the great scholar was doing in his house, and the rabbi answered him in the following way: 'I knew you are very busy studying Torah. I myself had some free time, so I decided to come and help at your home.' In running before the impoverished aristocrat, Hillel was practising the same line of teaching. He provided the poor man with his needs, while helping him in a deeper way, through personal example, to free himself from being dependent on status symbols as a source of honour and dignity.

Following the talmudic ruling, the principle of addressing subjective needs was embraced by later generations of halakhists, though they also struggled with some of the concerns that emerge from the adoption of such a standard. One interesting opinion claimed that the ruling of the Talmud relates exclusively to a person whose impoverishment is not yet known to the public. If his condition has become known, there is no obligation to provide him with such goods as a horse and a slave, and he is treated like any other poor person.[9] This opinion interprets the rule as limited to the protection of the impoverished person from the shame resulting from a loss of status. Thus, only the outward signs of status, such as a servant and a horse, must be addressed by providers of *tsedakah*, in order to allow the poor to hide their condition.[10] Such a

---

9. This opinion is quoted in the name of the *ge'onim* in R. Betzalel Ashkenazi, *Shitah mekubetset* on BT *Ket.* 67b.

10. Me'iri's formulation in relation to the story of Ukba is similarly sensitive to the concerns of shame: 'Even though we see a poor man who maintains himself at a high standard, this should not be a reason to avoid giving to him. On the contrary, we should extend our giving, since it is possible that such a poor person is concerned with his pedigree and status, and he is not living in such a lavish manner for the sake of pleasure, but by way of social elevation in order to hide his poverty from human beings' (*Beit habeḥirah* on BT *Ket.* 67b, s.v. *af al pi*). The parallel to the story of Ukba in the Jerusalem Talmud seems to provide a different reasoning: 'Aba bar Ba gave his son Shmuel money to distribute to the poor. He went and found one poor person eating meat and drinking wine. He came back and told his father. His father said to him: "Give him more since his pain is great"' (JT *Pe'ah* 8: 9, 21b). The

restrictive reading of the rule might also be supported by the fact that public knowledge of someone's dire economic condition may harm his prospect of recovery. This reading was not accepted by mainstream halakhah, which rightly interpreted the scope of the rule of addressing subjective needs as extending beyond the mere concern with shame and loss of status. As we saw in the stories above, it relates to habits and special needs. Providing a devoted musician with a well-tuned violin might be an expression of such sensitivity to unique loss and deprivation, which is ignored by generalized and impersonal definitions of the poverty line.

In analysing the mediaeval and later halakhic discussions of this principle, one particular controversy – between Maimonides and Rabbi Moses Isserles – emerges as immensely significant to contemporary debates on distributive justice and moral theory. The great sixteenth-century Ashkenazi scholar of Krakow, Rabbi Moses Isserles, upon reaching this ruling in his critical annotations to the *Shulḥan arukh*, made the following important remark:

> It seems that this ruling [concerning subjective need] pertains to the communal officer responsible for the allocation of *tsedakah* [*gabai tsedakah*] or to the public. But an individual is not obligated to provide the poor with what he [subjectively] lacks. He should rather inform the public of the poor's deprivation, and if there are no other people with him, the individual must provide for him if he can afford it.[11]

Rabbi Moses Isserles seems to add a reasonable reservation. Addressing such particular and sometimes expensive needs ought to be the domain of the public fund that has the resources for allocating such sums, as well as the means of inquiring into the unique conditions of the supplicant. The individual giver, encountering the poor, has to address

---

practice of doubling the supply to the poor was justified in this source as an attempt to comfort the poor person because of his miserable condition. It reflects a recognition that sometimes people who live in poverty might spend a lot on a particular purchase in order to provide immediate short-term relief from their mental stress.

11. Gloss on *Shulḥan arukh*, 'Yoreh de'ah' 250: 1.

only basic common needs of destitution and deprivation without being burdened with such costs.

Rabbi Isserles' view has its roots in sensitivity to the potentially overwhelming claim of a particular pain that ought not to be laid at the door of the individual donor. It is a striking position, since it stands against the simple reading of the talmudic text, a problem that was noted by some commentators who questioned Rabbi Isserles' position. The precedents and stories mentioned in the Talmud concerning such a practice pertain to individual givers such as Hillel, Ukba, and others. These individual scholars did not seem to address the poor as official representatives of the public communal fund; they acted as individuals.[12] Rabbi Isserles' reservation forced him to reread the Talmud as relating to a situation in which these individual providers had no opportunity to appeal to the public for support; only under such unique conditions were they required to address them alone.[13] Such a problematic reading of the authoritative text is proof of the pressing problem that was posed by the principle.

Maimonides presents a radically different position concerning the relation of the individual giver and the public funds in addressing subjective needs. In order fully to appreciate Maimonides' line of thinking, it is worthwhile to clarify the general way in which he organized the laws of *tsedakah* in his *Mishneh torah* code. The Torah obligates each individual to provide for the poor, yet there are no laws in the biblical material that aim at establishing institutional communal structures for care of the poor. The talmudic literature treated the nature of individual obligation in detail, and also developed a body of rules that established a full-fledged welfare community. It legislated norms of taxation, and defined the rules pertaining to the conduct and role of those officials responsible for collecting and distributing public funds. *Tsedakah* was, therefore, understood by the Talmud as a two-track obligation: an

---

12. See the criticism of R. Yoel Sirkis, *Bayit ḥadash*, 'Yoreh de'ah' 250:2, and the opinion of Eliyahu b. Shlomoh, the Vilna Gaon, *Hagahot hagra* on *Shulḥan arukh*, 'Yoreh de'ah' 250:3.

13. See the defence of R. Moses Isserles' position in R. Shabetai ben Me'ir Hakohen, *Siftei kohen*, 'Yoreh de'ah' 250:1.

individual obligation of each towards his or her fellow human being, and a communally-shared burden of caring for the vulnerable and the poor. The Talmud was well aware of cases in which these obligations might overlap, and addressed the question of the relationship between individual duty and collective responsibility.[14]

Maimonides deals separately with the individual dimension and the collective one. He begins his treatment of *tsedakah* with the individual obligation, and, after two chapters, shifts to the collective responsibility:

> In every city where Jews live, they are obligated to appoint faithful men of renown as trustees of a charitable fund. They should circulate among the people from Friday to Friday and take from each person what is appropriate for him to give and the assessment made upon him. They then allocate the money from Friday to Friday, giving each poor person sufficient food for seven days. This is called the *kupah*.
>
> Similarly, we appoint trustees who take bread, different types of food, fruit, or money from every courtyard from those who make a spontaneous donation, and divide what was collected among the poor in the evening, giving each poor person sustenance for that day. This is called the *tamhui*.
>
> We have never seen nor heard of a Jewish community that does not have a *kupah* for charity. A *tamhui*, by contrast, exists in some communities, but not in others. The common practice at present is that the trustees of the *kupah* circulate [among the

---

14. The question of such overlap emerges when the poor approach people individually for charity and the collective fund provides for them as well. See Tosefta *Pe'ah* 4: 8; BT *BB* 9a. It is no surprise that the wealthy members of the community would like to stress the individual obligation, and the middle class would prefer an organized progressive taxation for the purpose of welfare that would ease their own individual obligation. Such a communal clash is reported in Rashba, *Responsa* (vol. 3, 280). Rashba ruled that progressive taxation of the rich for the sake of welfare ought to be the rule, rather than leaving the matter of charity to individual initiative and good will. See also the interesting opinion of R. Moshe Feinstein, *Iggerot mosheh*, 'Yoreh de'ah' 1:149.

community and collect] every day and divide [the proceeds] every Friday.[15]

In these sections, Maimonides describes the communal responsibility and its basic institutional structure. The previous two chapters, however, are directed to the individual and his obligations, and they start with the following formulations:

> It is a positive commandment to give charity to the poor among the Jewish people, according to what is appropriate for the poor person if this is within the financial capacity of the donor, as [Deuteronomy 15:5] states: 'You shall certainly open your hand to him'. [Leviticus 25:5] states: 'You shall support him, a stranger and a resident and they shall live with you', and [Leviticus 25:36] states: 'And your brother shall live with you'.
>
> Anyone who sees a poor person asking and turns his eyes away from him and does not give him charity transgresses a negative commandment, as [Deuteronomy 15:7] states: 'Do not harden your heart or close your hand against your brother, the poor person'.
>
> You are commanded to give a poor person according to what he lacks. If he lacks clothes, we should clothe him. If he lacks household utensils, we should purchase them for him. If he is unmarried, we should help him marry. And for an unmarried woman, we should find a husband for her. Even if the personal habit of this poor person was to ride on a horse and to have a servant run before him and then he became impoverished and lost his wealth, we should buy a horse for him to ride and a servant to run before him. [This is implied by Deuteronomy 15:8 which] speaks [of providing him with] 'sufficient for his need in that which he wanteth'. You are commanded to fill his lack, but you are not obligated to enrich him.[16]

---

15. Maimonides, *Mishneh torah*, 'Hilkhot matenot aniyim' 9:1–3 (trans. Eliyahu Touger).
16. Ibid. 7:1–3.

In contrast to the later ruling of Rabbi Moses Isserles, it is clear that Maimonides makes the individual giver responsible for the subjective needs of the other. Maimonides postulates this definition of need before mentioning the communal fund and structure, and according to his opinion, the duty of *tsedakah* upon each individual encompasses caring for the needs of the poor in his particular situation, with sensitivity to his past habits and status. On the other hand, in the following chapter, which Maimonides devotes to communal structures of welfare, there is no mention of such an obligation to attend to subjective needs. The communal fund provides basic needs that each poor person deserves such as food, clothing, and shelter. The officials of the fund act as impersonal and general providers, focusing solely on an objective definition of needs. Maimonides therefore presents the opposite opinion to that espoused later by Rabbi Isserles. The subjective needs of the poor fall within the domain of the individual giver; they do not fall within the remit of communal obligation.

It seems that Maimonides' position has its source in a particular attitude towards the fundamental moral posture of the individual that addresses a fundamental philosophical concern with far-reaching implications. The question of the proper stance of the individual as a moral agent was raised in contemporary moral philosophy by Bernard Williams. Williams challenged the utilitarian maxim that moral and distributive decisions should be guided by the attempt to maximize overall utility. If, for example, an individual has resources that he plans to spend, utilitarians such as Bentham claim that he ought to spend them in a way that reflects a commitment to bringing the maximum happiness to the maximum number of people. Such a demand is based on a firm conception of equality that grants equal weight to each individual preference, a weight that has to be impartially assessed before acting. In following this utilitarian principle of impartiality, a person cannot spend money to buy his child a computer if he can instead use the money to buy clothing for ten poor children. He also ought not to invest in particular personal projects, such as cultivating literacy, when contributing to environmental change with that same investment would have resulted in greater overall utility. This basic principle of utilitarianism grants more weight to overall utility maximization than to agent-relative considerations in the moral calculus. Williams criticized such a norm, arguing that it undermines the integrity of the individual, since it prohibits him from pursuing the personal projects and aspirations which define his identity as a human being. Adopting such an impartial stance is wrong because it restricts our capacity to form the partial attachments and goals which are basic to the formation of genuine personal integrity.[17]

The debate between Maimonides and Rabbi Isserles concerning the way to address subjective needs triggers a more basic question concerning the impartial stance that does not relate to the problem of allowing space for individual partial projects and goals. Maimonides' ruling that it is the individual provider who must address the subjective needs of the poor implies a rejection of the idea that a moral agent has to adopt the impersonal and impartial moral point of view. When confronting the needs of an impoverished individual, which might be expensive, one should not act like an impersonal distributor who calculates the best overall use of the limited resources at his disposal in relation to global needs. Such an individual provider might spend a great sum of money in order to alleviate the chronic pain of someone who has appealed to him by helping him to buy expensive medicine, while realizing that the same amount of money given to Oxfam might maximize better the overall utility of his giving. This attitude rests on the conviction that a moral subject acting as an individual should address the subject whom he encounters, and that it would be morally wrong to pull out a calculator from his pocket before addressing such a need. The individual provider is not a distributive bureaucrat, but a subject confronting the pain and need of another subject.

The issue at stake is not the clash between the impersonal obligation and the capacity to form partial preferences and particular goals as raised by Williams. In providing for the subjective need of the other, the giver is not inclining towards his personal partial preferences or towards causes that are particularly dear to his heart. He is, rather, resisting the impersonal posture while embracing and responding to the actual relationship formed between him and the poor person whom he has

---

17. J.J.C. Smart and B. Williams, *Utilitarianism: For and Against* (Cambridge: Cambridge University Press, 1973), 108–17.

encountered. In this situation, it would be morally wrong for him to view himself as if he were an impersonal universal provider. The impersonal stance involves two different perspectives. The first, which is self-directed, demands that the moral agent assume an impartial and impersonal position, while transcending his own preferences and goals; the second is other-directed, expecting an impersonal attitude towards the claims of others. Williams challenged the first self-directed impartial stance; our discussion poses a challenge to the other-directed impersonal stance. The impersonal stance of justice is not always appropriate. The denial of the exclusivity of the impersonal stance is not only a challenge to the impartial general way of proper allocation of resources; it is also the denial of seeing the individual pain one confronts as a mere instance of a general obligation towards addressing the pain of others. The particular encounter itself, and the ensuing relationship that it creates, generate their own moral force.

On the other hand, following Maimonides' position, officials who are responsible for allocating communal resources must adopt the larger impersonal perspective. In providing for needs, they have to take into account the limited resources, the needs of the rest of the poor, and the hierarchy among such needs.[18] An individual, when acting as an official qua public figure, has an impartial obligation that stems from his particular institutional role and commitment. He would be betraying such a trust if he were to adopt the relational subjective stance when encountering the needs of others. It is for this reason that, while Maimonides obligates the individual giver to provide for subjective needs, no such expectation is raised in his dealing with the public fund.

It is a shortcoming of utilitarianism and some other moral theories that they call upon every individual to adopt an institutional posture by tying him to the impersonal general perspective. Maimonides' understanding, in opposition to Rabbi Isserles' ruling, seems to be sensitive to the interpersonal quality of such an encounter, and to the radical

---

18. The adoption of the impersonal stance by the communal fund does not necessarily assume taking into account global needs of all the poor in the world. It could be that, given certain associational obligations, it will rightfully restrict itself to the needs of its own community.

difference that is required when taking a personal, as opposed to an institutional, stance. The proper moral stance of justice in addressing the needs of others is therefore layered and contextual. In different roles, different postures will be adopted and different distributive policies and decisions will be called for.

Chapter 7

Access to Justice in Jewish Financial Law: The Case of Returning Lost Property

Michael J. Broyde

I. INTRODUCTION

Access to justice and theories of legal exclusion are among the most difficult of ideas for those outside any given legal system to grasp. They

---

In describing the quality that makes a Jewish sage, Rabbi Samson Raphael Hirsch writes, 'It is not by virtue of his knowledge that a man is recognized as being a Jewish sage, and it is not by means of his knowledge that he wins people's hearts to the Torah. The credential for his knowledge is the way he lives, and only a Godly way of living earns him the scepter of a herald of the Divine Word' (Samson Raphael Hirsch, *Collected Writings*, vol. 1 (New York: Feldheim, 1984), 315). Chief Rabbi Jonathan Sacks is recognized around the world as an ambassador for Jewry. He has won the hearts of all who hear his words, because he embodies the Torah that he teaches and he lives the Divine Word whose sceptre he holds. His sense of justice excludes no one, and his mission to return those who may be lost includes everyone. With deep respect and admiration, it is my honour to dedicate this article, regarding the obligation to return lost objects, to the Chief Rabbi.

appear to the foreigner as distinctly unfair, naked chauvinism by the system in favour of its own 'citizens'. Upon examination, however, one can see that all legal systems do in fact engage in some form or another of exclusion based on citizenship.[1]

Secular law is not alone; this article argues that in the area of financial rights, duties, and obligations, halakhah (Jewish law) frequently excluded gentiles from its full benefits. Ironically, because halakhah is an internally consistent system, wherein any exemption necessitates a corresponding loss of legal stature, it did so simply because it did not consider gentiles as bound by its obligations. Thus, for example, halakhah did not compel the return of the lost property of a gentile[2] precisely because he was not legally obligated to return the lost property of others. Exclusion was based on a failure of reciprocity – the privileges of halakhah were given only to those who were fully obligated in, and thus accepting of, halakhah, in this case the laws of lost property.

Halakhah rules that if a person loses an article in a location where most of the people are not legally obligated to return lost property (such as in an area where most people are gentiles), that person is assumed to have abandoned hope of ever reclaiming his object, and the item then belongs to the finder.[3] This is because halakhah assumes that gentiles do not return lost objects – they are not obligated to under halakhah and, indeed, halakhah posits that the typical gentile does not in *fact* do so, an assumption borne out by the common law's rule, which does not require one to stop and take possession of lost property.[4] Therefore, even

---

1. For example, the laws of the United States prohibit the ownership or operation of commercial fishing vessels under the American flag by non-American citizens. While the origin of this law might be based on security concerns, it is now used solely to ensure that certain economic opportunities go only to American citizens; see Catherine Bishop, '18th-Century Law Snares Vietnamese Fishermen', *New York Times*, 26 Nov. 1989, p. A1; anon., 'Of Citizens, and Poachers', *New York Times*, 18 Oct. 1989, p. A14.

2. See e.g. BT *BK* 113*b*, and R. Joseph Karo, *Shulḥan arukh*, 'Ḥoshen mishpat' 266:1.

3. *Shulḥan arukh*, 'Ḥoshen mishpat' 259:3.

4. R. Shlomo Yosef Y. Hunter (ed.), *Entsiklopediyah talmudit*, vol. 5 (Jerusalem, 1984), 359 (gentile); Shlomo Drimmer, *Teshuvot beit shelomoh* (Lvov, 1876), 'Oraḥ ḥayim' 57; Mordechai Gross, *Mishpat ha'avedah* (Benei Berak, 5742), introd., p. 11 and id., *Sha'arei tsedek: sefer mishpat ha'avedah* (Benei Berak, 1983), 47. If, in fact, most people

a Jewish loser of a lost object abandons hope for its return when he loses the object in such a community. Thus, because the Jewish person's lost object will most likely not be returned by the gentile, the Jewish person is not required to return the gentile's lost object.

The fairness of this rule can be demonstrated by a simple model of four possible societies:

(1) a society where all observe halakhah's rules in the area of lost objects, and return all property that is lost;

(2) a society where none observe halakhah's rules in this area, whether because they are not required to do so by non-Jewish law or by halakhah, or because they simply do not do so in practice;

(3) a society where 30% of the people observe halakhah's rules in this area;

(4) a society where 70% of the people observe halakhah's rules in this area.

In society (1) all lost, non-abandoned objects are returned to their owners. Integrated over time, all are treated equally, as everyone loses objects and everyone finds and returns them. In society (2), no lost objects are returned to their owners; either the owner finds them, or abandonment occurs and another finds them and keeps them. Integrated over time, all are treated equally, as everyone loses objects and everyone finds them.

In society (3) an injustice occurs if the 30% have to return the lost objects of all members of the population. Those 30% who faithfully return lost objects would not have their objects returned to them, while those 70% who do not return lost objects would benefit from the conduct of the 30%. The halakhic ruling in this case has two aspects:

returned such property, halakhah would not assume that one abandons hope of return upon losing property in a place where a majority of the people are gentiles. See Michael Broyde and Michael Hecht, 'The Return of Lost Property According to Jewish and Common Law: A Comparison', *Journal of Law and Religion*, 12 (1996), 225–54.

(A) one does not have to return the lost objects of people not legally obligated to return lost objects belonging to others; and,

(B) in an environment where *most* people do not return lost objects, one may assume that the person who loses property in such a society immediately abandons any hope of recovery, and thus the finder may keep the object.

In effect, these two rules turn society (3) into society (2), a society where no one returns lost objects to anyone. This second rule is needed just so as to release the 30% from the normal obligation found in halakhah to pick up these objects and to search for their true owners.

In society (4) an injustice also occurs, as the 70% who faithfully return lost objects would not have their objects returned to them by the 30%, while those 30% who do not return lost objects would benefit from the conduct of the 70%. In this society, halakhah accepts only the first rule promulgated in society (3), and maintains that one is not obligated to return the lost object of a person who does not feel obligated to return objects to others. This does not completely solve the 'free-rider' problem, as the 30% still benefit from the 70% who pick up lost property, advertise its loss, and return it to any who can prove original ownership. However, since most of society adheres to the 'rule of return', no other solution is reasonable. (Furthermore, while I have no data to support this claim, I suspect that in a society where 70% of the population returns lost objects, the members of this majority will harness the legislative process to compel the other 30% to adopt this rule.)

In sum, there is no fair way to run a society in the absence of reciprocal obligations or reciprocal non-obligations.

II. MONOTHEISTIC GENTILES

This, then, is the starting point of halakhah in this arena; no obligation is imposed on the Jew to restore the lost property of a gentile, or vice versa. Although at first glance one might be uncomfortable with this rule, as we have demonstrated above, in reality a strong case can be made that any other rule would have been bad jurisprudence and unworkable in practice. A legal system's civil law does not exist in the abstract. If the system is to promote justice, those who would benefit by its privileges must also accept its duties. Justice is not served if the burdens fall on one group and the advantages on another. It would be patently unfair to compel the return of lost property of another in the absence of the ability to compel reciprocity by the loser in the future. Proof of the fact that reciprocity (and not religious identity) is the legal key can be found in the fact that halakhah does not compel returning the lost property even of a Jew who deliberately declines to observe halakhah. This is because such a Jew lacks legal fidelity to the system, and would not necessarily accept as binding the halakhic rules that require one to take possession of and return lost property.[5] This case is to be distinguished from the talmudic ruling that 'one must return the lost object of a Jew, even if he is a sinner and eats non-kosher food when he succumbs to temptation.'[6] That passage is understood by nearly all of the commentaries as limited to the (occasional) non-ideological viola-tor of halakhah[7] who, when given the option of easily complying with Jewish halakhah, does so. This is someone who returns lost property to others as mandated by halakhah, even if he is not always entirely faith-ful to the Jewish dietary guidelines. Were this a Jew who announces that he does not return lost property to others, there would be no obligation to return his lost property; in that sense, he would be no different from a gentile who also does not feel bound by the halakhic requirements.[8]

---

5. *Shulḥan arukh*, 'Ḥoshen mishpat' 266:2.
6. Ibid.
7. See R. Menahem Me'iri, *Beit habeḥirah* on BT AZ, 26b; *Shulḥan arukh*, 'Ḥoshen mishpat' 266:1–2, and 'Yoreh de'ah' 151:1–2 and commentaries ad loc. See, particu-larly, the remarks of R. Moshe Sofer, *Ḥatam sofer* 6:67 (letters), R. Avraham Yitshak Kook, *Da'at kohen*, 'Yoreh de'ah' 8, and R. Eliezer Waldenberg, *Tsits eli'ezer* 8:18, all of whom reach this conclusion. This formulation forces one to accept that the state-ment of R. Karo (*Shulḥan arukh*, 'Ḥoshen mishpat' 266:2) requiring one to return property to a morally weak violator is limited to an occasional violator who remains loyal to halakhah even while sometimes violating it. It would not be applicable to a continuous public violator; this would be consistent with the ruling of R. Karo in *Shulḥan arukh*, 'Yoreh de'ah' 151:1–2.
8. I would also make the claim that, conversely, a gentile who thinks he is a Jew, and conducts himself as if he is bound by halakhah and thus returns lost property to Jews, must have his lost property returned to him. I am not aware of any discussion of this exact case in halakhic sources, but a close examination of R. Moshe Feinstein's letter

The general rule is expressed in its simplest form by Rabbi Eliezer Memitz (twelfth century), in his *Sefer yere'im*. He states:

> If a Jew deliberately sins in any of the commandments found in the Torah and does not repent, one is not obligated to preserve his life or to lend him money, since it states 'your brother shall live' and regarding loans it states 'one of your brothers [you shall lend to]' [Leviticus 25:36–7]. Once one sins deliberately one leaves the status of brother, since brotherhood means brotherhood in observance of the commandments.[9]

Indeed, a wide range of commentaries accept this approach.[10] Thus, the status of 'brother' appears to be limited to a Jewish[11] person who is generally observant of halakhah. One who routinely violates halakhah – even if he does so for non-ideological reasons – loses his status of 'one's brother'[12] even as he remains a full Jew for the purposes of many other laws within Judaism.[13]

To clarify, it is my view that a casual violator of halakhah for non-ideological reasons is still a fellow-Jew entitled to all the rights and privi-

---

(dated 26 Sivan 5444, shortly before his death, and soon to be published in the final volume of *Iggerot mosheh*, which is widely available on the internet) concerning the obligation to rescue Ethiopian Jewry indicates that he was of that view.

9. R. Eliezer Memitz, *Sefer yere'im* (Benei Berak, 2003), 156.

10. See *Teshuvot maimoniyot* on *Sefer mishpatim*, 36; R. Shabetai Hakohen (Shakh), *Siftei kohen*, 'Yoreh de'ah' 159:6, 251:1–2; 'Ḥoshen mishpat' 388:62; R. David Halevi (Taz), *Turei zahav*, 'Yoreh de'ah' 251:1; *Teshuvot rabenu ḥayim or zarua*, 116; Tosafot BT AZ 26b s.v. *ani* (one possibility); R. Nisson Aaronson, *Atsei levonah* (Zitmar: Isaac Moshe Baksht, 1870), 'Yoreh de'ah' 151:1.

11. See e.g. *Entsiklopediyah talmudit*, 1:434, which states without dispute that 'A gentile is not in the category of brother.'

12. R. Moshe Isserles, gloss on *Shulḥan arukh*, 'Yoreh de'ah' 251:2, comments of Shakh on this paragraph and comments of R. Moshe ben Yosef of Trani, *Teshuvot mabit* (Venice, 1689), 37; but see R. Avraham Karelitz, *Ḥazon ish*, 'Yoreh de'ah' 2:28. This person would be the equivalent of the monotheistic gentile for the laws of lost property – it is permissible to return his lost object, but it is not obligatory.

13. Thus, for example, the marriage of a Jew who is not a 'brother' is completely valid; see e.g. R. Eliezer Memitz, *Sefer yere'im hashalem*, ed. Yosef Rafa'el Hazon (Jerusalem, 1980), 156.

leges of being a member of the community. However, if he stops observing the reciprocal obligations of Jewish commercial law – for example, he does not return lost property to its rightful owner when required to by halakhah – then one is not required to return his lost property either (even though without a doubt he would still count in a prayer quorum and otherwise be 'Jewish'). Commercial law has to focus on reciprocity and not identity, even while other areas of halakhah focus on identity.

This theory of reciprocity can also find support from Rabbi Moshe Isserles' (1520–72) statement in his gloss on the *Shulḥan arukh* of Rabbi Joseph Karo (1488–1575), where he states that in a society where the general secular law (binding on all citizens) requires that one return lost property to its owner under all circumstances, halakhah, through the principle of 'the law of the land is the law', also requires that one do so.[14] It seems that, at least according to this approach, the governmental decision to mandate the return of lost property creates a general, *reciprocal*, obligation to do so according to halakhah as well. This makes it clear that the cardinal principle governing halakhic rules in this area is legal reciprocity. One must return the property of all who are legally compelled to return the lost property of others. Similar sentiments can be found in the writings of Rabbi Isser Zalman Meltzer (1870–1953), who states:

> It is obvious that the return of lost property…is subject to the laws of the land [*dina demalkhuta*] and the reason for this is that the decree made by the government is not contrary to halakhah…. Thus this matter is subject to the law of the king and under the rubric of 'Noahides obligated in laws [*dinim*]' since Noahides are also obligated to decree laws based on fairness and not theft or fraud.[15]

This, then, is one approach. There are, however, some authorities who rule that the talmudic rule exempting one from returning the lost property of a gentile applies only to idolatrous pagans and not to those

---

14. Isserles, gloss on *Shulḥan arukh*, 'Ḥoshen mishpat' 259:7.

15. R. Isser Zalman Meltzer, *Even ha'azel: hilkhot ḥovel umazik* (Jerusalem, 1975), 8:5, commenting on Maimonides, *Mishneh torah*, 'Nizkei mamon' 8:5.

gentiles who accept a monotheistic deity. The most complete statement of this position is that of Rabbi Menahem Me'iri, who lived in Provence during the fourteenth century:

> Whoever belongs to the nations which are disciplined by religio-moral principles and are worshippers of the Deity in some way, although the dogmas of their faith are far removed from those of ours … is like a full Israelite in respect of the law of lost property and of all such matters without any distinction whatsoever.[16]

So too, Rabbi Judah Hehasid (d. 1217) states that a gentile who accepts the seven Noahide commandments is to be treated as a 'brother' in regard to the law of lost property.[17]

However, as has been noted by Rabbi J. David Bleich,[18] Me'iri's opinion contains two distinct insights. The first is that gentiles of his day are not considered idol worshippers but rather are monotheists, even though their faith is not completely monotheistic. The second is that such a person is within the parameters of one's 'brother' for the purpose of the laws of lost property. This second insight is very difficult to accept, as the simple understanding of the Talmud is that Jewishness is a necessary (but not sufficient) requirement for 'brotherliness'.[19] Thus, even if one accepted without reservation Me'iri's theological insight, it provides no logical proof for the proposition that monotheistic gentiles have the status of 'brother' in halakhah. As cogently noted by Rabbi Bleich, the Tosafists reached the same conclusion as Me'iri concerning the status of the contemporary Christians as non-idol worshippers, without

---

16. Me'iri, *Beit habeḥirah* on *AZ* 2b; quoted in R. Betsalel Ashkenazi, *Shitah mekubetset* on BT *BK* 113b and translated in R. Yitshak Halevi Herzog, *Main Institutions of Jewish Law* (London: Soncino Press, 1980), p. 393 n. 2.

17. R. Judah Hehasid, *Sefer ḥasidim*, §355. See also the commentaries of R. Reuven Margalit, *Mekor ḥesed* (Jerusalem, 1958), R. Abraham Price, *Mishnat avraham* (Toronto, 1957), and R. Hayim Benevisti, *Keneset hagedolah* (Jerusalem, 1964) on *Sefer ḥasidim*.

18. J. David Bleich, 'Divine Unity in Maimonides, the Tosafists and Meiri', in Lenn E. Goodmann (ed.), *Neoplatonism and Jewish Thought* (Albany, NY: SUNY Press, 1992), 237–54.

19. BT *BK* 113b.

even considering the possibility that this gave them the legal status of 'brother'.[20] Indeed, Rabbi Isserles, and many other normative halakhic authorities, have little difficulty accepting the possibility that the opinion of Tosafot is correct without ever reaching the insight of Me'iri that such gentiles are 'brothers' for legal purposes.[21]

The recently published uncensored version of Rabbi Joseph Karo's *Beit yosef* clearly rejects Me'iri's second insight. Commenting on Rabbi Jacob ben Asher's (*c*.1269–*c*.1340) apparent assertion in his *Arba'ah turim* that one is not obligated to return lost property only in the case of an idol worshipper, Rabbi Karo states:

> It is obvious that all gentiles are the same for this law [in that one does not have to return their lost property] whether they worship idols or they do not, since they are not one's 'brother'. The reason [Rabbi Jacob ben Asher] wrote 'idol worshippers' is not mentioned specifically. It is possible that in the Edomite[22] lands the Jews were oppressed by the king because of this law or the like, and thus the wise men of Israel replied that this phrase was used by the writers of the Talmud to denote worshippers of idols who denied the single Creator of the world, but gentiles of this day who accept the existence of a single Creator do not have this status.[23]

In short, Rabbi Karo thinks that Me'iri's ruling that Jews must return the lost property of gentiles who are pious monotheists was apologetic, and written solely for the benefit of the antisemitic rulers of Christian Europe.

An additional factor inclining one to accept that Me'iri's point cannot mean what it literally claims to state – that one must return the lost property of all monotheistic gentiles – is that Me'iri himself, in his explanation of BT *Ketubot* 15*b*, asserts that the talmudic rules allowing

---

20. See Tosafot on BT *Bek.* 2*b* and BT *San.* 63*b*.
21. Isserles, gloss on *Shulḥan arukh*, 'Oraḥ ḥayim' 156:1; see Bleich, 'Divine Unity in Maimonides', 239–42.
22. This must be a synonym for Christian countries.
23. Karo, *Beit yosef*, 'Ḥoshen mishpat' 261:1 (in the Makhon Yerushalayim edition of *Tur*).

discrimination against gentiles in certain financial situations are limited to those gentiles whose laws of liability are not the same as halakhic rules. However, adds Me'iri, if the law is the same and the obligations are reciprocal, then there is no difference in treatment according to halakhah. Given Me'iri's inclination in this case to focus on reciprocity, it is difficult to accept that he would impose the obligation to return lost property *without a reciprocal obligation.*[24]

Whether or not Me'iri's assertion concerning returning lost property is authentic or the result of censorship, it is conceptually unrelated to the correctness of his first insight, namely that Christianity is a monotheistic religion. Even accepting the correctness of that insight, it is very difficult to rule that just because Christians are ethical monotheists, they must therefore have their lost objects returned. Rabbi Karo could not even consider the possibility that there was an authentic opinion within halakhah that considers a monotheistic gentile to be a brother, thus directing that his lost property be returned. It is also important to realize that Rabbi Karo clearly *did* consider the opinion of the Tosafists, that some contemporary gentiles were monotheists, to be tenable.[25]

Perhaps the reason nearly all authorities rejected this rule *obligating* one to return the lost property of a gentile – even for pious gentiles who clearly are monotheistic worshippers and fully in compliance with halakhah's understanding of the proper conduct for a gentile – is because of the theoretical problem of reciprocity; one cannot run a legal system equating the legal obligation of a Jew to a fellow Jew with the obligations of a Jew to a pious gentile and a pious gentile to a Jew. Such an approach can be found in Rashi's commentary on the Talmud,[26] which clearly focuses on the issue of reciprocity and the problem of one who harmonizes the obligations of halakhah to return lost property to a 'brother'. This can also be inferred from Maimonides' classification

---

24. One could thus understand Me'iri concerning lost property in a completely different light. One could argue that he is referring to 'nations which are disciplined by religio-moral principles and are worshippers of the Deity in some way', who also return lost property as a matter of religious belief or secular law.
25. Karo, *Beit yosef*, 'Oraḥ ḥayim' 156 and 'Yoreh de'ah' 147.
26. Rashi on BT *Ket.* 15*b*, s.v. *lehazkir avedah.*

of the commandments to return lost property.[27] Reciprocity was the guiding principle of most early authorities. Indeed, one is logically directed to accept the assertion of Rabbi Moshe Sofer (1762–1839) and the inclination of Rabbi Bleich, which is that Me'iri's view on this issue was placed in the text to placate the censor, and is not authentic even within the opinion of Me'iri[28] – even as Me'iri's opinion concerning the monotheistic nature of Christianity is authentic to Me'iri. Certainly that was the opinion of Rabbi Karo.

A different approach to Me'iri's point is also possible, although it is difficult to read this approach into his exact words. This approach further supports the basic theory of reciprocity. Maybe Me'iri's view is only that ethical monotheistic gentiles are entitled to have their property returned when they too return lost property belonging to all, and Me'iri is merely reinforcing the idea that ethical gentiles are no different from Jews; only if they agree to return lost property does their lost property need to be returned. The unstated sentence of course is that ethical monotheistic gentiles are no better than ethical monotheistic Jews – if they do not agree to return the lost property of others, their own lost property need not be returned.

III. SANCTIFICATION OF GOD'S NAME AND DESECRATION OF GOD'S NAME

So far, this article has addressed the rules relating to the return of lost property of a gentile independent of any rules not relating specifically to lost property. The practical operation of these basic rules is curtailed by the operation of two fundamental principles of halakhah unrelated to the rules of lost property: profanation of God's name, and sanctification of God's name. The former is the grave sin of causing people to think ill of God, Jews, and Judaism, and the latter is the commandment to sanctify God's name and Judaism.

---

27. See Maimonides, *Mishneh torah*, 'Hilkhot gezelah ve'avedah' 11:1, 3.
28. See R. Moshe Sofer, *Kovets she'elot uteshuvot ḥatam sofer*, 90, and J. David Bleich, 'One Who Has Circumcised But Not Immersed', in *Contemporary Halakhic Problems*, IV (New York: KTAV/Yeshiva University Press, 1995) 145–71.

The Talmud,[29] immediately following the passage which imposes no duty of restoration of the gentile's lost property, quotes the statement of Rabbi Pinhas son of Yair: 'Whenever the danger of causing a desecration of God's name exists, even the retaining of a lost article [of the gentile] is forbidden.' Both Maimonides and the *Shulḥan arukh* incorporate this statement into halakhah as limiting the general rule, and requiring one to return such property.[30] Moreover, the *Shulḥan arukh* states that the return of a gentile's lost property where such an act would be likely to result in sanctification of God's name, reflecting credit upon the Jew and his faith, merits the highest religious praise. In a situation where the gentile's property is going to be destroyed, rather than lost, halakhah imposes an obligation to salvage the property based on proper manners in a civilized society, a lower-level principle.[31]

Even the rules of sanctification or desecration of God's name have a clear element of reciprocity in them. A Jew who does not return the lost property of another, in a situation where halakhah allows the finder to keep the property, does not create a desecration of God's name in a society where no one returns lost objects, as no one will even notice the action or lack thereof – it is the norm. The desecration occurs when a Jew does not return an object in a situation where such objects are generally returned, or are encouraged to be returned, by society at large. This is reciprocity, in a way; it desecrates God's name to behave in a manner perceived to be less moral than the society one lives in. Indeed, one sanctifies God's name only when one returns lost objects in a situation where society looks on it as morally proper to do so, which is a form of reciprocity, as society would encourage the return of all such property.

IV. CONCLUSION

One can now fully comprehend the importance that personal status and reciprocity play in the halakhah of lost property. The unmodified talmudic rule for the property of a person who does not consider him-

---

29. BT BK 113b.
30. Maimonides, *Mishneh torah*, 'Hilkhot gezelah ve'avedah' 11: 3; *Shulḥan arukh*, 'Ḥoshen mishpat' 266:1.
31. *Shulḥan arukh*, 'Ḥoshen mishpat' 266:1.

self bound by halakhah is that one is under no obligation to return the lost property of such a person, since that person – honest as he might be – does not consider himself reciprocally legally obligated to return lost property to another. Halakhah ruled that one may – but need not – return this property anyway, just as the other may – but need not – return a legally bound Jew's property. Conversely, in the case of a person who does consider himself bound by halakhah to return lost property, one is obligated to return the property of such a person precisely because the person feels legally obligated to do the same. Indeed, the same rule is true for the lost property of a person who is legally bound according to secular law to return lost property to others. In that case, halakhah would require that his property be returned, as he would do the same to the property of a Jew.[32]

---

32. This must flow logically from R. Isserles' assertion that the laws of the land bind one to return lost property even in situations where its return is not compelled by halakhah; see Isserles' gloss on *Shulḥan arukh*, 'Ḥoshen mishpat' 259:7. It is analytically impossible to assert that R. Isserles means that the principle of abiding by the laws of the land requires that one return property to a Jew and not to a Noahide, as there can be no instance where this principle is a binding principle that governs Jew-Jew relations and not Jew-Noahide relations. The very essence of obeying the laws of the land would otherwise be destroyed.

Section III

Religion and Contemporary Society

Chapter 8

The Space of Exchange

Charles Taylor

Those who are confident in their faith are not threatened but enlarged by the different faith of others.'[1] I believe that this articulates a profound truth, of which there are many to be found in the work of Jonathan Sacks. I want to seize the occasion of this work in homage to him to try to embroider on this truth. I want to say why I find this claim convincing, in spite of what appears paradoxical in it.

This will be in part an account of how I came to believe this, first as a felt intuition, and then gradually with some articulated grounds (although I still have a long way to go on this score). So it will verge on the autobiographical, and since I am a Catholic Christian, it will also reflect this provenance. But I think this meshes well with one of Jonathan Sacks's central points, that we approach the transcendent, which we both call God, by rather different itineraries.

---

1. Jonathan Sacks, *The Dignity of Difference* (New York: Continuum, rev. edn. 2003), 65–6.

We have to start off recognizing that many will find the claim Jonathan Sacks makes in this statement very paradoxical, if not downright false. And the first thing we need to deal with is a (modern, Western, secular) misprision about religious faith, which is seen as just another word for 'belief', or perhaps for 'belief on rather slender evidence'. In the latter sense, it is in contrast to 'know': I know that $2 + 2 = 4$, but I believe that the present recession will not last many years (more perhaps as a matter of hope than of evidence). In this context, one could argue that the difference between believing and knowing is ultimately a matter of confidence. I have total confidence that $2 + 2 = 4$, and at that point my belief graduates to knowledge.

But now, if you feed this interpretation of faith (i.e. that it equals 'belief' in this sense) into Jonathan Sacks's claim, then it comes out something like: the things I really know are not shaken by the different beliefs of others, which is quite psychologically understandable but also clearly implies that these other beliefs aren't worth much. It hardly expresses the ecumenical openness which Jonathan Sacks espouses here.

How did this misprision arise in our Western history? We see it already with (what we can roughly call) the Deism of the seventeenth and eighteenth centuries. True religion was rational: one could reason to the existence of a wise and benevolent Creator from the existence of the world, and one could reason to the content of His law (which could also be called Natural Law[2]) from the obvious needs of human beings. Other, less acceptable religions demanded that one believe other matters (like God giving a Law on Sinai, or a man who was God) which could not be established by reason. So your religion was a matter of what you believed, rather than the rituals or practices you engaged in, or the things you hoped for. This grid of interpretation was then applied to non-Western religions with the predictable distortion.

The last and most absurd consequence of this misprision can be found in the arguments of today's angry atheists, where the core of biblical monotheism is thought to lie in the demand that one espouse

---

2. See John Locke, *Second Treatise of Civil Government*, ch. 2, section 6, in id., *Locke's Two Treatises of Government*, ed. Peter Laslett, 2nd edn. (Cambridge: Cambridge University Press, 1967), 288–9.

certain weird hypotheses about the origins of the world supposedly inspired by Genesis 1. And the surprising and distressing thing is that some people of faith are led to espouse the same view, and to assemble 'proofs' of 'Creation science'.

Faith and belief are complexly related. A faith can be inseparably connected to certain claims of fact, like the Sinai event, or the historicity of Jesus, or the historicity of Gautama Buddha; but the faith can't be reduced to these. Faith (or belief *in*, rather than belief *that*) incorporates an anticipatory confidence or hope in some further transformation. To have faith is to be on a path. To have confidence in one's faith is to be confident that this path leads to a destination that one dimly descries.

This last clause is crucial. Religious faith, unlike my strong anticipatory confidence that the recession will soon be over, points us to a transformation that we very imperfectly understand. We may hope and aspire to understand it better, but now we only see 'through a glass darkly' (1 Corinthians 13).

For some proposition that I believe in the ordinary sense, we could say that my confidence in it would be the greater the less doubt I feel about it. But with faith, the matter is quite different. Faith, even confident faith, doesn't exclude doubt. It may, indeed, even call for it, in the following sense. If we aspire to move beyond our very imperfect understanding of God (speaking now in a monotheistic context) and of what it means to be close to God, then we may find that the principal obstacle in our path is too great a credence in certain received images of God (the all-powerful avenger of transgressors of His will, or the too-distant Father who cannot really hear us, and so on). To borrow an expression from Wittgenstein (in another, but not wholly different context), a 'picture is holding us captive'.[3] To move forward in the path of faith is to get beyond these images, and for this, the solvent of doubt may be indispensable. A confident, strong faith is one which can live in doubt; and worse than doubt: in a sense of separation from God, in

---

3. 'Ein Bild hielt uns gefangen', *Philosophical Investigations*, i, para 115. See the bilingual edition of *Philosophical Investigations*, trans. Elizabeth Anscombe (Oxford: Basil Blackwell, 1953), 48.

a dryness, a sense of abandonment, of unreachable distance separating us from Him.

One of the more comic misunderstandings of our contemporary world came to light after the death of Mother Teresa, when her diaries were published, and showed that she had been through long periods of dryness, of a sense of distance from God, which naturally are food for doubt. Contemporary journalists were startled. So she didn't believe after all! Surely, they won't canonize her now! For those who know the lives of the two great Teresas, of Avila and Lisieux, and of John of the Cross,[4] these experiences rather place her in their lineage.

People of course differ, as also do saints, but for a given individual, there may be no way to move forward in faith without facing doubt, even doubts which threaten to be crippling, and which seem to separate us from God. So let's get back to Jonathan Sacks's statement: that meeting the different faith of others doesn't need to threaten, but can enlarge our own faith. The meeting I'm talking about here is the kind of exchange (which can take place through reading, as well as through actual conversation) where we come to see what makes another's faith really powerful and inspiring for him or her. The attempt is to come to understand the fullness of the promise that another faith points to, to see it in its most convincing light.

This may of course lead to conversion. But it doesn't need to. On the contrary, it may greatly assist me in travelling my own path of faith, for a number of reasons. The first is a negative one, that this kind of encounter can remove obstacles. One of the things we are all tempted to do when we suffer doubt about our own faith is to reflect: well at least I'm not subscribing to an absurd, irrational, inhuman, violent creed like those Christians (or Jews, or Muslims, or Bolshevik atheists, etc.). The trick is to start off from a caricature of the possible alternative to which

---

4. Teresa of Avila, Spanish Carmelite reformer of the 16th-cent.; St John of the Cross (1542–97), a Spanish priest, poet, and mystic, who was a follower of Teresa, originator of the expression 'the dark night of the soul'; Thérèse de Lisieux (1873–97), a French nun who was inspired by Teresa of Avila.

one's faith is contrasted, and a rosy picture of one's own, and then one can feel the confidence in one's own option flooding back into one's depleted soul. Things are even better if the deficient other is painted as the opponent of one's own faith, so that one is showing devotion to this latter in maximally maligning, even perhaps attacking the Other. This is a variant of the well-known device whereby one stokes up one's own sense of purity by cranking up the repudiation, even persecution of the Other. For much of Western history, Jews were the scapegoats of choice serving Christian self-congratulation. Today, Islamophobia seems to be playing this role for Christians and secularists alike. We are constantly being told that real liberals are hostile to Muslims; the way to refurbish your liberal or feminist credentials is to shout ignorant calumnies of Islam.

This operation can only work if one operates with a caricature of the Other who is being used to restore our confidence. So we were told that Judaism was a kind of mindless legalism; and now we are told that Islam is inherently violent, and so on. The demeaning caricature of the Other works together with the idealized version of the self. The first is punctured by a real exchange with the Other, which aims to understand the fullness of the promise as he or she lives it. Once the exchange expands to include different perspectives on our common history, the idealized sense of self also begins to crumble.

This kind of exchange can have a liberating effect, in that it knocks away a crutch that can be used to shore up our confidence and still our doubts, whereas in fact, the way forward, the way to grow in faith, is to face and live through these doubts. This is the main negative benefit. It is a negation of a negation, if I can lapse into Hegel-speak for a moment.

But learning about the Other also has a positive content. We come to understand a new (to us) mode of spiritual life, where this term is used very broadly so as to include atheists and agnostics as well. And we may find this very impressive, powerful, even admirable. How to respond to this? At this point, it would help to stop talking in general terms, which become extremely cumbrous, just because faith positions are so different, and so I shall try to articulate the reaction as it naturally formulates itself for someone like me, a Catholic Christian.

To meet a Jew, a Buddhist, an agnostic, whose spiritual stance, faith, and/or struggle with this I find truly admirable, is to discover a fact about the world God made, that such lives are possible. This, of course, is something that couldn't happen according to certain traditional formulations of Catholic faith which I may have been brought up to accept. 'Extra ecclesiam, nulla salus' (There is no salvation outside the church) has often been given that gloss. But now I not only know that such people exist, I can see that they contribute to what I understand to be God's purpose in healing the world. (I am here jumping the track of strictly Catholic language and borrowing a Jewish term, *tikun olam*, mending the world. This kind of borrowing is one result of the encounters I am trying to describe, and I will return to this below).

I may see these people at work in overcoming long-standing rifts and mutual hostilities between different faith communities. I may even have met them in the course of one such common endeavour. This is a widespread experience in today's world, and is one of the positive fruits of the ecumenical spirit which has been growing in the last half-century.

Speaking from the Catholic perspective, this is a feature of the world God made, and of His work in healing it. It cannot be a faith-full response to deny it, or belittle it. It must be integrated into my faith.

This may happen in different ways. One is the negation of the negation I mentioned above, whereby I overcome the caricatures and stereotypes of the Other that I have been brought up on. There may be horrible and violence-prone ways of living this (to me, up to now) unfamiliar faith, as there are certainly distressingly violence-prone ways of living my own, but I no longer define the Other essentially by such negative forms. I can no longer repeat slogans like 'Islam is violent', while continuing, of course, to criticize sharply certain Muslim individuals and movements.

But beyond this, my sense of the spiritual landscape of our world and of God's work in it has been enlarged and this will lead me to see my faith in a new light. I may be led to borrow insights and forms of expression (as in my example of *tikun olam* above). Understanding Buddhist *karuna* (compassion) will make us understand *agapê* (Christian 'charity') in a new light. Or I may be led to integrate various disciplines, modes of meditation or prayer (as we see with John Main and the Christian Meditation movement he founded, which has been important in my life).[5]

But apart from such borrowings, I will have been made aware of a much richer variety of spiritual paths, and this has to enrich and enlarge my sense of the possible ways of being Christian. My understanding of the range of Christian vocations that have to come into communion in the Church will have been transformed by this exchange with the non-Christian Other. To understand and accept greater diversity outside is also to acknowledge a greater diversity within. My faith will have been, in Jonathan Sacks's term, 'enlarged'.

But those who feel the paradox in Jonathan Sacks's principle will want to object here. What if your admiration for the Other leads you simply to desert your own faith, and go over to theirs? In that case, you will have enlarged your views, but hardly your faith.

Of course, that can happen. No one can guarantee that encounter will not simply produce conversion. But this will seem a much more likely, even logical step, if one starts off with the view that an adequate, mature faith must provide one with a complete and consistent understanding of things. For someone who comes out of a certain Catholic tradition that would want to claim that such an understanding is to be found in Catholic theology supplemented by Catholic philosophy, encountering the Other may be very challenging, requiring recourse to such formulae as 'implicit Christians',[6] and the like. But a very common reaction over the last century has been to try to move beyond particular faiths to some universal understanding of God, or even beyond to some impersonal Force, or Ground of Being. The various theologies and philosophies of historical faiths are then seen as just first approximations to this core doctrine, and the scandal of the plurality of incompatible

---

5. John Main (1926–82), Benedictine monk who founded and inspired what has become the World Community of Christian Meditation.
6. Karl Rahner's concept of people who are not Christians, and may not even have heard of Christianity, but can nevertheless be considered part of the Church because of the lives they lead.

views is overcome. All spiritual people are the saints, or *tsadikim*, or wise or holy men of the one true, universal understanding of ultimate reality.

But this hope springs from an illusion, which is nourished by the misprision described above that reads faith as belief. Faiths are like paths, on which people enter with anticipatory confidence, and then travel. These paths are shaped by a whole host of things, including rituals, sacraments, stories, exemplary figures, modes and disciplines of prayer, meditation, devotion, which can also be disciplines of the body, and of course also (sometimes) beliefs. Each faith consists of a different combination of some of these elements, and others that I haven't been able to enumerate. One doesn't unite the different faiths by flattening out their doctrinal story into some core elements. Such a stripped-down common story doesn't yet constitute a faith that one can practise. It can, of course, become one, by incorporating practices of prayer, meditation, chanting, devotion to exemplary figures, and so on. But then it becomes another faith, perhaps very profound, and capable of bearing fruit in deeply spiritual lives. But this doesn't take it beyond the many into the one all-embracing One. The scandal of particularity is not in any way overcome. And that's because it can't be overcome.

And this is what Jonathan Sacks has been telling us all along. This can come as news to us Christians, but as he argues, it doesn't to Jews. This was built into their faith from the beginning.

Besides this, the attempt to construct a new faith by bricolage among existing practices of the traditional ones is not likely to open a path as deep and powerful as these have been. An integrity and coherence can emerge among the practices of a long-standing tradition, which may be lost in mixing and matching. As the Dalai Lama once put it, 'You can't put a sheep's head on a yak's body.'

The move to the synthetic super-religion is tempting if one feels strongly the scandal of particularity. One will feel this if one thinks that there ought to be, indeed must be somewhere, available to be discovered, one religion which will satisfy everyone intellectually and touch everyone spiritually. This would be rationally satisfying, and is certainly the way the One God of Deism would have disposed things. He is the God of the Philosophers, to speak in the voice of Pascal. But the world actually made by the God of Abraham, Isaac, and Jacob doesn't work that way.

For someone rooted in his or her faith, who doesn't accept the a priori demand for universality, the experience of the Other can enlarge faith. If faith is a journey, often through recurrent doubt, towards a deeper and fuller embedding in its end point, be this God, or Nirvana, or *amor fati*,[7] then this kind of exchange, which opens new horizons and makes new demands, will be the motor of growth, of enlargement. It can only seem a betrayal of faith if any admission that something is incomprehensible (at least for now) from one's faith standpoint is deemed unacceptable. If faiths compete against each other, and the prize goes to the one that understands the whole, and hence understands the others better than they do themselves, then such an admission is tantamount to a withdrawal from the race. But by such a standard all faiths fail, and a little realism might suggest to us that they are always bound to fail. A little humility will help us all pursue our several paths.

This means an admission on all sides that we cannot understand how it all fits together. And this, even though all faiths are based on powerful intuitions about the whole. This is the paradox. Buddhism has an overall conception of humans making their way through many lives, ultimately to attain Nirvana; Christianity is based on a story of how the world is brought back to God through the Incarnation. And these understandings are not optional extras to faith; they are essential to its practice. When I follow the liturgies of Holy Week and Easter, my prayer and meditation focus on the Crucifixion and Resurrection, and their significance for all humanity. Practising my faith is not separable from my sense of this significance.

So we, all of us, whatever our position, work and live out of our respective understandings of the whole, as felt or (partly) understood, even while we are aware that we can't make sense of everything in their terms. The journey of faith is not like a course in metaphysics, even if some journeys may include deep metaphysical thinking.

At this point, one might be tempted to invoke the word 'mystery'. This is often an unhelpful thing to do, because the word is frequently used very vaguely to apply to something incomprehensible or impenetrable.

---

7. 'The love of fate'. I am referring here to the ability to will and affirm whatever happens, which Nietzsche saw as the highest goal.

But the term has, in fact, many levels of meaning, which are worth sorting out. I want to distinguish three facets of the meaning of this widely used word, not all of which are always in play, of course. (1) We use it to designate something which defies understanding, something we can't explain, which even seems impossible given how we (think we) know things work, but nevertheless happens. This is the sense in which a novel is a 'murder mystery'. (2) It can also mean something which is (1), but also given a great importance, because the puzzling matter is something of great depth and moment; what is still barely understood here would reveal something of great moment about us, the cosmos, God, or whatever. (3) If we draw on the etymology, which relates the word to what is hidden, and then also to the process of initiation, in which secrets are revealed, then another facet comes to the fore: here we are dealing with the way that we could come to know more about the matter in question. Something is a 'mystery' in this sense when we can't come to understand it by taking a disengaged stance to it, applying already articulated concepts, but when we have to open ourselves to our experience of it, explore it by immersing ourselves in it. For example, the behaviour of people of another culture can be mysterious, but we can learn to understand it by immersing ourselves in it, interacting with the people, remaining open to their values, norms, ways of talking. If we remain fixed within our initial judgements about them: strange, coarse, barbaric, etc., we will impede the learning, and never grasp what they're about. Or the appeal of a work of art can be baffling, until we allow ourselves to be led by the articulations of a helpful friend and give our full attention to it.

This third sense is the one that is appropriate here. Moving along the path of faith is something one can only do by further immersion, in the prayers, the rituals, the practices, the images, stories, and thoughts.

Mystery in this third sense connotes a way of knowing, and not just as in the first sense, something that defies knowledge – knowledge, that is, of the other, disengaged kind. There are, as it were, two registers of knowing, participatory and objectifying; one can sometimes 'translate' between them, but the renditions are always approximate and imperfect. So whatever advances in understanding we make in the first may never allow us to answer certain questions we pose in the second. And questions about how to make final sense of the whole may fall into this latter category.

Perhaps we have a distant analogy in natural languages. One can be bilingual in languages A and B, and yet be unable to offer a perfectly adequate translation from one to the other.

The kind of encounter and exchange I have been describing here is, I believe, a mark of our time.[8] They are becoming more and more frequent in our ecumenical age. And along with them grows a resistance in many if not all faiths among those who fear these encounters, who are worried about the loss or contamination they might entail. So there is very often a rift within a faith or confession around the issue of ecumenical exchange.

Both sides have seen something real; there are both gains and dangers here. I have been talking in the above pages about the gains of enlarged faith for the participants in these exchanges. But other far-reaching changes result from them.

They in fact can create a new situation in which many of us live our faith no longer primarily in the closed circle of fellow believers, but largely in this space of exchange. Real friendships grow across the boundaries, and a sense of fellowship, even solidarity, arises. How many of us have felt a bond of closer understanding with people of another faith than we feel with many of our co-religionists?

And therein lies a danger: of alienation from, even contempt for some of the latter. And this estrangement may be intensified by our struggles with them on a host of issues, including those of ecumenical contact. The costs of this may be high. The rift may undermine our common life; switching back to a Catholic language, there is a danger to our Church as a sacramental union. Many churches seem to be threatened today with schisms. These do not usually arise around this issue, but it can play a role.

Beyond that, there is a danger that we fail to extend to our

---

8. See Anthony Carroll's insightful description of this new situation, 'Church and Culture: Protestant and Catholic Modernities', *New Blackfriars*, 90 (no. 1026), March 2009, 163–77.

alienated fellow members the hermeneutical charity which has just yielded such fruit in our relations with another faith. We may indeed, disagree with the conservative stance which shies away from such contacts, but the people who take up this stance invariably have richer spiritual lives than can be captured by their ideological position. To revert to my familiar context, 'conservative' Catholics very often practise more intensely than others types of prayer which connect profoundly to the tradition. Even when they seem to cede to a 'Donatist'[9] temptation and want to get rid of the rest of us, we must never reciprocate. The communion of the Church is at stake.

So there are dangers here as well. But we should never lose from sight the immense gain that trans-faith friendship and solidarity represent. To speak once more in my own voice, I feel that I am living a bit more fully my vocation as a Christian when I can engage in this kind of exchange. This, too, counts for me as an enlargement of faith.

I have been trying in this essay to embroider Jonathan Sacks's profound phrase with which I began, by adding what could be thought of as a series of personal footnotes, which I am glad to offer in homage to his work.

9. The Donatists were a 4th-cent. breakaway church, which held that the Christian Church should be a small gathering of the really pure, as against a larger body including many sinners and back-sliders. St Augustine argued strongly against them.

Chapter 9

We Are Not Alone

Menachem Kellner

OUR WORLD

Each of us lives at the centre of his or her universe, but few of us mean that literally. Not too very long ago, however, that human beings literally lived at the centre of the universe was a given, at least in Western culture. From our perspective, that universe was very small. It was a sphere which in today's terms was smaller than our own solar system. It was small in other ways as well: spiritual entities aside, all that was thought to exist could be seen by the naked eye (or inferred to exist) – nothing microscopic, nothing telescopic. The world was small in another sense as well: it had no history, either because it was uncreated and basically unchanging (as Aristotle taught) or because since creation the natural world (miracles aside) was as it was meant to be, with no evolution. In this world, populated by only a few million human beings, people's lives were often nasty, brutish, and short since so many of their fellows were often nasty and brutish (and often short as well, given available nutrition). In such a world, it made immediate intuitive sense to think that one's own group had been specially chosen by God: all other groups believed in arrant nonsense, behaved outlandishly, and were often thought to be barely human.[1]

The universe we live in is dramatically larger than that of our fore-bears. Looking outward, we discover that we orbit the sun, not the other way round, and live on a planet which is one of many that orbit the sun. The sun itself is a star of no particular distinction, tucked into a galaxy of no particular distinction. Our Milky Way galaxy is part of a galactic cluster, which itself in turn is part of a super-galactic cluster, and so on, with no end in sight. Zooming back into ourselves, we discover that we are composed of molecules, composed of atoms, composed of atomic particles, composed of sub-atomic particles, and so on. When Jews look at the world around them, we discover that in numerical terms we do not even constitute a statistical error in the Chinese or Indian censuses.

Looking at the world in this way, it becomes harder and harder to take seriously those who read Rashi's comment on Genesis 1:1 to the effect that all that exists was created only so that God could reveal the Torah to Moses, in order that the Jewish people could live according to it in a small patch of real estate on the eastern shores of the Mediterranean Sea. Looking at the billions of human beings who surround us, we discover that a huge percentage of them are no less moral and no less sophisticated than we are.[2]

The challenge to Jewish self-importance constituted by alterna-

---

1. Anthony D. Smith has shown that the notion of chosenness is endemic to Western culture (and not just the West) – but, of course, the Jews get blamed for the idea more than do other peoples. See Anthony D. Smith, *Chosen Peoples* (Oxford: Oxford University Press, 2003).

2. Rashi opens his commentary on the Torah by paraphrasing from *Midrash tanḥuma* ('Bereshit' 11) as follows:

   Rabbi Isaac said: It was not necessary to begin the Torah [the main object of which is to teach commandments] with this verse, but from 'This month shall be unto you [the first of the months]' [Exod. 12:2], since this was the first commandment that Israel was commanded to observe. But what is the reason that the Torah begins with 'In the beginning'? Because of the verse, 'The power of His works He hath declared to His people in giving them the heritage of the nations' [Ps. 111:6], for if the nations of the world should say to Israel: 'You are robbers, because you have seized by force the lands of the seven nations [of Canaan],' Israel could reply to them: 'The entire world belongs to the Holy One,

tive faiths and cultures is not new, but it does have a beginning point in time. The biblical authors were confident that the idolaters against whom they struggled were barbarians. The talmudic sages seem not to have been overwhelmed with admiration for the cultures of the people among whom they lived. Living in an Islamic world, however, Sa'adiyah Gaon (882–924), Judah Halevi, and, pre-eminently, Maimonides realized that they confronted a challenge that could not be brushed aside with a broken reed. Samuel ibn Tibbon (*c*.1150–1230) and Menahem Me'iri each showed that they found much in contemporary Christianity to admire.

It is against this background that I would like to comment on Rabbi Jonathan Sacks's challenging observation, 'Those who are confident in their faith are not threatened but enlarged by the different faith of others.'[3] There is much to admire in this statement, although, if it is true, it would appear that very few religious people in the pre-modern West were confident enough in their faith to feel enlarged, rather than threatened, by the faith of others – such would appear to be the evidence of wars of religion, crusades against infidels and heretics, and the persecution of religious, cultural, and ideological others. Even in our relatively enlightened age, it would appear that more people are threatened than enlarged by the faith of others.

All this is true, but there is still much to be learned from Rabbi Sacks's observation. I believe that it provides a new angle for understanding an 800-year-old debate in Jewish sources. Bluntly, I want to make the case that attempts to ground Jewish chosenness in the claim that Jews are distinguished from others by some sort of innate characteristic,

---

blessed be He; He created it, and gave it to whomever it was right in His eyes. Of His own will He gave it to them [the seven Canaanite nations] and of His own will He took it from them and gave it to us.'

Rashi here expands on the *Tanḥuma* text, but, so far as I can judge, in no way distorts it. Emphasizing what I take to be a central focus of his gloss here, Rashi continues, this time paraphrasing *Genesis Rabbah* 1:1:

'In the beginning He created': This passage cries out for a midrashic interpretation, as our rabbis have interpreted it: [God created the world] for the sake of the Torah since it is called 'the beginning of His way' [Prov. 8:22] and for the sake of Israel, since they are called 'the beginning of His crops' [Jer. 2:3].

3. Jonathan Sacks, *The Dignity of Difference* (New York: Continuum, rev. edn., 2003), 65–6.

which makes them both different from and superior to other human beings, reflects a lack of religious self-confidence. Not to beat around the bush, the alternative view is that of Maimonides, according to which all human beings are equally made in the image of God. What distinguishes Jews from other human beings is nothing innate, ontological, metaphysical, or however you might want to characterize it, but the truth of the Torah. This view is neither pluralist nor liberal, but it does save Maimonides from the charge of a lack of religious self-confidence, and from the charge of racist particularism.

We do not have to remain bound by Maimonides. He takes us many steps on the way towards enabling us to be enlarged by the faith of others, but certainly does not take us all the way – that we will have to do on our own.

THE WORLD OF HALEVI AND THE HALEVIANS

Two facts about the earliest statement that Jews are in some actual sense distinguished from non-Jews are significant. The first is that it dates from the twelfth century, not earlier,[4] and the second is that it occurs in a book titled *The Book of Refutation and Proof on Behalf of the Despised Religion*. Judah Halevi's *Kuzari*, as the book is better known, was written as a defence of rabbinic Judaism in the face of attacks by Karaites, Christians, Muslims, neo-Aristotelian philosophers writing in Arabic, and, I would add, by the kind of Judaism soon to be found in the writings of Moses Maimonides (1138–1204; Halevi died in 1145). It is note-

---

4. I am more than painfully aware of the (thankfully very small number of) rabbinic passages which could be construed as teaching that Jews are not only God's chosen people, especially beloved first-born sons, as it were (Exod. 4:22), but in some inherent sense truly distinct from and superior to non-Jews. But even such statements as BT AZ 22b, according to which only non-Jews carry the pollution which the Edenic snake cast into Eve (a statement the outer meaning of which Maimonides, *Guide*, ii. 30, says is deeply disgraceful), and the various misanthropic statements attributed to R. Shimon bar Yohai, need not be read literally (indeed, that is the general approach to R. Shimon bar Yohai's famous statement in BT *Yev*. 60b–61a – see especially Tosafot ad loc.). Even if one insists on reading them literally and anachronistically, as if they reflected views that found general expression only in the Middle Ages, they still remain a tiny and wholly unrepresentative set of texts.

worthy that Halevi's defence of Judaism involves unprecedented claims about the special nature of the Jews.[5]

We have thus a fairly late book, written by a poet-philosopher who was clearly affronted by the disdain he felt on the part of the majority cultures then warring over his homeland (born in Christian Spain, Halevi spent his maturity in the Muslim South). He also lived in a world in which Muslims of pure Arab descent saw themselves as superior to other Muslims and in which some Christians cast doubt upon the simple humanity of Jews, who had every reason to know better, but stubbornly persisted in rejecting the messiahship of Jesus, despite its 'obvious' truth. It is hardly surprising that Halevi chose not only to emphasize the truth and beauty of the Torah, but also the special nature of its recipients.

What did Halevi claim in this regard? In light of later iterations of the claim that Jews are significantly distinguished from and superior to non-Jews, Halevi's claims are restrained, and, as was pointed out to me by Rabbi Daniel Korobkin, perhaps wholly theoretical.[6] Halevi maintained that in the ten generations from Noah to Abraham, a line of descent developed (or, perhaps more accurately, was caused to develop by God) of individuals capable of achieving prophecy. This special subset of humanity continued to develop through Abraham (but not through his brother Haran), through Isaac (but not through his brother Ishmael),

---

5. I am writing on the assumption that the Zohar postdates Halevi and that its doctrines were, by and large, unknown to him. Contemporary scholarship usually ascribes authorship of the Zohar to the 13th-cent. Spanish kabbalist R. Moses de Leon and his circle, even if some scholars see it as the outgrowth of a long mystical tradition that preceded it. For a recent analysis of rabbinic views which qualify or reject the traditional ascription of the Zohar to R. Shimon bar Yohai, see Marc Shapiro, 'Is there an obligation to believe that R. Shimon bar Yohai wrote the Zohar?' (Heb.), *Milin havivin*, 5 (2010–11) Heb. section, 1–20. On zoharic doctrines concerning the special nature of the Jews, see Moshe Hallamish, 'The Kabbalists' Attitude to the Nations of the World' (Heb.), in Aviezer Ravitsky (ed.), *Joseph Baruch Sermonetta Memorial Volume* (*Jerusalem Studies in Jewish Thought*, 14) (Jerusalem, 1988), 289–311. Hallamish's interest in this article is in the image of non-Jews in kabbalah, but its picture of the Jew is made clear along the way.

6. The differences are only theoretical since no one achieves prophecy any more. However, there are those who interpret a late poem of Halevi's as explaining his resolve to reach the land of Israel in order to achieve a prophetic experience. See Yosef Yahalom, *Shirat hayav shel r. yehudah halevi* (Jerusalem: Magnes, 2008), 93–106.

and through Jacob (but not through his brother Esau) and finally to all of Jacob's descendants, the children of Israel/Jacob. For Halevi, this special subset of humanity is related to the rest of the human race as the heart is related to the rest of the body: the core organ (and the seat of thought for mediaevals, following the Bible), without which the other organs cannot survive and which itself, if we take the analogy further, cannot survive without them.[7]

Halevi's intellectual honesty is such that he accepts the consequences of his position. Flying in the face of received halakhah, he maintains that converts to Judaism remain inferior to born Jews (*Kuzari*, i. 26): 'whoever joins us from among the nations especially will share in our good fortune although he will not be equal to us'.[8] Halevi's honesty is further evidenced by his astounding admission (*Kuzari* i. 113–15) that Jews in practice all too often fail to live up to their divine potential, and, if given the chance, could be as brutal as the nations among whom they live.

Writers coming after Halevi tended to be more absolute in their claims about the special nature of the Jews, most often rooting their claims in kabbalistic notions. Historically, the various forms of Jewish ontological particularism have been purely theoretical discussions, with no concrete consequences in the lives of their authors, or those who read their works. One hopes that the same will be true for what appears to be a truly blood-thirsty contemporary expression of the view that Jews are ontologically distinct from and profoundly superior in every fashion to gentiles. The book *Torat hamelekh* purports to be a disinterested and entirely theoretical halakhic discussion of the circumstances under which it is permissible to kill innocent gentiles. I do not mean to blame Halevi or his successors in the Jewish tradition for this book,

---

7. See Halevi, *Kuzari*, i. 27–8, 96, 101–03, and 115.
8. See further Daniel J. Lasker, 'Proselyte Judaism, Christianity, and Islam in the Thought of Judah Halevi', *Jewish Quarterly Review*, 81 (1990), 75–91. The inferiority which Halevi attaches to converts to Judaism relates not to matters of *yiḥus* ('descent'; a convert may not become a king of Israel, for example, nor marry a *kohen*), but to their very nature – in effect, they are no longer gentiles, but not entirely Jewish either.

but do want to insist that it is one possible consequence of their ontological particularism.[9]

Moving from the immoral to the ridiculous, Jewish ontological
particularists always remind me of a joke I like to tell, along the lines of
the country mouse and city mouse, only in this case the mice are Jews
in late nineteenth-century Tsarist Russia.

A Jew from a small *shtetl* meets a Jew from the great city of Odessa.
The big-city Jew, trying to be polite, asks about the *shtetl* and
inquires, how many people live in your village? The *shtetl* Jew
replies with pride, at least two thousand. And how many of them
are Jews, continues his interlocutor. Oh, about 1,800, he is told.
Not to be outdone, the country Jew asks the city Jew, how many

---

9. Yizhak Shapira and Yosef Elitzur, *Torat hamelekh* (Yitshar: Yeshivat Od Yosef Hai,
2009). Some of the 'pearls' found in this book include the claim that the existence of
a gentile who is not a 'resident alien' (and in this day and age, no gentiles can achieve
that status) 'has no legitimacy' (p. 43); Jews and gentiles share *nothing* in common,
but, in effect, belong to different orders of reality (p. 45); a gentile who violates one of
the seven Noahide commandments (stealing, for example, even something of slight
value, or, in the eyes of the authors of the book, undermining Jewish sovereignty
over any part of the land of Israel) is to be executed without advance warning. The
Jew who witnesses the act can serve as judge and executioner (pp. 49–51); and so
it goes in depressing and blood-curdling detail. *Torat hamelekh*'s views are based on
readings of kabbalistic texts mediated through the teachings of R. Yitshak Ginzberg,
cited as direct inspiration by the authors of the book. I regret to note that the idea
that Jews and gentiles do not share the same human essence is found in circles which
identify with modernity and enlightenment, far from R. Ginzberg and his morally
twisted views. See, for example, Hershel Schachter, 'Women Rabbis?', *Hakirah: The
Flatbush Journal of Jewish Law and Thought*, 11 (2011), 19–23. On p. 20, R. Schachter,
distinguished professor of Talmud and Rosh Kollel at Yeshiva University, writes, as
if it is totally uncontroversial: 'Hashem [God] created all men *B'Tzelem Elokim* [in
the image of God], and *Bnai Yisrael* [Jews] with an even deeper degree of this *Tzelem
Elokim* – known as *Banim LaMakom* [Children of the Omnipresent].' I hasten to
add that R. Schachter (who bases himself here, apparently, on a [mis-]reading of
Mishnah *Avot*, 3:14) would be horrified to have his views connected to *Torat hamelekh*.
I cite him only as an example of the casual way in which many Jews assume some
sort of ontological divide between Jews and gentiles. (R. Schachter expands on his
particularist views on the nature of Jewish uniqueness in a lecture, which can be
accessed at: http://www.torahweb.org/audioFrameset.html#audio=rsch_050204.)

people live in Odessa? He is impressed with the reply, at least 3 million. He then asks, and how many of them are Jews? Flabbergasted by the answer (about half a million), he asks in amazement, 'really? Why do you need so many *goyim*?

The doctrine concerning the special innate ontologically superior nature of the Jews is, on the face of it, so obviously insane, so observably false in the real world (as Judah Halevi himself had to admit), and so totally unsupported by the overwhelming majority of biblical and rabbinic texts (and to my mind both immoral and fundamentally un-Jewish), that one is driven to wonder how anyone could take it seriously, and how it could have become so dominant a theme in mediaeval and contemporary Judaism. Two answers spring to mind, the second of which will bring us back to Rabbi Sacks's observation about confidence in one's faith.

Jewish history may not be exclusively lachrymose but the survival of the Jews in the face of exile and persecution is indeed remarkable. Persecuted individuals and peoples often develop a common defence mechanism, to wit, that their persecutors are themselves inferior. Is it any wonder that the Jews adopt that view? All people need to feel special; persecuted individuals and peoples (when they do not succumb and internalize the views of the persecutors – a syndrome which appears particularly widespread today among Jewish enemies of Israel) will often and understandably claim moral and even innate superiority over their persecutors. This is perhaps one way of understanding how a religious tradition that begins with the insight that all human beings are created in the image of God could spawn a book like *Torat hamelekh*. This matter is so basic, so fundamental, that I am not familiar with any Jewish thinker, no matter how liberal and universalist in his or her views, who manages without some interpretation or other of the idea of Jewish chosenness. Even Mordecai Kaplan – whose view of God is basically that of George Lucas's Obi-Wan Kenobi, namely, an unself-conscious natural force in the universe – arrives in his last book (*The Religion of Ethical Nationhood*) at the unexpected conclusion that it is only the special nature of Jewish nationalism which stands between the world and nuclear Armageddon.

Thus, even those who try to naturalize everything (such as Mordecai Kaplan) end up with some notion of Jewish chosenness.

The issue achieves added urgency in the light of a comment I once heard the late Emil Fackenheim make: Jews were murdered in the Holocaust because their great-grandparents refused to assimilate. From this it follows, I add, that the decision to remain Jewish in the face of great assimilatory pressures and inducements is a *moral* choice, one which might be fraught with unimaginably horrible consequences for one's grandchildren, God forbid. One must have good reasons for remaining Jewish.

Given all this, it is hardly surprising that Jews and Judaism have developed mechanisms for keeping Jews Jewish. One mechanism which appears to have proved effective is the claim that Jews constitute a metaphysical kind, distinct from and superior to other humans. This is certainly one way to encourage loyalty in the face of fierce persecution, and in the face of the blandishments of the contemporary world, which, in the USA, at least, seem to be wiping out the Jewish people through kindness, not murder.

The view that Jews are in some serious way innately different from and superior to gentiles is deeply rooted in contemporary Judaism.[10] This is so much the case that after I literally wrote a book to convince one of the members of my synagogue that for Maimonides, there is no inherent difference between Jews and non-Jews (my *Maimonides on Judaism and the Jewish People*), he read the book, admitted the cogency of my arguments, and then said that in consequence, his admiration

---

10. In my experience, so-called liberal and secularist Jews are no less particularist than are the Orthodox; indeed, when it comes to the full acceptance of proselytes, Orthodox Jews in Israel are typically much more open than their secularist counterparts. I often check the 'particularism-level' of audiences to which I speak by telling the following joke: an Eastern European Jew in the nineteenth century, tired of the discrimination to which he was subjected, converts to Christianity. The following morning he starts to put on tefillin. His wife says, 'Idiot, what are you doing? Just yesterday you converted!' The man strikes himself on the head and says 'Goyishe kop!' The last expression means 'gentile head' – in my experience many people who laugh at the joke think that conversion out of Judaism makes a person dumber. Invariably, almost everyone in the audience laughs.

for Maimonides had diminished. Another member of my synagogue, a lawyer, sought to convince me that when Maimonides used the talmudic expression *kol ba'ei olam* (all human beings), he could not mean to include non-Jews, since the term is found in the liturgical poem, *'Unetaneh tokef'*:[11] for him it was a given that God neither judges nor even listens to the prayers of non-Jews! For people like my two fellow synagogue-goers, billions of gentiles are like static, background noise, of no possible interest to God.

This is certainly not the view of Maimonides and his contemporary followers, as I will suggest after making one more point.

Biblical authors, and to a great extent the rabbis of the Talmud, appear to have been convinced that idolaters were brutal and corrupt. As much as idolatry was a religious deviation, it was also a cause of profound moral corruption and in that sense was truly a source of *tumah* (ritual impurity). But what happened when the gentiles among whom the Jews lived, and with whom they conducted business, and with whom they often had social ties (otherwise, why forbid the consumption of gentile wine, oil, and bread, for fear that it might lead to intermarriage?) turned out to be moral individuals, trustworthy in their personal dealings, and sophisticated in their religious beliefs? People confident in their faith would be untroubled by such a situation. But perhaps people not so confident in their faith would seek to bolster their identities by denigrating the others as, in effect, not fully human, not truly made in the image of God to the fullest extent possible, not only different, but also innately inferior? There is no way to perform psychoanalysis on long-dead Jews, but looking at those Jews among us today who most disdain gentiles, is it far-fetched to see the results of a persecution complex (as paranoids may really have enemies, so also, as it were, one can acknowledge persecution without justifying a persecution complex), the results of a lack of self-confidence?

Again, there is no way of knowing, but it does help set the stage for

---

11. A central element in the liturgy of the High Holidays. For a recent study, see Reuven Kimelman, 'U-N'Taneh Tokef as a Midrashic Poem', in Debra Reed Blank (ed.), *The Experience of Jewish Liturgy: Studies Dedicated to Menahem Schmelzer* (Leiden: Brill, 2011), 115–46.

a wholly other way of looking at the difference between Jews and gentiles, one which grows out of untroubled confidence in the truth of Torah.

MAIMONIDES AND THE MAIMONIDEANS

There are many ways of proving that Maimonides rejected the idea that Jews are in some innate sense distinct from and inherently superior to non-Jews.[12] One of the most direct texts is his letter to Obadiah the Proselyte.[13] In this letter, he writes that Abraham is as much the father of proselytes as he is of born Jews. That this is no rhetorical flourish is evidenced by the fact that Maimonides makes this statement in a halakhic responsum and that he derives halakhic consequences from this claim. Indeed, he goes on to say (as if he were directly controverting Halevi, which is not beyond the pale of possibility) that the proselyte is actually closer to God than the born Jew.[14] In further contradistinction to Halevi, Maimonides points out that the children of Israel at Sinai were themselves all converts to Judaism: the Jews are a nation constituted by a religious act, not by shared descent. This point was made by a prominent twentieth-century Maimonidean, Rabbi Joseph Kafih (1917–2000), but before turning to his comments, I want to elaborate just a bit on Maimonides' position.

My friend Hayim Shahal pointed out to me that the Hebrew expression *kedoshim tihiyu* (Leviticus 19:2: 'You shall be holy') can be read in the future tense (as a promise) or in the imperative (as a commandment or challenge). Maimonides read it in the latter sense, Halevi in the former. Another way of putting the same point: for Halevi, the Torah

---

12. Much of my academic writing has been devoted to this issue. In particular, see *Maimonides on Judaism and the Jewish People* (Albany, NY: SUNY Press, 1991); *Maimonides' Confrontation with Mysticism* (Oxford: Littman Library of Jewish Civilization, 2006); and *Science in the Bet Midrash: Studies in Maimonides* (Brighton, MA: Academic Studies Press, 2009).

13. For an English translation of much of the letter, see Franz Kobler, *Letters of Jews through the Ages* (New York: East and West Library, 1978), vol. 1, pp. 194–6; for discussion, see James Diamond, *Converts, Heretics, and Lepers: Maimonides and the Outsider* (Notre Dame, IN: University of Notre Dame Press, 2007).

14. In a certain sense, converts are more Jewish than born Jews, since born Jews may or may not know truth while converts (at least in a Maimonidean *beit din*) only become Jewish by virtue of knowing the truth.

was given to the Jews, for only the Jews could receive it; for Maimonides, it was receipt of the Torah which created the nation of Israel out of a motley collection of ex-slaves and hangers-on. Maimonides' views in this regard are so extreme that I believe it is fair and correct to say of him that the history recorded in the Torah could have been different (had Abraham been a Navajo, for example) and that the commandments which reflect that history (the festivals, the sacrificial cult, etc.) could also have been different. For Maimonides, in other words, the Torah records what actually happened, not what had to happen. History could have worked out differently (but, of course, it did not).

In 1958, the then-Prime Minister of Israel, David Ben-Gurion, wrote to about fifty Jewish intellectuals asking for help in defining who is a Jew. One of the answers he received was from Rabbi Joseph Kafih, then at the beginning of a magnificent career of translating and explaining Maimonides' works. Rabbi Kafih wrote to Ben-Gurion:

> What is the meaning of the term 'Jew'? It must be stated that the term does not denote a certain race. Perhaps it is wrong to use the word 'race' so as not to mimic the modern-day racists and their associates, as according to the perception of the Torah, there are no different races in the world. In order to uproot this theory, the Torah felt compelled to provide extensive details of the lineage of all the people in the world so as to attribute them to a single father and a single mother. Thus it might be more proper to say that the term 'Jew' does not denote a certain tribe, or in other words, does not indicate the descendants of Abraham, Isaac, and Jacob in the limited sense of the phrase. We know beyond any doubt that throughout the generations, many people of different nations became intermixed with the Israelites.[15]

But Jews are not just followers of a religion, Rabbi Kafih writes, since at their core is a nation; anyone who accepts the religion becomes so deeply interwoven in the nation that he or she becomes

---

15. R. Kafih's letter may be found in Eliezer Ben-Rafael, *Jewish Identities: Fifty Intellectuals Answer Ben-Gurion* (Leiden: Brill, 2002), 247–53.

indistinguishable from born Jews. Rabbi Kafih also makes the very interesting point that the detailed accounts of the 'descent of man' in the book of Genesis were included in the Torah to emphasize that all the nations of the earth are essentially one family, all descended from one source.

Maimonides does not need to posit the superiority of Jews over non-Jews since he is convinced of the truth of the Torah. Since the Torah is true, and since all humans are essentially the same, there is no reason why all humanity will not someday accept the Torah. His messianism, following that of Isaiah and of Amos, is universalist.

Fine and good, for Maimonides, non-Jews are made in the image of God, just as Jews are. What of non-Jewish religions? Can one find truth in them? Maimonides clearly held that there was some truth in Christianity and Islam, since he tells us that they each have a role to play in making the world ready to accept the messiah. Christianity teaches the sanctity of the Written Torah, acknowledges that the Torah's commandments were at least once normative, and looks forward to a messianic redemption. Islam professes a no-nonsense version of austere monotheism.

Let us now recast our discussion in terms common to contemporary Jewish discourse: why be Jewish? For Halevians the answer is simple: you are Jewish. Remaining Jewish means remaining what you are; you can fool yourself into thinking that you can cease being Jewish and the attempt means that you are untrue to your innermost essence. For Maimonides the answer is also simple: one should remain Jewish because Judaism is true (a view which Halevi and those in his camp would, of course, heartily endorse). That is enough for Maimonides, but not, it appears for Halevi – it is here that I detect the lack of Jewish theological self-confidence that I suggest is to be found in Halevi, but very clearly not in Maimonides.

It is because of that self-confidence that Maimonides has no trouble acknowledging the partial truth of Christianity and Islam. That made sense in his world in his day...does it make sense in ours? Maimonides lived and thought in a world in which truth was one, objective, unchanging, and *accessible*. This made excellent sense in his finite, static universe. While I have no desire to admit to any version of epistemological relativism, it cannot be denied that our confidence in what we can know has been shaken. The appropriate response to this situation seems to me not to be relativism, which makes a mockery of truth and of the possibility of actual communication; nor pluralism, which makes a mockery of truth and of revelation; but, rather, the appropriate response to our predicament ought to be modesty.[16] A person who is modest about his or her claims to truth, as opposed to absolutist about them, is open to the possibility of being inspired, enlarged in Rabbi Sacks's term, by other people whose claims to truth are equally restrained and modest.[17]

WE ARE NOT ALONE

While not giving up on the idea that revelation (be it Jewish, Christian, or Muslim) teaches truth in some hard, exclusivist sense, putative addressees of revelation ought to be modest about how much of it they understand, and restrained in the claims they make on behalf of revelation and about adherents of other religions. Admittedly, it may be easier for a Jew to advance this position than for a Christian or a Muslim. This is so for several reasons. First, until the Middle Ages, at least, Jews sought to understand how God instructs them to inject sanctity into their lives, and paid very little attention to the question of how God expects them to think. Given the notion that the Torah contains many levels of meanings, and the profound differences among Jewish thinkers about the nature and content of those meanings, a stance of theological modesty *ought* to be easier for Jews to maintain than for adherents of more clearly theologically-based religions. Second, given the nature of Jewish-gentile relations over the last two millennia, Jews had very little reason to look to gentiles for spiritual enrichment. We, however, live in a different world, and I thank God for that.[18] Last, Jews, not thinking

---

16. My wife and I have argued for this position in 'Respectful Disagreement: A Response to Raphael Jospe', in Alon Goshen-Gottstein and Eugene Korn (eds.), *Jewish Theology and World Religions* (Oxford: Littman Library of Jewish Civilization, 2012), pp. 123–33.

17. Here we go beyond Maimonides, who was much more optimistic than we can be about accessing truth, both of reason and of revelation. One need not be a postmodernist to admit that access to absolute truth is more problematic than many of our mediaeval forbears thought.

18. The Lord of all the Universe is not too great to have revealed the Torah to us, but is certainly too great to be captured by our puny understanding of Torah. To claim

that one must be Jewish in order to achieve a share in the world to come, have traditionally paid little attention to the beliefs and practices of others. But, having left the ghetto and the mellah, we live in a world very different from that of our forebears and, looking around, discover admirable gentiles from whom we can learn much. We are no longer alone.[19]

otherwise is to be guilty of cosmic hubris, and to close ourselves off to the possibility of being enlarged by meetings with others who also seek God and whom God does not ignore.

19. My thanks to James Diamond, Jolene S. Kellner, Eugene Korn, Ariel Meirav, and Avram Montag for helpful comments on earlier drafts of this essay.

Chapter 10

Halakhic Authority in a World of Personal Autonomy

Jacob J. Schacter

I

In a 1985 study, Robert Bellah pointed to the growing ubiquity of the principle of personal autonomy and individual choice in American culture. He presented the memorable example of a nurse, Sheila Larson, who had 'actually named her religion (she calls it her "faith") after herself'. Larson defined this faith – 'my own Sheilaism', as she called it – in these words: 'It's just try to love yourself and be gentle with yourself.

I am honoured to present this essay in honour of Chief Rabbi Lord Jonathan Sacks, a highly gifted teacher, writer, and orator, and an outstandingly articulate spokesman for the enduring relevance of Jewish ideals and values in the world at large. My thanks to Neal Kozodoy for his kind and gracious help in preparing this essay for publication and to the editors of this volume for their many useful suggestions.

You know, I guess, take care of each other. I think He would want us to take care of each other.'[1]

For sociologists of religion, Bellah's 'Sheilaism' took hold as a shorthand way of describing an increasingly widespread American phenomenon.[2] By the end of the century, Robert Wuthnow was able to show that organized religion, which earlier had 'dominated [Americans'] experience of spirituality, especially when it was reinforced by ethnic loyalties and when it was expressed in family rituals', had devolved into something else entirely; now, he reported, 'growing numbers of Americans piece together their faith like a patchwork quilt... in which each person seeks in his or her own way'.[3] The result, mourned an author in the *Chronicle of Higher Education*, was 'a world increasingly populated by Zen-leaning Lutherans, or Buddhists turned Catholic, or Jews turned Quaker' – a world in which individuals 'are so mired in the self that we are losing sight of the sacred'.[4]

By the turn of the twenty-first century, the replacement of the vaguely prescriptive word 'religion' by the word 'spirituality', with its connotations of something wholly personal and unencumbered by obligations, had progressed to the point where an entire book on the subject could be entitled *Spiritual But Not Religious: Understanding Unchurched America*.[5] And it was only a brief matter of time before established houses

1. Robert Bellah et al., *Habits of the Heart: Individualism and Commitment in American Life* (Berkeley, CA 1985), 221. Imagine what she would have called her faith if her name had been Judy.

2. Bruce A. Greer and Wade Clark Roof, '"Desperately Seeking Sheila": Locating Religious Privatism in American Society', *Journal for the Scientific Study of Religion*, 31/3 (1992), 346–52. For an earlier formulation of this point, see Louis Dupre, 'Spiritual Life in a Secular Age', *Daedalus*, 111 (Winter 1982), 24–5.

3. Robert Wuthnow, *After Heaven: Spirituality in America Since the 1950s* (Berkeley, CA, 1998), 2. See also id., *Growing Up Religious: Christians and Jews and their Journeys of Faith* (Boston, MA, 1999), esp. pp. 162–93; Wade Clark Roof (ed.), *Contemporary American Religion* (New York, 2000), p. viii.

4. Donna Schaper, 'Me-First "Spirituality" Is a Sorry Substitute for Organized Religion on Campus', *Chronicle of Higher Education* (18 Aug. 2000), p. A56.

5. Robert C. Fuller, *Spiritual But Not Religious: Understanding Unchurched America* (New York, 2002). See also below, nn. 43, 50.

of worship caught up with their errant parishioners and began to adopt 'Sheilaistic' practices of their own.

In 2002, the *Wall Street Journal* reported on the growth of 'flexible praying' and 'moveable holidays' as some churches switched 'the pre-Easter "Maundy" service from the traditional Thursday to Tuesday (for less-hectic Easter weekends)' or added 'a combined Good Friday and Palm Sunday double-header service so members [could] get key elements of the Easter story all at once'. For worshippers disposed to sleep late on Easter morning, the *Journal* noted 'a Sunday-evening option where liturgy scripted on PowerPoint is projected up on a screen and a band plays everything from ancient Christian tunes to rock music'.[6] Three years later, an article in the *New York Times* described 'a number of Christians [who] are regularly attending different churches in the course of a week or a month, picking and choosing among programmes and services, to satisfy social and spiritual needs. They are comfortable in participating in multiple churches' – and, evidently, the churches were comfortable in accommodating them.[7]

What was true for America was no less true for Europe. *Newsweek* reported in 1999, 'Young Europeans, in particular, are creating mix-and-match faiths, forging moralities where they can find them. Stalls in the Spanish pilgrimage town of Santiago de Compostela sell Rastafarian hats, Hindu incense, and Kurt Cobain T-shirts along with the crucifixes.'[8]

Whether in America or in Europe, it is not only a matter of the young – although the young are conspicuous, and the adolescent young especially so. According to Christian Smith:

American youth, like American adults, are nearly without exception profoundly individualistic, instinctively presuming autonomous, individual self-direction to be a universal human norm and life goal. Thoroughgoing individualism is not a contested

---

6. Nancy Ann Jeffrey, 'Religion Takes a Holiday', *Wall Street Journal* (15 Mar. 2002), pp. W1, W12.

7. Neela Banerjee, 'Going Church to Church To Find a Faith That Fits', *New York Times* (30 Dec. 2005), p. A18.

8. Carla Power, 'Lost in Silent Prayer', *Newsweek* (12 July 1999), 53.

orthodoxy for teenagers. It is an invisible and pervasive doxa, that is, an unrecognized, unquestioned, invisible premise or presupposition.[9]

The essence of that 'doxa' is, as paraphrased by Smith, 'If you don't choose it, it's not authentic for you.'[10]

Back in 1985, taking note of the new religious realities, Bellah and his co-authors had foreseen 'the logical possibility of over 220 million American religions'.[11] Today, over twenty-five years later, with the American population at the 300 million mark, the figure needs to be revised upward commensurately. Indeed, according to an August 2006 report in the *New York Times*, every year sees the emergence of 40 to 45 new religious groups.[12] 'Ritual' has given way to 'ceremony', as personal autonomy reigns ever more supreme.

II

Which brings us to the Jews. Far from being unaffected by the general trend, American Jews appear to be at its forefront. In '"Desperately Seeking Sheila"', Bruce A. Greer and Wade Clark Roof reported that 'Jews were considerably more privatized than either Protestants or Catholics', being more likely than either group to exercise their freedom of choice in defining the substance of their religion.[13] To adopt the suggestive terminology of Jonathan D. Sarna, where once Jewish cultural identity was determined largely by religious and ethnic 'descent', today it is largely based instead on 'consent'[14] – or, as I prefer to put it, on 'assent'.[15]

9. Christian Smith, *Soul Searching: The Religious and Spiritual Lives of American Teenagers* (New York, 2005), 143.
10. Banerjee, 'Going Church to Church'.
11. Bellah et al., *Habits of the Heart*, 221.
12. Michael Luo, 'Seeking Entry-Level Prophet: Burning Bush, Tablets Not Required', *New York Times* (28 Aug. 2006), p. B1.
13. '"Desperately Seeking Sheila"', 350.
14. Jonathan D. Sarna, 'The Secret of Jewish Continuity', *Commentary*, 98/4 (Oct. 1994), 57.
15. For a very different, indeed opposite, understanding of the notion of 'communities

Steven M. Cohen and Arnold Eisen have summarized the current situation well:

> The principal authority for contemporary American Jews, in the absence of compelling religious norms and communal loyalties, has become the sovereign self. Each person now performs the labor of fashioning his or her own self, pulling together elements from the various Jewish and non-Jewish repertoires available, rather than stepping into an 'inescapable framework' of identity (familial, communal, traditional) given at birth. Decisions about ritual observance and involvement in Jewish institutions are made and made again, considered and reconsidered, year by year and even week by week. American Jews speak of their lives, and of their Jewish beliefs and commitments, as a journey of ongoing questioning and development. They avoid the language of arrival. There are no final answers, no irrevocable commitments.[16]

This conception of Judaism has been compellingly championed by the Jewish Renewal Movement, as indicated in the following description of a 'Living Waters Weekend' it sponsored in 2000:

> Optional sunrise walk and meditation. Musical workshop service at the ocean. Guided conscious eating at breakfast. Water exercises for body toning. Yoga with Kabbalah. Outdoor games, time for massage. Sacred gathering for men and women. Poetry readings and music. *Havdalah* ritual on the beach. Sunrise co-ed *mikvah* ritual in the ocean. Breakfast celebration with new affirmation. Kabbalistic meditation. Sacred sharing ceremony.[17]

---

of assent and descent', see Paul Morris, 'Community Beyond Tradition', in Paul Heelas et al. (eds.), *Detraditionalization: Critical Reflections on Authority and Identity* (Cambridge and Oxford, 1996), 238–45.

16. Steven M. Cohen and Arnold Eisen, *The Jew Within: Self, Family, and Community in America* (Bloomington, IN, 2000), 2.

17. See the *Jerusalem Post*, 20 Feb. 2000.

The references to yoga and other vaguely Eastern-sounding rituals are not coincidental. In its 2001 coverage of this general phenomenon, *Fortune* adduced the example of Ricardo Levy, a Jew 'long interested in philosophy and religion, particularly the Eastern traditions; he has, for example, practiced tai chi, a physical discipline rooted in Taoism. Like many baby-boomers, Levy has fashioned his own brand of spirituality, which draws from a number of religious traditions.'[18] But the appeal to external sources of spiritual nourishment is not limited to Eastern traditions. A 2006 feature in the *Forward* described, among others, a 'new generation of "Chavurah Jews", meeting in lay-led prayer groups and retreats in a collective and "DIY" [do-it-yourself] way; what might be called "OMG! Jews" [who] pick and choose from multiple sources of religious and cultural identity rather than look to a single source (such as a synagogue) for communal and spiritual life; Online Jews, such as the Jewschool and Jewlicious communities', and still more. The page where this story appeared featured a description of a *minyan* led by a rabbi who studied for two years at the very traditional Yeshivat Chaim Berlin and then spent 'most of the next decade pursuing practices that read like a menu of the contemporary holistic movement: yoga, tai chi, shiatsu, Reiki, Alexander Technique, Feldenkrais, gyrotonics, Zen meditation, martial arts, integrative body psychotherapy and postural integration.'[19]

In October 2006, *Jewish Week* readers were introduced to Israelis gathered on Yom Kippur in a Tel Aviv pub stocked with cigarettes, beer, and platters of food, and emitting 'sounds of merriment'. In the words of one Israeli at the party, 'I devoted time to Yom Kippur this morning, asked for forgiveness, and now I'm enjoying myself.'[20] In the *New York Times* two months later, a Jewish woman gushed about the joys of celebrating Christmas: 'My husband and I were consenting adults. This was our house. Why couldn't we celebrate whatever we wanted?' While 'pretty sure' that she would also want her children to appreciate

18. Marc Gunther, 'God & Business', *Fortune* (9 July 2001), 76.
19. Jay Michaelson, 'Exploring the New Jewish Spiritualities' and Jennifer Bleyer, 'Rabbi's Journey Leads to "Ecstatic" Minyan', *Forward* (12 May 2006), 15. The third article on the page deals with new, non-traditional uses for the *mikveh*.
20. Jonathan Mark, 'Yom Kippur's Moveable Feast', *Jewish Week* (6 Oct. 2006), 16.

the centrality of Hanukah, she concluded: 'On the other hand, maybe it's nice to teach children that holidays can be done à la carte. Every religion, every culture, has so many beautiful rituals and traditions to choose from. Maybe celebrating is a step toward tolerating. I can hardly wait for Hanukwanzaa.'[21]

As the above suggests – and there are many more examples – the 'unlimited choices' available to today's seekers hardly exclude a (selective) dip into Jewish as well as non-Jewish sources – or even, for some, a conditional look into the world of traditional Jewish learning. Thus, at an Israeli institution called the Secular Yeshiva, students devote themselves to the study of authoritative Jewish texts – minus the authority. As one of its founders explains the school's philosophy, 'We don't see any text as an authority, but as an inspiration.' Since, in the words of the school's director, 'the idea is to expose [students] to many worldviews', at this yeshiva 'there is no prayer service, no kosher kitchen, and no separation between the sexes. There is', he adds, 'a period in the morning called *shaḥarit*, the name given to morning prayers, but rather than pray, the students meditate or read poetry.' On Yom Kippur one year, 'several students decided to fast for the first time in their lives, *not because it was a mitzva* [emphasis added], but because for them it was a physical manifestation of their spiritual learning process.'[22]

In fact, choice extends not only to the fashioning of one's Judaism but even to the possibility of abandoning it altogether. In this context, it is instructive to study how various Jewish encyclopaedias published in the twentieth century dealt with the appropriateness of including someone who converted out of the faith. Does such an act disqualify that person from inclusion in a 'Jewish' encyclopaedia or not? While the editors of the *Jewish Encyclopedia* (1901) and even the *Encyclopaedia Judaica* (1972) felt that anyone born of a Jew 'who was sufficiently distinguished' merited inclusion, 'because the present work deals with

---

21. Cindy Chupack, 'Jewish in a Winter Wonderland', *New York Times, Sunday Styles* (24 Dec. 2006), Section 9, p. 2.
22. Erica Chernofsky, 'Not in Search of God', *International Jerusalem Post* (18–24 May 2007), 17.

Judaism as a race',[23] the editors of *Jewish Women in America: An Historical Encyclopedia* expressed the following rationale for including such women: 'Conversion to another religion, a path chosen by a few women in the encyclopedia, was treated as part of a woman's Jewish biography, that is, her explicit rejection of Judaism. Conversion is, after all, an aspect of the modern Jewish experience.' For these writers, choice is so much a part of Judaism that one can actually exercise one's 'Jewishness' in the very act of rejecting it![24]

III

Yet, at the heart of traditional Judaism stands a diametrically opposite set of values and assumptions. As a divine document, the Torah – and the Oral Law as well (вт *Shabat* 31a) – represent the will of God, which Jews are bidden to obey. The word 'mitzvah' does not mean a 'good deed', to be performed or avoided at will, but a 'commandment', a non-negotiable, uncompromising requirement or obligation. When it comes to belief and practice, all choices are not equally valid. In particular, religious observance cannot be defined by whatever I may want it to be at any given moment. 'Commandment' means that there is a Commander, God, and that every Jew is commanded. It is a total system. Picking and choosing, mixing and matching, buffet-style selectivity – these are out of the question.

Juxtaposing the word 'rights' – 'a highly evocative one…in the post-Enlightenment secular society of the West' – to the word 'mitzvah', the legal scholar Robert Cover wrote:

---

23. Cyrus Adler et al., 'Preface', *Jewish Encyclopedia* (New York, 1901), pp. ix–x; anon., 'Introduction', *Encyclopaedia Judaica*, vol. 1 (New York, 1972), 7.
24. See Paula E. Hyman and Deborah Dash Moore, 'Editor's Preface', in eaed. (eds.), *Jewish Women in America: An Historical Encyclopedia*, vol. 1 (New York, 1997), p. xxii. For comparisons of the respective criteria of inclusion/exclusion in these encyclopaedias and others, see Susan A. Glenn, 'In the Blood? Consent, Descent, and the Ironies of Jewish Identity', *Jewish Social Studies*, NS 8/2–3 (2002), 139–52. For the role of 'Sheilaism' in the Modern Orthodox community, see Steven Bayme, 'New Conditions and Models of Authority: Changing Patterns within Contemporary Orthodoxy', in Suzanne Last Stone (ed.), *Rabbinic and Lay Communal Authority* (New York, 2006), 113–28.

The principal word in Jewish law, which occupies a place equivalent in evocative force to the American legal system's 'rights', is the word 'mitzvah', which literally means commandment but has a general meaning closer to 'incumbent obligation'.... All law was given at Sinai, and therefore all law is related back to the ultimate heteronomous event.[25]

In placing a premium on the concept of 'incumbent obligation', traditional Judaism places a premium on submission, which is to say on the absence of personal autonomy and the multiplicity of equally valid choices that is at the centre of contemporary religious life. Do we not recite a few times a week in the prayer prior to the reading of the Torah, *Ana avda dekudsha berikh hu*, 'I am a servant of the Holy One, may He be blessed'? *Shalaḥ et ami veya'avduni*, 'Send forth My people that they may serve Me', is the divine message delivered through Moses to Pharaoh in the book of Exodus (7: 26). Freedom is not an end in itself; it is valued only as a means towards heeding the Creator's call to be His servants.

The fullness of what it means to be commanded – to the point of knowing which shoe to put on first and which fingernail to cut first[26] – is reflected in a variety of talmudic statements. One central example is the teaching *Gadol hametsuveh ve'oseh mimi she'eino metsuveh ve'oseh*, 'One who is obligated [to perform a commandment] and does so is greater than one who is not obligated [to perform it] and does so' (BT *Bava kama* 38a; *Kidushin* 31a, 87a). This teaching has normative halakhic implications; it serves, for example, as the basis for considering the meal at a bar mitzvah – and, for some, a bat mitzvah as well – as a religiously significant act, a *se'udat mitsvah*.[27]

The indispensability of obedience in halakhic commitment is stressed in a number of the writings of Rabbi Joseph B. Soloveitchik

25. Robert Cover, 'Obligation: A Jewish Jurisprudence of the Social Order', in Martha Minow, Michael Ryan, and Austin Sarat (eds.), *Narrative, Violence, and the Law* (Ann Arbor, MI, 1995), 239–40.

26. R. Joseph Karo, *Shulḥan arukh*, 'Oraḥ ḥayim' 2:4; R. Moses Isserles, gloss on *Shulḥan arukh*, 'Oraḥ ḥayim' 260: 1.

27. R. Shlomoh Luria (Maharshal), *Yam shel shelomoh*, BK, no. 37; R. Ovadiah Yosef, *Yabia omer* 6:29; id, *Yehaveh da'at* 2: 29.

(the Rav, 1903–93). Take the Rav's discussion of the law that a religious holiday cancels the practices of mourning – a law that, as he makes clear elsewhere, keenly affected his own being as a Jew grieving the death of a spouse. He presents the following scenario:

> The mourner, who has buried a beloved wife or mother, returns home from the graveyard where he has left part of himself, where he has witnessed the mockery of human existence. He is in a mood to question the validity of our entire axiological universe. The house is empty, dreary, every piece of furniture reminds the mourner of the beloved person he has buried. Every corner is full of memories. Yet the halakhah addresses itself to the lonely mourner, whispering to him: 'Rise from your mourning; cast the ashes from your head; change your clothes; light the festive candles; recite over a cup of wine the *Kiddush* extolling the Lord for giving us festivals of gladness and sacred seasons of joy…join the jubilating community and celebrate the holiday as if nothing had transpired, as if the beloved person over whose death you grieve were with you.' The halakhah, which at times can be very tender, understanding, and accommodating, may, on other occasions, act like a disciplinarian demanding obedience.[28]

This same connection between submission and struggle was expressed by the Rav in a number of other contexts. For example:

> The religious experience does not always free man from care and pain, as many religious leaders assert. The believer is not always without sorrow and at peace with himself and the world. We find him quite often *torn by inner conflicts and doubts, groping in the dark, wrestling with his own conscience and convictions* [emphasis added]. The transcendental experience weighs heavily upon him.

---

28. R. Joseph B. Soloveitchik, 'Catharsis', *Tradition*, 17/2 (1978), 49. For a poignant description of his personal connection to this experience – the holiday of Purim fell during the *shiva* week for his wife – see Aaron Rakeffet-Rothkoff, *The Rav: The World of Rabbi Joseph B. Soloveitchik*, vol. 2 (n.p., 1999), 7–8.

He tries to cast it off and rid himself of that great burden, under whose impact he walks humbly and slavishly, committed to duties that he dislikes, to restraints and sacrifices that he resents, without being able to lift his head in full dignity and to regain his freedom and independence of living.[29]

So central is the idea of religious submission that it is required, according to Maimonides, even of the gentile who has committed himself to the Seven Noahide Laws:

A heathen who accepts the seven commandments and observes them scrupulously is a 'righteous heathen', and will have a portion in the world to come, provided that he accepts them and performs them because the Holy One, blessed be He, commanded them in the Law and made known through Moses our Teacher that the observance thereof had been enjoined upon the descendants of Noah even before the Law was given.[30]

And so the issue is clearly drawn. In the words of Jonathan Sacks, 'From the perspective of the autonomous self, then, halakhic existence is

---

29. R. Joseph B. Soloveitchik, 'The Absence of God and the Community of Prayer', in *Shalom Carmy* (ed.), *Worship of the Heart: Essays on Jewish Prayer by Rabbi Joseph B. Soloveitchik* (Jersey City, NJ, 2003), 73–4. This notion lies behind the Rav's response in the famous fourth footnote of his *Halakhic Man* to those who perceive religious faith as 'simple and comfortable' or as 'tranquil and neatly ordered, tender and delicate'. See id., *Halakhic Man* (Philadelphia, PA, 1983), 139–43. See also id., 'Catharsis', 46; Abraham Joshua Heschel, *God in Search of Man* (New York, 1955), 282–3. My thanks to R. David Shapiro for bringing this text to my attention.

30. Maimonides, *Mishneh torah*, 'Laws of Kings' 8: 11. The translation is from Isadore Twersky, *A Maimonides Reader* (New York, 1972), 221. For some literature on this difficult and controversial Maimonidean text, see Jacob Katz, *Exclusiveness and Tolerance* (New York, 1969), 175–6; Isadore Twersky, *Introduction to the Code of Maimonides (Mishneh torah)* (New Haven, CT, 1980), 455 n. 239; Mikhael Tsevi Nehorai, 'Ḥasidei umot ha'olam yesh lahem ḥelek le'olam haba', *Tarbits*, 61/3–4 (1992), 465–87; Eugene Korn, 'Gentiles, the World to Come, and Judaism: The Odyssey of a Rabbinic Text', *Modern Judaism*, 14 (1994), 265–87. See also my 'Rabbi Jacob Emden: Life and Major Works' (PhD diss., Harvard University, 1988), 739–41. (See also n. 3 of Alasdair MacIntyre's essay in this volume [eds.].)

inauthentic because it flees from making personal choice the centre of its universe. From the perspective of tradition, much of contemporary ethics is inauthentic precisely *because* it makes personal choice the measure of all things.'[31] Therefore, given the absolute premium placed upon personal autonomy and individual choice in contemporary culture – a culture in which Jews as a group, including many observant Jews, are deeply rooted – is it possible to construct a compelling argument for Jews to *choose* obedience and submission to the discipline of halakhah? Can one convince Jews that, in the words of a prominent Reform rabbi, they 'must choose to be commanded again'?[32] Even the typical Modern Orthodox Jew, writes Rabbi Aharon Lichtenstein, while recognizing 'that authority, and submission to it, is critical...bridles at the thought of constricting his autonomy.'[33]

Can anything be done to help resolve this dilemma?

IV

We may begin by noting that even the most meticulously observant halakhic Jew does not always view unquestioning submission to God as appropriate. Take the daring argument of Abraham to God: 'Shall not the Judge of all the earth do justly?' (Genesis 18: 25) or Moses' bold retort to God over a similar case of contemplated collective punishment: 'Shall one man sin and You be angry with the entire assembly?' (Numbers 16: 22). And what about the famous line put into God's mouth by the talmudic rabbis: 'My children have defeated Me, My children have defeated Me' (BT *Bava metsia* 59b)?

In the realm of the mind (as opposed to practice), one fruitful

---

31. Jonathan Sacks, *One People? Tradition, Modernity, and Jewish Unity* (London and Washington, DC, 1993), 158.

32. The phrase comes from R. Arnold Jacob Wolf, 'Reclaiming Shabbat', *Reform Judaism*, 12/1 (Fall 1983), 14. It is cited in Marc Lee Raphael, 'The Emergence and Development of Tradition in Reform Jewish Worship, 1970–1999', *Jewish History*, 15 (2001), 121. This article presents the Reform Movement's struggle with the very issue being presented here, the notion of mitzvah as commandment.

33. R. Aharon Lichtenstein, 'Legitimization of Modernity: Classical and Contemporary', in Moshe Z. Sokol (ed.), *Engaging Modernity: Rabbinic Leaders and the Challenge of the Twentieth Century* (Northvale, NJ and Jerusalem, 1997), 3.

source for finding a place for autonomy is the Rav's emphasis on the 'creativity' and 'individuality' of halakhic man, a figure whose 'autonomy asserts itself more and more'. The halakhic individual, he writes,

> relies upon his intellect, he places his trust in it and does not suppress any of his psychic faculties in order to merge into some supernal existence. His own personal understanding can resolve the most difficult and complex problems. He pays no heed to any murmurings of intuition or other types of mysterious presentiments. Halakhic man is a spontaneous, creative type. He is not particularly submissive and retiring, and is not meek when it is a matter of maintaining his own views....
>
> Even the Holy One, blessed be He, has, as it were, handed over His imprimatur, His official seal in Torah matters, to man; it is as if the Creator of the world Himself abides by man's decision and instruction....
>
> Halakhic man received the Torah from Sinai not as a simple recipient but as a creator of worlds, as a partner with the Almighty in the act of creation. The power of creative interpretation (*ḥiddush*) is the very foundation of the received tradition.... The essence of the Torah is intellectual creativity.[34]

With certain exceptions like Rabbi Avraham Karelitz (the Hazon Ish, 1878–1953) and Yeshayahu Leibowitz (1903–94) who, in different ways, took the principle of submission to an extreme,[35] many others have

---

34. Soloveitchik, *Halakhic Man*, 78–82.
35. For the position of the former, see Lawrence Kaplan, 'The Hazon Ish: Haredi Critic of Traditional Orthodoxy', in Jack Wertheimer (ed.), *The Uses of Tradition: Jewish Continuity in the Modern Era* (New York and Jerusalem, 1992), 145–73. Leibowitz for his part maintains that religious behaviour can only be based on worshipping God as His faithful servant. Even searching for 'meaning' in mitzvot is inappropriate because it shifts the focus from God to the individual. See id., 'Religious Praxis: The Meaning of Halakhah', in id., *Judaism, Human Values, and the Jewish State* (Cambridge, MA, 1992), 3–29.

reached similar conclusions, seeking to wrest a measure of autonomy from the all-encompassing nature of halakhic obedience.[36]

But I want to move in a different direction. First, a closer look at contemporary notions of autonomy yields the inescapable conclusion that they are, in fact, bankrupt and empty of meaning. All people make decisions to limit their autonomy – and do so all the time – to get through life. All people abide by laws, whatever they may be; the dream of unbridled liberty and autonomy is a foolish one. The choice made by Jews committed to halakhah to serve God is a choice to move to a higher form of freedom, an 'ordered freedom', if you will, and one more tested and longer lasting than any other notion of 'ordered freedom' or 'ordered liberty' (to use phrases often attributed to George Washington and at the heart of the American constitutional order). The life of the halakhic Jew represents, I would argue, the highest human expression of this freedom, deeply creative and exercised in the context not of isolated individuals but of an entire community. In the words of the sages (*Kalah rabati* 8), *Ein ben ḥorin ela mi she'osek batorah*, 'There is no one as free as one who is involved with Torah', and I take 'involved with Torah' to go beyond solely the study of Torah. And, if this is the case, when I personally make a conscious choice to 'abdicate' my freedom of choice in the service of God, I am not abdicating anything of value at all but rather gaining something of infinitely greater value.[37]

---

36. See, for example, R. Aharon Lichtenstein, '*Mitzva*: A Life of Command', in id., *By His Light: Character and Values in the Service of God* (Jersey City, NJ and Alon Shevut, 2003), 49–60, esp. p. 57; Moshe Z. Sokol, 'Personal Autonomy and Religious Authority', in id. (ed.), *Rabbinic Authority and Personal Autonomy* (Northvale, NJ and London, 1992), 169–216, which differentiates between 'hard autonomy', which is rejected and 'soft personal autonomy', which is affirmed. For other approaches, which do not share the fundamental assumptions of the present article about the binding nature of halakhah, see Eugene B. Borowitz, 'Autonomy Versus Tradition', *CCAR Journal*, 15/2 (April 1968), 32–43; id., 'The Autonomous Self and the Commanding Authority', *Theological Studies*, 45 (1984), 34–56; id., 'The Autonomous Jewish Self', *Modern Judaism*, 4/1 (1984), 39–56; Emil Fackenheim, 'The Revealed Morality of Judaism and Modern Thought', in Arnold J. Wolf (ed.), *Recovering Judaism: Reflections on a New Theology* (Chicago, IL, 1965), 51–75.

37. I thank Neal Kozodoy for helping me formulate and sharpen this very important point. It is, in fact, interesting to note that the overabundance of choice in America

I plan to deal with this point at much greater length in a forthcoming publication. Here I want to make a more focused point, albeit one unlikely to resonate with anyone who is not already, at least to some extent, committed to halakhah, even most broadly conceived, as essential to Jewish identity and Jewish meaning. Above all, I address myself to those who, while valuing halakhic behaviour as an important if not indispensable component of their lives, are struggling to find personal meaning in it and/or to commit themselves to it in its entirety.

My core proposition is this: one need not give up one's autonomy in order to understand, appreciate, and submit to the divine authority of Torah and mitzvot. Even as a life of halakhah rests on a set of objective requirements that do not generally allow for individual expression, much in that life not only allows for but encourages – nay, even requires – such expression. Indeed, I hope to demonstrate that the halakhic system itself provides its adherents with multiple opportunities to exercise personal autonomy; 'pockets of autonomy' exist and, in fact, are central in the world of halakhic authority. In short, one need not check one's individualism at the door of halakhic commitment.

Borrowing the terminology of a Dutch gentile scholar, although presenting it in a very different way, Isadore Twersky once characterized halakhah, or 'Jewish religious consciousness', as consisting of two elements simultaneously: both 'religion in manifestation' and 'religion in essence'.[38] In the Jewish context, the former term refers to the outward act: the performance of the mitzvot. One *manifests* one's commitment to God and Torah by *acting* in a certain public, visible, obvious, and identifiable way. Holding the 'four species' (*arba minim*) on Sukkot, eating matzah on Passover, lighting sabbath candles, donning tefillin and reciting kiddush: all are examples of this category. Anyone seeing an individual performing such acts knows exactly what she or he is doing.

---

has also generated something of a backlash. See Barry Schwartz, *The Paradox of Choice: Why More is Less* (New York, 2004). The subtitle of the book is, 'How the Culture of Abundance Robs Us of Satisfaction'. My thanks to Dan Cohn for bringing this book to my attention. In a different context, see John Tierney, 'To Choose is to Lose', *New York Times Magazine* (21 Aug. 2011), 33–7, 46.

38. Isadore Twersky, 'Religion and Law', in S.D. Goitein (ed.), *Religion in a Religious Age* (Cambridge, MA, 1974), 69–70 and p. 78 n. 2.

By contrast, the latter term, 'religion in essence', refers to the inner, personal, subjective, and hidden component of observance, what Twersky calls the 'interior, fluid spiritual forces and motives…internal sensibility and spirituality'. Here we mean to designate what the adherent of halakhah is *feeling* or *experiencing* while performing the act – the fundamental assumption being that God does not want halakhic practitioners to be robots or monkeys but rather to be affected, inspired, elevated, and even transformed by the acts they perform.[39]

Each of these elements is necessary, and each coheres with the other. 'The true essence of halakhah', writes Twersky, consists in both 'prophecy and law, charisma and institution, mood and medium, image and reality, normative action and individual perception, objective determinacy and subjective ecstasy'.[40] Elsewhere, he refers to halakhah as 'a tense, vibrant, dialectical system which regularly insists upon normativeness in action and inwardness in feeling and thought',[41] and to its aim as a 'composite act which is subjective though quantified, inspired and regular, intimate yet formal'.[42] One without the other is incomplete; both are necessary. 'For many religious traditions', writes an expert in Christianity, 'ancient texts, beliefs and rituals do not replace experience as the vital center of spiritual life, but instead provide the means for engendering it.'[43] This statement pertains to Judaism as well.

---

39. During a visit to the Metropolitan Museum of Art in New York in September, 2005, I saw on a wall a quotation attributed to Henri Matisse that is relevant here: 'I do not literally paint the table but the emotion it produces in me.' I suggest that 'table' is 'religion in manifestation', 'emotion' is 'religion in essence'.

40. Twersky, 'Religion and Law', 70.

41. Isadore Twersky, 'The Shulḥan Aruk: Enduring Code of Jewish Law', *Judaism*, 16/2 (1967), 157.

42. Isadore Twersky, 'Some Aspects of the Jewish Attitude toward the Welfare State', *Tradition*, 5/2 (1963), 144–5. For Twersky's formulation of some late mediaeval examples of this phenomenon, see id., 'Talmudists, Philosophers, Kabbalists: The Quest for Spirituality in the Sixteenth Century', in Bernard Dov Cooperman (ed.), *Jewish Thought in the Sixteenth Century* (Cambridge, MA, 1983), 431–57; id., 'Law and Spirituality in the Seventeenth Century: A Case Study in R. Yair Hayyim Bacharach', in Isadore Twersky and Bernard Septimus (eds.), *Jewish Thought in the Seventeenth Century* (Cambridge, MA, 1987), 447–67.

43. Amy Hollywood, 'Spiritual But Not Religious', *Harvard Divinity Bulletin*, 38/1–2 (Winter-Spring 2010), 21.

The Rav repeatedly stressed this dual nature of the halakhic obligation; in fact, I would characterize this as one of the central motifs of his lectures and writing. A few examples:

> I learned from [my mother] very much. Most of all, I learned that Judaism expresses itself not only in formal compliance with the law but also in a living experience. She taught me that there is a flavor, a scent and warmth to *mitzvot*.... The laws of Shabbat, for instance, were passed on to me by my father.... The Shabbat as a living entity, as a queen, was revealed to me by my mother.... The fathers *knew* much about the Shabbat; the mothers *lived* the Shabbat, experienced her presence, and perceived her beauty and splendor.[44]

> There are two aspects to the religious gesture in Judaism: strict objective discipline and exalted subjective romance. Both are indispensable....
>
> Judaism has always believed that wherever actions are fair and relations are just, whenever man is able to discipline himself and develop dignified behavioral patterns, the latter are always accompanied by corresponding worthy emotions. Feelings not manifesting themselves in deeds are volatile and transient; deeds not linked with inner experience are soulless and ritualistic. Both the subjective as well as the objective component are indispensable for the self-realization of the religious personality.[45]

---

44. R. Joseph B. Soloveitchik, 'A Tribute to the Rebbitzen of Talne', *Tradition*, 17/2 (1978), 77. For another formulation of the 'distinction between mother's and father's mission within the covenantal community' along these same lines, see id., 'Parenthood: Natural and Redeemed', in id., *Family Redeemed: Essays on Family Relationships*, ed. David Shatz and Joel B. Wolowelsky (Jersey City, NJ, 2000), 114–15.

45. R. Joseph B. Soloveitchik, 'Marriage', in id., *Family Redeemed*, 40. For additional references to this theme in the works of Rabbi Soloveitchik, see his 'Al ahavat hatorah vege'ulat nefesh hador', originally published in *Hado'ar* 39/27 (27 May 1960), 519; id., 'Letter to Morris Laub', 23 Jan. 1972, in R. Nathaniel Helfgot (ed.), *Community, Covenant and Commitment: Selected Letters and Communications by Rabbi Joseph B. Soloveitchik* (Jersey City, NJ, 2005), 337–8; id., *The Lonely Man of Faith*, 56; id., 'Uvikashtem misham', in id., *Ish hahalakhah: galui venistar* (Jerusalem, 1979), 210–11

V

It should thus be clear that one's experience of mitzvot is very personal and subjective. As Isadore Twersky notes:

[W]hile there are established modes of religious behavior, there are no established modes of religious sensibility, religious experience, or measures of moving ever closer to God. Here uniqueness reigns. Every halakhic act is accompanied by 'practice of the

---

n. 19, and id., *Shiurim lezekher aba mari z"l*, vol. 2 (Jerusalem, 2002), 198–206 (regarding *avelut* and *simḥat yom tov*); id., 'Ra'ayonot al hatefilah', in id., *Ish hahalakhah: galui venistar*, 239–43; id., 'Mah dodekh midod', in id., *Divrei hagut veha'arakhah* (Jerusalem, 1982), 79; id., 'Peleitat sofreihem', in id., *Divrei hagut veha'arakhah*, 137–40; id., 'Zemanei hateshuvah veyiḥudam', in id., *Yemei zikaron* (Jerusalem, 1989), 233; id., *The Halakhic Mind* (New York, 1986), 78–81, 85; id., 'Kibbud u-Mora: The Honor and Fear of Parents', in id., *Family Redeemed*, 126–30; id., 'Petition, Prayer and Crisis', in Carmy (ed.), *Worship of the Heart*, 13–19, 21; id., 'Intention (Kavvanah) in Reading Shema and in Prayer', in Carmy (ed.), *Worship of the Heart*, 87–106; id., 'Reflections on the Amidah', in Carmy (ed.), *Worship of the Heart*, 146–7; Aaron Rakeffet-Rothkoff, *The Rav: The World of Rabbi Joseph B. Soloveitchik*, vol. 2 (n.p., 1999), 147–8, 170, 175–80, 210–12; B. David Schreiber, *Sefer noraot harav*, vol. 9 (n.p., 1998), end of book; Pinhas Peli, *Al hateshuvah* (Jerusalem, 1975), 40–1, 58 n.; Abraham R. Besdin, *Reflections of the Rav: Lessons in Jewish Thought* (Jerusalem, 1979), 143–4 on the sin of Korah, 163; Arnold Lustiger, *Before Hashem You Shall be Purified: Rabbi Joseph B. Soloveitchik on the Days of Awe* (Edison, NJ, 1998), 17–22.

Secondary literature on this theme includes Lawrence Kaplan, 'Rabbi Joseph B. Soloveitchik's Philosophy of Halakhah', *Jewish Law Annual*, 7 (1988), 193–5; id., 'The Multi-Faceted Legacy of the Rav', *Bekhol derakhekha da'ehu*, 7 (1998), 63–4; R. Elyakim Koenigsberg, *Sefer shiurei harav al inyanei avelut vetishah be'av* (Jerusalem, 1999), 1–2, 78–82; id., *Sefer shiurei harav al inyanei sheḥitah, meliḥah, basar beḥalav, veta'aruvot* (Jerusalem, 2005), 5–6; R. Yosef Blau, 'Hesped for the Rav', in Michael A. Bierman (ed.), *Memories of a Giant: Eulogies in Memory of Rabbi Dr. Joseph B. Soloveitchik* (Jerusalem and New York, 2003), 122–4; Shlomo Zev Pick, *Mo'adei harav* (Ramat Gan, 2003), 24–6; id., 'Memories of Rav Joseph B. Soloveitchik', *Bekhol derakhekha da'ehu*, 15 (2004), 70; Alex Sztuden, 'Grief and Joy in the Writings of Rabbi Soloveitchik', *Tradition*, 44/3 (2011), 9–32. It is also highlighted by R. Aharon Lichtenstein in his appreciation of the impact of his father-in-law. See his 'R. Joseph Soloveitchik', in Simon Noveck (ed.), *Great Jewish Thinkers of the Twentieth Century* (Clinton, MA, 1963), 294–7. See, too, R. David Shapiro, *Rabbi Joseph B. Soloveitchik on Pesach, Sefirat ha-Omer, and Shavuot* (Jerusalem, 2005), 53–67, and the bibliography on pp. 66–7; Jeffrey R. Woolf, 'Time Awareness as a Source of Spirituality in the Thought of Rabbi Joseph B. Soloveitchik', *Modern Judaism*, 32/1 (2012), 54–75.

heart' – a personal, subjective religious component. The objective act is standard and unchanging; the practice is various and multifaceted.[46]

Nor is this view a modern innovation. As Michael Stanislawski writes in a very different context, 'we have countless expressions of individuality, individuation, and richly idiosyncratic interiorities not circumscribed by [particular] views of God and Torah – no one could confuse Maimonides' interior life with Judah Halevi's, or the Vilna Gaon's with the Baal Shem Tov's.'[47]

In this experiential, 'religion in essence', realm of halakhic observance, individuality is central. There is much room for autonomy in the personal and subjective way each individual experiences the mitzvah she or he performs; 'religion in essence' is central to the mitzvah act. It is a simple and obvious fact that, for example, different people experience taking the 'four species' differently, that the mitzvah of sukkah means different things to different people, that not all women have the same thoughts during Friday night candle-lighting, and so on. Some people are more rationally oriented, some more mystical; some are more intellectual, some more emotional; some like to say, some love to sing. The structure of the law is given, it is constant; the experience of the law is personal and subjective, various and multifaceted, individual and fluid.

This leaves the way open for modern individuals, rooted in the values and assumptions of Western culture, to enter the worldview of halakhic commitment and, I would submit, to accept the authority inherent in it. The yoke of the law lies lighter on those aware of the degree to which the law itself makes room for the expression of their individuality.

To be sure, I hardly mean to underplay the nuances and complexities of this suggestion. One issue concerns guidelines or boundaries to legitimate individual religious experience. Rabbinic texts attach symbols

---

46. Isadore Twersky, 'What Must a Jew Study – and Why?', in Seymour Fox, Israel Scheffler, and Daniel Marom (eds.), *Visions of Jewish Education* (Cambridge, 2003), 52.

47. Michael Stanislawski, *Autobiographical Jews: Essays in Jewish Self-Fashioning* (Seattle, WA, and London, 2004), 13.

to the 'four species', suggesting that they represent different parts of the body or different types of Jews.[48] These traditional possibilities for a 'religion in essence' for this mitzvah are well known and meaningful. But what about someone immersed in Eastern religions for whom, let us say, the concentric shape of the *etrog* and the linear shape of the *lulav* represent the primal forms of woman and man, achieving their highest spiritual level when brought together (*igud*) as one? Many would hesitate to accept this as Jewishly valid, and I am not sure that I would disagree with them.[49] Even so, I stand by the basic point. Despite limitations to what may be considered appropriate religious experiences, a great deal of room exists for both autonomy and individual expression in the overall world of religious authority. Jewish observance was not meant to be mechanical, monotonous, simply performed by rote. On the contrary, it is meant to be lived and experienced. Therein, precisely, lies the rationale for strict punctilious attention to halakhic details and structure.

VI

Finally, and most strikingly, if measures of autonomy, individuality, and choice are possible in the realm of 'religion in essence', there is also a case to be made for their applicability even in the realm of 'religion in manifestation', a realm where one might expect religious practice and ritual behaviour to be fully scripted, structured, 'standard and unchanging'.

Clearly, Jewish observance needs structure and form. 'Without the traditions and legal structures of marriage to contain and sustain it, romance is always in danger of flaming out or heading down blind alleys, extinguished as quickly as it first appeared.'[50] Those words, uttered by a Unitarian minister, could just as easily have been uttered by a traditional Jew. And marriage is only one example of this central point.

---

48. *Leviticus Rabbah* 30: 12, 14. For other associations, see Arthur Schaffer, 'The Agricultural and Ecological Symbolism of the Four Species of Sukkot', *Tradition*, 20/2 (1982), 128–40.

49. My thanks to Dr William Kolbrener who suggested a version of this possibility to me (personal communication via email, 23 Nov. 2005).

50. Cited in Elizabeth Debold, 'Spiritual But Not Religious', *What is Enlightenment Magazine*, 31 (Dec. 2005–Feb. 2006), 105–10. It can be found online at www.wie.org. My thanks to David Landes for bringing this article to my attention.

How so? Take the rituals of Sukkot again, as scripted and regulated a collection of requirements as any 'religion in manifestation' could demand. The Talmud and the codes instruct us in exactly what is involved and what is to be done: what elements comprise the 'four species', how to hold and shake them, the practice of first holding the *etrog* upside down in order to fulfil the requirement of reciting the blessing prior to fulfilling the mitzvah, what a sukkah looks like, how many walls it must have, what materials may be used to cover it, and more, much more.[51] Or take other examples of carefully defined rules and behaviours: how many fringes comprise the *tsitsit*, what is recited during kiddush, how much wine is necessary to fulfil the obligation, how to bake matzah for Passover, in what time-frame must it be eaten, at which point is the *berakhah* (blessing) over the candles on Friday night recited, and so forth. All these details are carefully and meticulously described – and many more like them, thousands more, govern every aspect of every festival, of the sabbath, of prayer, and of the totality of an observant Jewish life.

And yet, even into this world of 'religion in manifestation' a measure of autonomy and choice is constantly allowed to intervene and, indeed, is meant to intervene. Examples of this would include decisions by a man as to whether or not to wear his *tsitsit* over his shirt, wrapped around his belt loops, visibly protruding from his shirt, or tucked into his pants, with *tekhelet* (blue thread) or not.[52] Decisions of whether or not to sleep in the sukkah, make personal additions to different blessings in the Shemoneh Esreh, stand for the Torah reading or repetition of the Amidah, or put on Rabbenu Tam's tefillin would fit into this category. Also, according to Rabbenu Hananel and Ritba, it is the personal prerogative of every individual to decide whether or not he or she wants to act

51. See BT *Sukah*; *Shulḥan arukh*, 'Oraḥ ḥayim', 'Laws of Sukkah', nos. 625–44; 'Laws of Lulav', nos. 645–67. On holding the *etrog* upside down, see the various approaches in Tosafot on BT *Sukah* 39a, s.v. *over*; *Arba'ah turim* and *Shulḥan arukh*, 'Oraḥ ḥayim' 651.

52. On *tsitsit*, for example, see R. Eliezer Y. Waldenberg, *Tsits eli'ezer* 8:3; R. Ovadiah Yosef, *Yeḥaveh da'at* 2: 1; R. Alfred Cohen (ed.), *Tekhelet: The Renaissance of a Mitzvah* (New York, 1996). See also David J. Landes, 'Traditional Struggles: Studying, Deciding, and Performing the Law at the Rabbi Isaac Elchanan Theological Seminary' (PhD thesis: Princeton University, 2010), 239.

lifenim mishurat hadin, beyond the letter of the law.[53] In all such instances, one's personal decision will clearly affect one's halakhic behaviour. Under this same heading, we may add the diverse ritual practices adopted in recent years by some women in more Modern Orthodox communities and considered appropriate by some *poskim* or recognized halakhic authorities: bat mitzvah ceremonies, reciting kaddish or *birkat hagomel* (blessing on an escape from danger) in the synagogue, and many more.[54]

What I hope to have made clear is that Jewish tradition not only allows for, and even encourages, a 'variety of religious experiences', to borrow from William James, but also recognizes the validity of a variety of religious behaviours. Jewish authority speaks in a multiplicity of voices. A fundamental awareness of these facts can, I believe, help light the way to a greater readiness on the part of God's children to submit to His will and accept with joy the blessing and the privilege of His commandments.

---

53. See their respective commentaries on BT *BM* 24*b*. This question of whether acting *lifenim mishurat hadin* can be required or not is, in fact, the subject of debate among mediaeval Jewish halakhic authorities, and many disagree with the position taken by R. Hananel. See Shmuel Shilo, 'On One Aspect of Law and Morals in Jewish Law: *Lifnim Mishurat Hadin*', *Israel Law Review*, 13 (1978), 359–90, esp. pp. 365–9; R. Aharon Lichtenstein, 'Does Jewish Tradition Recognize an Ethic Independent of Halakha?', in Marvin Fox (ed.), *Modern Jewish Ethics: Theory and Practice* (Columbus, OH, 1975), 62–88.

54. There is a large, and growing, literature on these matters. For references to halakhic authorities allowing and, in some cases, even encouraging these practices, see R. Yehiel Ya'akov Weinberg, *She'elot uteshuvot seridei esh*, vol. 3, 93; R. Ovadiah Yosef, *Yabia omer* 6:29; R. Ovadiah Yosef, *Yehaveh da'at* 2:29 (bat mitzvah); R. Ahron Soloveichik, *Od yisra'el yosef beni ḥai* (Chicago, IL, 1993), 100, no. 32 (kaddish); R. Ovadiah Yosef, *Yehaveh da'at* 4:15 (*birkhat hagomel*). I am not dealing here with other current women's synagogue ritual practices.

Section IV

Leadership

Chapter 11

Operating Across Boundaries: Leading Adaptive Change[1]

Ronald Heifetz

Judaism is about the miracle of unity that creates diversity.[2]

– JONATHAN SACKS

Human beings have long known how to create productive relationships across group boundaries. As hunters and gatherers, we knew how to trade and marry across bands and collaborate seasonally on hunting herds for food. When we began to settle into agricultural communities

---

1. Adapted from Ronald Heifetz, 'Operating across Boundaries', in Todd L. Pittinsky (ed.), *Crossing the Divide: Intergroup Leadership in a World of Difference* (Boston: Harvard Business Press/Center for Public Leadership, 2009), ch. 10.
2. Jonathan Sacks, *The Dignity of Difference: How to Avoid the Clash of Civilizations* (London: Continuum, 2002), 54.

ten to fourteen thousand years ago, creating large social systems with multiple group boundaries, we applied that know-how to more complex arrangements. We used ceremony and celebration, feasts and gift-giving, extended family bonds through marriage between clans and tribes, norms of trade and reciprocity, shared history, tradition, and sometimes language and faith. We developed ramified authority structures in which those who were given authority identified and generated complementary goals for their groups and superordinate goals for groups of groups.

We know from studies of traditional hunter and gatherer societies like the !Kung people in Botswana (! pronounced with a click) that cultural norms provide the knowledge and guide the behaviours needed in normal times to co-ordinate interactions inside and between groups. In challenging times, however, those with authority must be able to step in and co-ordinate problem-solving on problems for which usual norms of social operation are insufficient to provide direction and decision. Someone or some subgroup of authorities, often elders and specialists, must dip into a deeper reservoir of knowledge and wisdom to make decisions and resolve conflicts both within their community and between communities. The variety of instruments to promote productive exchange across group boundaries had to be learned and practised by authorities within each group whose trust from their own group was based, in part, on their competence in managing routine, yet critically productive, transactions across group boundaries.[3] Practices of authority accumulated and were passed down through generations. For example, early in the journey of the Israelites from Egypt to the Promised Land, Jethro warns Moses, his son-in-law, that he will wear himself thin unless he organizes his society. Jethro tells Moses to create an authority structure consisting of leaders in charge of groups of a thousand, a hundred, fifty, and ten (Exodus 18:21).

In our day, successful relationships between groups of people are ubiquitous. One can simply walk down the street to any set of neighbourhood shops and listen to a store owner describe the many arrangements with

---

3. See Ronald A. Heifetz, *Leadership Without Easy Answers* (Cambridge, MA: Belknap/ Harvard University Press, 1994), ch. 3, 'The Roots of Authority'.

vendors and suppliers that sustain a business. Indeed, perhaps no commercial entity functions without successful daily intergroup transactions. In a sense, any organization's current authority structures, expertise, processes, and cultural norms can be seen as adaptations to a past set of challenges that demanded innovation in managing complex activity across boundaries. Having enabled the organization to thrive, these once-creative adaptations became routine. People learned, by and large, what they were supposed to do.[4] Those with the greatest adaptability thrived, passing on their lessons to posterity, whereas many organizations and communities failed and perished in the face of new adaptive pressures.[5]

One of the key adaptive pressures of our time is the challenge of collaboration across the boundaries of religious communities. The unresolved traumatic histories and competition for legitimacy, primacy, and market share among religious communities threaten our world. Even were we to win the 'war on terror', not only militarily, but also by establishing a universally accepted international norm that delegitimizes the targeting of innocent people for any reason, the Crusades have not been laid to rest. The prevailing view among fundamentalist traditions that their one religion captures all necessary human truth has become unsustainable in a globally interdependent world. Weapons are too destructive, national borders in a world of vast international trade are too permeable, and information is too easily manipulated. Our religious communities and our theological understandings face enormous adaptive pressure. Clashes between peoples across religious boundaries threaten to destroy the fruits of humanity's richly diverse cultural history. Chief Rabbi Jonathan Sacks provides the theological basis for relations across boundaries beyond sterile tolerance, anchored in an appreciation of the diverse wisdoms of many peoples, struggling to live divinely inspired and guided lives. Making the theological argument that God intended diversity rather than uniformity in the design of human living,

---

4. See Philip Selznick, *Leadership in Administration: A Sociological Interpretation* (New York: Harper and Row, 1957).

5. See, for example, the case of Easter Island, in Heifetz, *Leadership Without Easy Answers*; Selznick, *Leadership in Administration*, ch. 2; or Jared Diamond, *Collapse: How Societies Choose to Fail or Succeed* (New York: Viking Penguin, 2005).

Rabbi Sacks gives us a theological basis for relationships of respect, curiosity, and learning across historically inflamed boundaries.

As skilled as humanity has become over many millennia in collaborating and competing with civility across boundaries, we remain challenged in so many arenas for which our current repertoire of strategies remains insufficient. Beyond the clash of religious communities, we face the daily wastes of social division, the demands of economic and environmental co-operation, and, in less dramatic but key ways, the failures to achieve synergy across divisions within an organization or between companies rendered one entity after an acquisition.

This essay presents an initial exploration of the kind of leadership work required when our communities and organizations face problems across boundaries requiring some degree of new organizational or cultural adaptation. We focus on three aspects of adaptive work: the commonality of loss, the politics of inclusion and exclusion, and the task of renegotiating loyalties. But first, we briefly explore the metaphor of adaptation itself as it applies to our collective lives.

ADAPTABILITY

The term *adaptation* comes from evolutionary biology. As with any metaphor, particularly one as abused as Darwin's theory of natural selection, we need to be cautious with the insights it offers and the ways we use them. In biological systems, adaptive pressures arise outside an individual organism: the ecosystem generates new challenges and opportunities. In cultural systems, however, pressures to change may emerge exogenously from external sources (changes in taste, competition, technology, and public policy) or endogenously from internal sources (shifts in orienting values, organizational priorities, balances of power, and competencies). In both cases, an adaptive challenge routinely generates conflict between groups in which the gap between goals and actual conditions is perceived differently – internally by different groups within a larger organization, or externally between separate groups, organizations, factions, communities, or societies.

These gaps cannot be closed with routine behaviour and existing know-how. To meet an adaptive challenge, groups must change some of their own priorities, loyalties, and competencies as they develop a set of responses and relationships that enable them to thrive anew, collectively, in the face of new external challenges, or to achieve a new internally-generated normative conception of what thriving may mean in their environment, or both. For example, external challenges posed by competition from Japanese car companies demanded new intergroup behaviour of all sorts among engineering and business units within American and European car companies. Internal challenges posed by civil rights activists in the United States demanded new intergroup behaviour among many factional groups within US national boundaries.

In biology, evolution has three key tasks: (1) to identify the DNA to conserve; (2) to identify the DNA to 'discard', and (3) to innovate new DNA. In evolution, most of an organism's core processes are *conserved*. More than 98 per cent of human and chimpanzee DNA is identical; a less than 2 per cent difference accounts for our dramatically increased range of function. Similarly in cultures, adaptive leadership is only in part about change: successful change is likely to build on the past. Rarely does success seem to be the result of a zero-based, ahistorical, start-over approach, except perhaps as a deliberate exercise in strategic rethinking. Most radical revolutions fail, and those that succeed have more, rather than less, in common with their heritage. The American Revolution, for example, created a political system with deep roots in British and European political philosophy, experience, and culture. New, thriving businesses such as Google have much more in common with their antecedents than less, both technologically and organizationally.

Yet we cannot lose sight of the fact that in biology, as in culture, new adaptations generate loss, and for human beings, a host of emotions associated with those losses; not many people like to be displaced, rearranged, or reregulated. No one likes their theology tampered with. One group's innovation can make the people in another group feel incompetent, disloyal, or irrelevant. New adaptations can threaten and disturb individual identity, anchored in past and current group loyalties. As students of leadership and change have long known from their explorations, adaptive pressures often generate a defensive reaction as people in groups try to ameliorate the disruptions and pain associated with their losses.[6] The practice of leadership therefore requires first the diagnostic ability to recognize these losses and identify predictable defensive patterns at both group and intergroup systemic levels. Second, it requires the know-how to counteract these defences in order to keep people engaged: facing the challenge within and across group boundaries, accepting losses on behalf of collective necessity and gains, and developing new integrative capacity.

The Hebrew Scriptures offer an archetypal example of how new challenges and aspirations threaten group identity. Leading the Israelites out of Egypt, Moses did not face a technical challenge, but an adaptive one. He knew where to go and how to get there. Indeed, he arrived at the threshold of the Promised Land within eighteen months of the Exodus. However, when he sent scouts to investigate the land, all except Joshua and Caleb reported not only a fruitful land but also cities with people who looked like giants: 'We seemed like grasshoppers in our own eyes, and we looked the same to them.' The Scriptures tell us that, lacking faith in themselves and in God, the Israelites demanded that Moses take them back to Egypt, enslaved but secure.[7]

This was not the first time that Moses fell on his face in despair. He had recently pleaded with God to put him out of his leadership misery and put him to death. God refused, suggesting that Moses organize himself better instead.[8] Moses was discovering in the Sinai desert that the hardest part of his job was not the Exodus itself and the challenge of gaining the trust of his people and persuading Pharaoh to let them go. The toughest challenge for his leadership was located in people's hearts and minds, beyond any expert solution he or even God could provide. With the support of God and a small faction that included Joshua, Caleb, and Aaron, Moses prepared himself for the long haul. Identity, anchored in slave–master intergroup relationships, had to evolve into a new identity anchored in new institutional and spiritual relationships among the

---

6. See, for example, the works of Chris Argyris; also Ronald A. Heifetz and Marty Linsky, *Leadership on the Line: Staying Alive through the Dangers of Leading* (Boston, MA: Harvard Business School Press, 2002).
7. Num. 13–14.
8. Num. 11.

Israelites themselves and with God. Moses spent nearly thirty-nine more years leading people on a journey towards a society that could govern itself with faith in God and law beyond any king.[9]

Adaptive challenges stress the organism. If the species is lucky, it will have variant individuals in its population who are capable of surviving (albeit under stress) in the more-challenging environment, buying time for further variations to emerge and consolidate more robust adaptations. Joshua and Caleb can be seen as the variant, adaptive individuals among the group of scouts sent into Canaan. In biology, human beings living at low altitudes can move to high altitudes, but they are stressed. Over time, however, the stresses select new variants among the next generations of progeny that enable the species to thrive, unstressed, in that environment. We know, for example, that the physiology of mountain people differs adaptively from that of sea-level people. But it takes generations to consolidate new adaptive capacity to thrive in the new environment.

One strategy of leadership, therefore, is to identify the sources of *positive deviance* in the population, sources of more adaptive innovation already emerging in some groups in the culture, from which to build new capacity.[10] But building on and consolidating these adaptive variants takes time, because people in different groups must learn, across boundaries, how to take advantage of them. Thus, the practice of leadership involves orchestrating conflict and discovery across group boundaries, regulating the disequilibrium those differences generate in the organization, and holding the parties through a sustained period of stress. During this period, they sift out what is precious from what is expendable

---

9. Num. 13–14; Aaron Wildavsky, *The Nursing Father: Moses as a Political Leader* (Tuscaloosa, AL: University of Alabama Press, 1984).

10. See Richard Pascale, Jerry Sternin, and Monique Sternin, *The Power of Positive Deviance: How Unlikely Innovators Solve the World's Toughest Problems* (Boston: Harvard Business Press, 2010); and M. Sternin, J. Sternin, and D. Marsh, 'Scaling Up a Poverty Alleviation and Nutrition Program in Vietnam', in T. Marchione (ed.), *Scaling Up, Scaling Down: Capacities for Overcoming Malnutrition in Developing Countries* (Amsterdam: Gordon and Breach, 1999), 97–115.

within their own groups, and they identify and run new experiments in variation to determine which innovations will work collectively.[11]

In organizations, the stresses of change are, therefore, both the stimulant for and the bane of adaptive change.

THE COMMONALITY OF LOSS

What then inhibits our collective ability to respond to adaptive challenges in a timely fashion with innovation and courage? Sometimes, of course, the challenge is beyond our capacity. Vesuvius erupts, and we simply cannot do anything about it, hard as we might try. But sometimes, even though we might have it within our collective capacity to respond successfully, we squander the opportunity. Leadership becomes dangerous when the losses and fear generated by the need for change trigger efforts to neutralize the disturbance and anyone associated with it.

Losses come in many forms among individuals, organizations, and societies, from direct losses of goods such as wealth, status, authority, influence, security, and health, to indirect losses of loyalty and competence. In our experience, the common aphorism that people resist change is more wrong than right. People do not resist change per se; they resist loss. People usually embrace change when they anticipate a clear net benefit. Rarely does anyone return a winning lottery ticket. People resist change when change involves the possibility of giving up something they hold dear.

Leadership, then, requires reverence for the pains of change. One has to know what the challenge of change means to people, in terms of loyalty, competence, or direct stakes, in order to fashion a strategy of rhetoric, pacing, alliances, and social learning. One may need the patience and compassion that Moses, in the end, developed through meeting the challenges of despair, both personally and on behalf of his people.

We find two common pathways in the patterns by which people resist losses and risk adaptive failure: diversion of attention and displacement of responsibility. These take a wide variety of forms in organizations and politics, including the use of decoys and distracting issues, tackling

---

11. See, for example, Pascale et al., *Power of Positive Deviance*, ch. 4, 'Hospital Infections', pp. 83–119.

only the aspects of the problem that fit a group's competence, jumping to solutions without adequate diagnosis, misusing consultants, blaming authority, scapegoating, personalizing the issues, launching *ad hominem* attacks, and externalizing the enemy. Religious communities elevate religious authorities who reinforce historical prejudices by reinforcing traditional interpretations of sacred text and collective history. Those religious leaders who try to refashion narratives to help their peoples see that options adaptive to the realities they face are endangered.

These protective patterns may restore internal group stability and *feel* less stressful than facing the changes that adaptation would require. However, they also enable people within groups to avoid engaging in the often-disruptive process of sifting through their cultural DNA in order to decide what to keep and what to leave behind.[12] They end up trading off the long-term on behalf of the short-term. Many people who worked for General Motors in the decades before its bankruptcy in 2009 perceived risks in their company's strategic commitment to producing big cars with large fuel appetites and hefty emissions. They could see the skyrocketing demand for oil in vibrant new economies in Asia and growing urgency about climate change. But they could not engage their colleagues, senior management, unions, and workers sufficiently to mobilize a timely change in the cost basis and kinds of cars GM produced. Joseph Schumpeter is mainly right in his analysis of free-market economies and the demise of established companies as new ones with better products

---

12. For analyses of both the adaptive and the self-defeating aspects of defensive behaviour at the individual level, see Anna Freud, *The Ego and the Mechanisms of Defense*, rev. edn. (New York: International Universities Press, 1966); and George E. Vaillant, *The Wisdom of the Ego* (Cambridge, MA: Harvard University Press, 1993), ch. 1. At the group and organizational levels, see Wilfred R. Bion, *Experiences in Groups* (New York: Basic, 1961); Chris Argyris, *Strategy, Change, and Defensive Routines* (Boston, MA: Pitman, 1985); Larry Hirschhorn, *The Workplace Within: Psychodynamics of Organizational Life* (Cambridge, MA: MIT Press, 1988); Chris Argyris, *Overcoming Organizational Defenses: Facilitating Organizational Learning* (Boston, MA: Allyn and Bacon, 1990); Heifetz and Linsky, *Leadership on the Line*; and Ronald A. Heifetz, Alexander Grashow, and Marty Linsky, *The Practice of Adaptive Leadership; Tools and Tactics for Changing your Organization and the World* (Boston, MA: Harvard Business Press, 2009).

emerge and compete: creative destruction comes with the territory of adaptive change, and few if any welcome it in their own lives.[13]

Sometimes defensive behaviours provide important protection against the threats of loss and change; but sometimes they squander the time an organization or community needs to meet adaptive pressures before the situation becomes far more costly or impossible to retrieve. Reality testing – the effort to grasp the problem fully – is an early casualty of the reaction to social and personal disequilibrium associated with adaptation. People may initially assess and address problems realistically; but if that assessment does not pay early dividends, moving into a protective posture may take precedence over enduring both the prolonged uncertainty associated with weighing divergent views and running costly experiments, and the pain of refashioning loyalties and developing new competencies.

With sustained distress, people often produce misdiagnoses: a society may scapegoat a group because so-called leaders reinforce the dominant perception that the group is indeed responsible for the problem, or worse. A classic study of thirty-five dictatorships showed that all of them emerged in societies facing crisis.[14] The Great Depression of the 1930s generated such deep yearnings for quick and simple solutions in many countries around the world that groups in them lost the capacity to operate across boundaries to reality-test different strategies for restoring their own local and national economies in a critical and open-minded way. A reversion to narrower identity groups took hold. Charismatic demagoguery, repression, scapegoating, and externalizing the enemy were all in play, leading to the catastrophes of World War II.

One group's innovation may be another group's loss, and even a history of innovation in an organization or community does not ensure ongoing creativity. By the 1980s, IBM had lost the formidable adaptability that earlier had generated breakthroughs in mainframe hardware and software systems. The few at that time who saw the emergence of microcomputers (PCs) had to go around rather than collaborate with

---

13. Joseph Schumpeter, 'The Process of Creative Destruction', in id., *Capitalism, Socialism, and Democracy* (1950), (Routledge: Taylor & Francis e-Library, 2003), 81–7.

14. J.O. Hertzler, 'Crises and Dictatorships', *American Sociological Review* 5 (1940), 157–69.

their colleagues, who were deeply invested in the previous generation of innovations. They had to go outside the company and seek external partners in constructing the first IBM PCs, mainly from outside vendors. Similarly, in the same era, Xerox failed to exploit the breakthrough technologies developed at its own Palo Alto Research Center (laser printing, personal computers with a graphical interface and the mouse, local area networks, etc.) – technology then seized upon by Apple and others. Orchestrating productive group conflict within Xerox between innovators and groups wedded to the company's previous products and brand identity would probably have required leadership that could identify and distribute losses and counteract the patterns of resistance to it.

Though they may differ according to the culture, patterns of avoidance seem to operate in any social context. In an organization, people may follow standard operating procedures even when they know they do not fit the situation. In an election, voters may choose good-news candidates when progress on pressing problems requires hard, distributed group losses and innovation. For example, the task of liberalizing protected economies often generates social disruption and economic loss, not only in the short term at the macro level, but also for a generation or more at the micro level, with the disruption of whole communities and their families, reinforcing the pressures on politicians to create barriers to foreign competition.

When an organization faces a routine challenge, however critical it may be, the structures, processes, and authoritative expertise currently in place often suffice to meet the situation. But when people face an adaptive challenge, problems and solutions do not fall so neatly into the current structure and processes. Discovering what DNA to keep, what DNA to discard, and what innovation will enable people to thrive into the future, bringing forward the best of their history, demands collaborating across boundaries.

People do not learn by staring in the mirror; people learn by engaging different points of view. An adaptive challenge outstrips current group knowledge and norms of interaction, and pieces of the puzzle and the variants that may lead to solutions are often scattered across divisions, functions, interest groups, and segments of the community. Solutions often require discovery, experimentation, and new working relationships across group boundaries, and the leadership to foster those new relationships. Ironically, the disequilibrium caused by tough adaptive challenges also increases the pressure to seek easy answers from those in authority, rather than draw on the distributed intelligence of people across groups. The pressure to restore equilibrium quickly leads to the common mistake of treating adaptive challenges as if they were technical problems amenable to authoritative solutions.

THE POLITICS OF INCLUSION: DEFINING THE GROUPS IN PLAY

Adaptive work consists of the learning required either to resolve internal contradictions in people's values and strategic priorities or to diminish the gap between these priorities and the realities people face. This work entails spurring groups to clarify what matters most, in what balance, with what trade-offs. What will it mean for us to thrive? And who is 'us', anyway? Where do we set the boundaries of the system? In the case of a local industry that pollutes a river, people want clean water, but they also want jobs. In the long run, given the spread of environmental values, an industrial polluter will deeply harm its reputation or even fail if it neglects the health of its host community. Conversely, a community may lose its economic base if it overlooks the needs of its industry. Do we delimit the system at the level of the business organization, or the local community it inhabits?

Determining which parties and issues to include in cross-boundary consultation is a strategic decision. Leadership requires asking the critical question, who should play a part in the deliberations, and in what sequence? Including too many parties can overload people's capacity to learn and to accommodate one another. However, social systems that fail to be inclusive may devise an incomplete solution or a solution to the wrong problem. At a minimum, those who lead must keep track of missing perspectives. Not only can lack of information undermine the quality of collective work among the included groups, but also excluded parties may sabotage the process of sustainable change.

Deciding who should play a part in the deliberations is not a given, but is itself a critical strategic question. Strategy begins with asking, who needs to learn what in order for the group to make progress on this challenge? How can one build a holding environment and strengthen the bonds that join the stakeholders together as a community of interests so that they withstand the divisive forces of problem-solving? Is a concern so critical that it threatens the community's survival? Does a party represent a constituency that must accept change if the larger community is to make progress? Does the party's perspective generate so much distress that including it would disrupt the work of building any kind of coalition within the functioning cross-boundary working group? If the party is important in the medium or long term but not in the short term, one might initially exclude it from a working group.

This is one of the pains of leadership. People must sometimes be excluded and the issues they represent put aside, regardless of their validity. Consider the issue of slavery when the US Constitution was being drafted during the Federal Convention of 1787. During that summer, many divisive issues had to be resolved by framers representing very different perspectives on the nature of government and the balance between liberty and order, local and national control, and the division and sharing of powers. To prevent fragmentation into North and South, the framers made a deliberate decision to avoid a strong stand on the institution of slavery – but they did not reach that decision until after some effort. In August 1787, they tried to tackle slavery, but James Madison quickly sensed that if they persisted in doing so, they would unravel the whole tapestry of union and lose the opportunity to form a more coherent federal government than that provided by the Articles of Confederation.[15]

This decision, however brutal in its effects, made sense even to some who abhorred slavery. 'A more perfect union' mattered more, and some seventy-five years later when slavery was finally abolished, in 1863, the union tested by war was strong enough to survive. But the experience

---

15. At most, the framers gave Congress the power to outlaw the importation of slaves after 1808. They initially chosen the year 1800, but that date was set back. In any case, the constitutional clause meant little. By the time of the federal convention, Virginia and Maryland had already stopped importation of slaves, because the birth of US-born slaves proved sufficient for their economic aims. See James Madison, *Debates in the Federal Convention of 1787*, vol. 2 (Buffalo, NY: Prometheus, 1987), sessions of 21, 22, and 25 Aug. 1787, pp. 442–7, 467–9.

of the Civil War also illustrates the extraordinary danger of leaving a tough issue on the back burner for too long. Although the issue may go away, it may also explode into a future crisis, generating trauma that continues to linger for generations.

Running the risk of delay may be necessary. But when adaptive capacity increases as the community successfully addresses its initial set of problems, prudence demands reintroducing the neglected issues. Perhaps had politicians done so more vigorously and skilfully in the first decades of this nation, and before cotton became central to the South's economy and social and cultural life, the Civil War could have been averted. Indeed, for a moment in 1790 Northern politicians explored in the first Congress the option of distributing equitably the pains of change by sharing the capital losses of Southern plantation owners, but the losses seemed inconceivably high. The North refused to pay the costs of eliminating slavery at that time, only to pay far greater costs in the Civil War itself in the losses of life, money, and the nation's long-term political health.

Leadership is at once the grand art of engaging the polity in its work, tolerating high levels of conflict among factions and across boundaries, and holding people's attention and responsibility within and across groups to issues in a timely fashion. It is also the personal art of staying alive to fight another day. In both senses, leadership is a distinctly political activity. Although the benefits and costs of exclusion and inclusion fluctuate, a bias towards the inclusion of issues and parties gives those who lead more options for diagnosis and action. Developing the network of group relationships also creates resources and builds resilience for future crises.

The Jewish people began to develop extraordinary adaptability after the Babylonian conquest in 586 BCE. Academies sprang up both to preserve and to continue the development of the nation in exile, drawing from Greek and Persian know-how in evolving its own methods of discussion, debate, and inquiry. These lessons were tested to the extreme in 70 CE, less than forty years after the crucifixion of Jesus, when the Romans destroyed Jerusalem, enslaving and dispersing the Jewish people. Now the Temple lay in ruins, and Jews were forced to meet this adaptive challenge or die as a people. They had to distinguish what was precious from what was expendable. They then had to devise wholly new adaptations that would enable future generations to preserve from the past what was most essential to their faith and identity.

This adaptive work meant facing a host of conflicts for which no sage knew the way. Only well-handled but hotly contested dialogue over many months and years among different schools of rabbinic thought could generate the required next steps. The rabbis needed to be both innovative and conservative at the same time. Indeed, many deeply meaningful customs, ceremonies, and laws underpinning the previous culture had to be transformed, or simply accepted as irrelevant and lost (for all practical purposes), in order for the Jews to survive, let alone thrive, in the new Roman world. In creating a portable people, for example, the rabbis had to invent a substitute for the Temple and the priesthood had to accept its obsolescence. Though rabbis differed sharply about which texts were most essential, they had to canonize a Bible from an assortment of holy texts so that a scattering community could carry with them those lessons that were most valuable and sustaining.

REFASHIONING LOYALTIES ACROSS BOUNDARIES

Working groups that come together to address an adaptive problem nearly always consist of representatives of factions communicating across boundaries. Like a legislative group, working groups are likely to mirror the complexity of the larger system.

To forge such a group of groups, those who lead must understand the relationships among the factions and the pressures from each representative's constituents. Each faction has its own grammar for analysing a situation in ways that make sense to its members. Shaped by tradition, power relationships, and interests, this internal language of problem-solving is used largely unconsciously, but members of the faction know intuitively when it is misused. In leading multiparty groups, leaders therefore need to sense the separate languages and identify the loyalties that anchor how each group makes sense of its current situation. Every first-rate diplomat and negotiator has an ear for groups' styles of discourse and subtexts of interest.

More difficult is the need to convince participants to refashion elements of their in-group loyalties as they work across boundaries to forge a coalition as a working group that produces a proposed adaptive solution. In leading such a process, in essence, leaders seek to form a new coalition with these people, where the coalition entity – the working group – has a purpose that redirects the narrower purposes of the factions. If leaders succeed, then the working group will achieve a new, self-perceived boundary of identity and cohesion of self-interest. New loyalties emerge among representatives working across boundaries, a process that often takes many months of confidential meetings. We call this Phase I of adaptive work. New loyalties anchor a new collective identity.

However, the most difficult challenge often lies ahead, in Phase II, when the members of the working group must go back to their constituents to promote the new adaptive arrangements. It is at this point that many negotiations and adaptive intergroup processes falter. After a working group succeeds in coming up with integrative ideas, each 'representative' member must lead his or her own constituents in incorporating and refining the results of the group process, or else the deal unravels. Confronting what negotiation theorists call the *constituency problem*, the working group coalition can be pulled apart when members face accusations from their constituents that they have sold out.[16] Claiming they have been betrayed, constituents demand a return to previous postures.

To succeed in Phase II, representatives must consult with each other on how best to communicate new shared understandings to their organizations, and together they must develop a problem-solving infrastructure that helps build each faction's capacity to adapt to change. A co-ordinated strategy across factional boundaries – with many opportunities for midcourse corrections by working-group members as they encounter resistance, and new information, within their own factions – increases the odds that constituents will accept and implement the proposed solutions achieved in Phase I of problem-solving negotiation.

Yet collaborative leadership consultations between working-group members on implementation strategy and tactics may be the most neglected phase of multiparty negotiations, and a common source of breakdown. Leading the process requires constructing relationships that

---

16. William Ury, personal communication, September 1993.

hold these factional representatives together despite the accusations of betrayal that will pull them apart.

For example, Israeli and Palestinian negotiators spent many hours and days in Oslo in 1993 refashioning deep personal loyalties to achieve common ground. It is probably fair to say, however, that they did not sufficiently prepare themselves to engage their own people in a parallel process of adaptive compromise and innovation. They did not have a flexible and adaptive joint strategy with which to make repeated mid-course corrections in their efforts to reshape the entrenched perspectives of their own peoples. Accused of disloyalty, they were overwhelmed by the backlash within each of their communities. They began to damage their newly formed alliances, and they allowed the progress they had made to be derailed by extremists.

Experiencing and being accused of disloyalty generate extraor-dinary dissonance, because negotiators risk rupturing the primary relationships that anchor their identity and power. Sometimes, their constituents would rather die or kill than face the emotional pain of experiencing ruptured ties, accusations of betrayal from their peers, and the imagined dismay of their ancestors, and they hold their politicians responsible for preserving these loyalties rather than challenging them. Refashioning loyalties lies at the heart of adaptive work, and it explains why it is so dangerous and difficult. Rabin and Sadat were assassinated by their own people. Egyptian president Muhammad Hosni Mubarak apparently warned Arafat, after the Camp David negotiations in the summer of 2000, that any proposal that asked refugees to give up a return to their ancestral homes would lead to Arafat's assassination, too.

To orchestrate multiparty conflict, one must create a containing vessel, a holding environment of structures and processes to sustain each representative in a heated set of interactions. Such was the functioning of the academies that held together the intense debates of the rabbis and their schools of disciples and thought after 70 CE. This may take months or years, because the process of enrichment among the leading negotiators also means a loosening of some of the habits of thought and loyalties that each brings to the process from being at home with his own kind. But constituent pressures can be more powerful than these new bonds of understanding and collaboration. Tested, then, with various kinds of loyalty tests, and confronted with dangers that can include the risk of death, expulsion, or loss of influence and authority within one's own faction, working-group members may be inclined to regress, cleanse themselves of the contaminating influences, reject the learning that came from engaging with other groups, and default to their individual cultural narrative once again.

Thinking politically, then, one would view any cross-boundary working group as a kind of legislature in which one is dealing, not simply with individuals, but with people who, regardless of their personal preferences, serve in representative roles and depend on the good will of their constituents for formal and informal authority (job, credibility, affiliation). Constituents' capacity to absorb changes that involve a mix of potential benefits and losses does far more to determine the representative's latitude for variability and innovation than do the personal preferences of the representative.

Therefore, in managing multiparty conflict, leading negotiators need to create a political map that identifies the perceptions of benefit and loss in each constituent group. A factional analysis is critical to strategic planning, because implementation ultimately requires adjustments of the hearts and minds in the periphery, and without such an analysis, those leading a process often become blindsided when presenting their innovative plan as they encounter constituencies who have not been through the same kind of process the representatives themselves went through to formulate the plan and its priorities. Benefits and losses need to be assessed, not simply in the usual tangible terms of property negotiation, but also in terms of the loyalties that need to be renegotiated, both in current professional relationships and in the hearts of constituents in relationship to their friends, families, and ancestors. Moreover, real losses include the additional challenges to identity associated with changes in responsibility and competence.

Let's examine these more closely to comprehend the power of these ties and their potential to generate adaptive failure. In the case of Israeli settlers and Palestinian refugees, the task of refashioning loyalties within each faction, which continues to block factions from reaching any peace agreement, has been central and profound. Many Jewish settlers grew up being told by their grandparents, 'You are the miracle generation. For the first time in one hundred generations, you can return to live on the same sacred ground as our ancestors. You can fulfil the dream to return our people to the land God gave us more than three thousand years ago.' And many Palestinian refugees have been told by their grandfathers on their deathbeds, 'Here is the key to our home. Guard this key, and return our family to our land.' Growing up in squalor, they have sustained themselves and their families by stories of those houses amid groves of olive trees.

A peace settlement will quite probably require each faction to give up part of these dreams. The settlers and refugees will have to say in their hearts and among themselves, 'We have failed, at least in part, to fulfil the legacy of our ancestors.' Israeli settlers will have to move off those stones. Palestinian refugees will have to mourn and memorialize their keys. Experiencing disloyalty towards ancestors and accusations of failure and betrayal from living family generates extraordinary dissonance; people contemplating such compromise risk the rupture of the primary loyalties that anchor identity. The internal personal negotiation, and the intra-factional negotiation, bring with them the pain of feeling that one has betrayed the people whose love and dreams one carries, individually and collectively.

Loyalties are internalized 'object relations', i.e. the key people in our lives who initially are 'objects' in our world become part of us and part of our identity as we incorporate their voices and perspectives and make them our own. We come to believe, largely unconsciously, that who we are is, in part, them. Therefore, the refashioning of loyalties changes one's individual and relational identity. Although difficult, it is, of course, possible to do so. In small ways, many of us grew up, having 'fallen some distance from the tree', and felt the disappointed expectations of friends and family, but we have also discovered that, over time, a new equilibrium is achieved through conversation and renewed familiarity in which these loyalties are refashioned. A successful effort to refashion loyalties enables one to become sufficiently secure and at peace in one's relational identity that one can say in one's heart, 'Ancestor, I can fulfil much of your dream, but I wrestle with realities that you did not foresee. I have to give up some of your dream to help our family thrive in the complexities of today's world.'

Few tasks in life, perhaps, are more difficult and more violently resisted than facing the emotional pain of ruptured ties and accusations of betrayal. Refashioning loyalties is at the heart of the adaptive work that must happen at the personal and in-group level if new solutions are to emerge collectively among groups.

CONCLUSION

Human communities have always had to acquire new adaptive capacity. With each new wrinkle of complexity, often generated by competition and new technologies, people have had to invent and discover new ways to transact life and business across boundaries. New ways to create bonds of affiliation and trust that could withstand the divisive emotions generated by difficult negotiations must have evolved over millennia. So it should not surprise us that in the face of our extraordinarily interdependent, changing, and globalizing world, we continue to face challenges that outstrip our current repertoire.

In drawing on the metaphor of biological adaptation, I have suggested that progress has three basic elements: identifying the cultural DNA to conserve, identifying the DNA to lose, and developing innovative DNA that will enable the organization or society to thrive in new and challenging environments. I describe this as a largely conservative process that honours the accumulated capacity of previous generations.

Applied to cultures, politics, and individual lives, we can see that even what appears from a distance to be a minor loss may constitute significant disloyalty and a potential rupture of key relationships that anchor our relational identities. In retrospect, we might see continuity with heritage and past, but in the present, the pains of change have an immediacy that makes it easy for people to lose perspective on the value of compromise and innovation, and the benefit of accepting losses now rather than later. Leadership, then, begins with respect for these direct and indirect losses so that partners across boundaries can engage in Phase II of their work, developing and refining in operation a strategy with appropriately conserving rhetoric, so that people can imagine bringing the best of their history into the future.

The adaptive work itself is done both internally within groups and externally among groups. If progress is to be made, some set of allies across boundaries from each group must step forward and provide leadership internally, generating and orchestrating internal group tensions and dynamism, importing the challenge from the environment and bringing it home. Thus human rights activists have often looked for allies *within* opposing factions to generate internal dissonance and thus dynamism towards change.[17] Of course, the loyalties within any group are usually stronger than those between groups, and, therefore, the likelihood that loyalties will be renegotiated increases when people are placed in tensions of loyalty with those they trust within their own group. It may, for example, be easier for a doctor who is sympathetic to alternative therapies to persuade more conservative doctors to try an alternative therapy than it would be for the alternative practitioner to do so. In a sense, then, the politics of leadership is the intimate art of collaborating across boundaries with allies who can lead internal group change back home.

Adaptability depends upon the capacity of a community to learn from differences. These resources lie within the diversity of a group, across sub-groups within a community, and across boundaries with other communities. Particularly in a world of rapidly increasing interdependence among communities with deep religious traditions and loyalty, Rabbi Sacks provides us with an extraordinary example of leadership in religious life in his own struggle and success in refashioning some of our collective narratives to enable us to learn from these differences. In a world desperately hungry for ecumenical wisdom, his success across faith communities provides a historic foundation for the work of peacemaking in our towns, cities, countries, and world. Not only does he propose in *The Dignity of Difference* a theology to promote curiosity and collaboration across faith boundaries, but his active work in Britain has created bridges of appreciation among Jewish, Christian, and Muslim communities.

---

17. See Ellen Chesler, *Woman of Valor: Margaret Sanger and the Birth Control Movement in America* (New York: Simon and Schuster, 1992); Ronald A. Heifetz, *Leadership Without Easy Answers*, ch. 8.

Chapter 12

Texts, Values, and Historical Change: Reflections on the Dynamics of Jewish Law

David Berger

The image of Jewish law as a self-contained fortress impervious to the slings and arrows of external fortunes or extra-legal ideologies and values has been nurtured by two very different forces. For centuries,

I am pleased to present this overview of a topic central to the work of any Orthodox rabbi to a man who has exercised his unique rabbinic responsibilities with surpassing eloquence and exceptional insight. The article had its origins in a paper presented at a conference of the Cardozo School of Law in October 2006. Subsequently, Daniel Sperber published two books of considerable relevance to this theme: *Darkah shel halakhah* (Jerusalem: Reuven Mass, 2007), and *Netivot pesikah* (Jerusalem: Reuven Mass, 2008). While I have not incorporated material from these works into the article, readers will profit from consulting them and some of the literature that they cite.

even millennia, Christian authors depicted Judaism as a legalistic religion indifferent to considerations of loving-kindness and grace. As Paul succinctly puts it, 'The letter kills, but the spirit gives life' (2 Cor. 3:6). An early Protestant joke told of a Catholic priest who mistakenly placed an inedible object in the mouth of a communicant; after waiting an intolerably long time for it to melt on his tongue, the parishioner exclaimed, 'Father! You have made a mistake. You have given me God the Father. He is so hard and tough He will never dissolve.'

Under the impact of religious and intellectual transformations in the late nineteenth and early twentieth centuries, Christian scholars contrasted the legalism and ethical backwardness of rabbinic Judaism with the spiritually refreshing and ethically sensitive message of Jesus. Jews from across the religious spectrum denounced these assertions, contending that they were rooted in both ignorance and anti-Jewish bias.[1] As I have noted in earlier essays, some of these denunciations were not without their irony, since Reform Jews, who had abandoned many of the rituals of Judaism for reasons by no means alien to the rhetoric of Christian critics, now composed paeans of praise to the spiritually uplifting character of the minutiae of rabbinic law.[2] Now, however, we confront a very different irony. Some Orthodox Jews, acting out of the deepest loyalty to Jewish law and angrily rejecting hostile evaluations of Jewish ethics, respond to what they see as the utter abandonment of legal discipline advocated by Reform and even Conservative Judaism by reinforcing the view that halakhah is marked by a self-contained analysis of

---

1. I have discussed the latter development along with the responses of Jewish apologists in David Berger, "The Jewish Contribution" to Christianity', in Jeremy Cohen and Richard I. Cohen (eds.), *The Jewish Contribution to Civilization: Reassessing an Idea* (Oxford: Littman Library of Jewish Civilization, 2007), 80–97, repr. in Berger, *Persecution, Polemic and Dialogue: Essays in Jewish-Christian Relations* (Boston, MA: Academic Studies Press, 2010), 312–32.

2. David Berger, 'Religion, Nationalism, and Historiography: Yehezkel Kaufmann's Account of Jesus and Early Christianity', in Leo Landman (ed.), *Scholars and Scholarship: The Interaction between Judaism and Other Cultures* (New York: Yeshiva University Press, 1990), 154 (repr. in Berger, *Persecution, Polemic, and Dialogue*, 296); and id., '"The Jewish Contribution"'. See also Christian Wiese, *Wissenschaft des Judentums und protestantische Theologie in wilhelminischen Deutschland: Ein Schrei ins Leere?* (Tübingen: Mohr-Siebeck, 1999), 162.

texts allowing for very little consideration of changed historical circumstances, external pressures, ideological concerns, and human sensitivities. To a large degree, the debate about halakhic flexibility is carried out on both sides by recourse to straw men. On the one hand, a legal system whose practitioners have sincerely believed in its divine origin cannot reasonably be expected to have treated it as potters treat their clay; on the other, no legal system could have remained viable from the period of the Talmud to the contemporary age had it not responded to human needs and even ideological transformations in ways that looked beyond the straightforward meaning of its inherited texts.

In this overview, I will attempt to depict certain patterns of halakhic re-evaluation that emerged in response to new economic, humanitarian, and religious concerns. The significant variables determining such re-evaluation include, inter alia, the seriousness of the need, ideological convictions, the susceptibility of the text to reasonable reinterpretation, the severity of the prohibition in question, popular instincts regarding that prohibition, and the attitude of the decisor and his community to the likelihood that popular practice may be in error.

At the risk of classifying myself as the *golem*, or boor, of Mishnah *Avot* 5:7, who does not proceed in order but addresses the last point first, let me begin with the final variable. Practices of a purely ritual nature developed in various Jewish communities and sub-communities that stand in stark contrast to the apparently unambiguous requirements of Jewish law. Thus, Rabbi Moses Isserles testified that, in sixteenth-century Poland, only exceptionally pious Jews slept in a sukkah.[3] Similarly, most hasidic and many non-hasidic Jews in the diaspora do not eat in a sukkah on the festival of Shemini Atseret even though the standard major authorities ruled that one must.[4] In the months preceding Passover, a large majority of observant Jews eat grain that should presumably be classified as newly grown and hence prohibited; a generation ago, the vast majority of observant Jews in the United States were not even aware of the prohibition despite its explicit appearance in Leviticus. In these

---

3. Gloss on *Shulḥan arukh*, 'Oraḥ ḥayim' 639:2.
4. See Aaron M. Schreiber, *Yesodot hanohag lehimana miyeshivah besukah bishemini atseret beḥuts la'arets* (Jerusalem: Netiv Haberakhah, 2004).

and similar cases, no broader issues are at stake; rather, the assumption that extensive sectors of pious and learned Jews would be engaging in blatant violations of the Torah was so unacceptable to rabbinic authorities that justifications were sought and found.

Haym Soloveitchik has argued that in the Middle Ages the self-image of a community was a central factor in determining whether or not popular custom would be maintained or overridden. Ashkenazi authorities were more likely to defend prevailing practice because they perceived their communities favourably, while Sephardi rabbis were more willing to assume that their fellow Jews were sinners out of either ignorance or indifference.[5] In a celebrated article, Soloveitchik applies this insight to contemporary Jewry, arguing that in the last few generations, Orthodox Jews have lost confidence in the traditions that they learned from their parents, so that they have replaced a mimetic society with one that tests all prevailing practices against the standards established by texts.[6]

Ideological considerations have played an interesting and sometimes ironic role in the reception of that article. Many Modern Orthodox Jews have expressed satisfaction with its thesis because Soloveitchik's examples of deviation from traditional behaviours tend to involve text-based stringencies such as the increased size of the required measure of matzah, and such innovations are ideal grist for mockery directed at the Orthodoxies of the right. Modernist ideology, however, can also trump mimesis. Thus, some of those who lionize the mimetic society as they savour the anti-haredi uses of Soloveitchik's analysis are simultaneously impelled by feminist convictions to change generations of synagogue practice on the basis of textual analysis far more tenuous than the con-

---

5. Soloveitchik formulates this point vigorously in his *Halakhah, kalkalah vedimui atsmi: hamashkona'ut bimei habeinayim* (Jerusalem: Magnes Press, 1985), 111–12, 116–19, seeing it as so central that he incorporates it into the book's title. Nonetheless, a key chapter (pp. 59–81) establishes and analyses a significant distinction between twelfth-century French and German authorities, where the argument about contrasting communal self-perceptions does not appear to apply. Recently, Soloveitchik has expressed reservations about the universality of the mediaeval Ashkenazi inclination to defend problematic popular practice. See his *Hayayin bimei habeinayim* (Jerusalem: Zalman Shazar Centre for Jewish History, 2009), 369.

6. Haym Soloveitchik, 'Rupture and Reconstruction: The Transformation of Contemporary Orthodoxy', *Tradition* 28/4 (1994), 64–130.

siderations that lead the traditionalist Orthodox to their usually more stringent deviations from the practices of the past. Affirmation or rejection of a mimetic ideal can depend very much on whose ox is being gored. I shall soon return to women's issues in even more sensitive contexts, but let me first make some observations about the much-studied reactions of rabbinic decisors to serious economic pressures that beset Jews in the Middle Ages. When facing a prohibition of rabbinic rather than biblical status, the difficulties of ruling leniently in the face of economic necessity were substantially mitigated. Thus, in a particularly striking illustration of this point, Rabbi Yom Tov ben Avraham of Seville (Ritva, 1250–1330) made the frontal assertion that the rabbinic prohibition against business dealings with idolaters on pagan holidays lest they thank their gods was never intended to apply in cases where economic survival was at stake.[7] The Tosafists appealed to a principle that can sometimes overcome even a biblical prohibition: that observing this restriction could generate hatred towards Jews. In this instance, they were able to cite compelling talmudic evidence that such a concern is decisive. Rabbenu Tam (1100–71) dealt with the challenge by restricting the prohibition to ritual objects.

Even more strikingly – and with consequences the mediaeval authorities were not likely to have foreseen – new assertions about the Jewish evaluation of Christianity, which has legal ramifications beyond its theological significance, emerged out of the crucible of these mediaeval economic realities. Thus, the Tosafists made the modest assertion that their Christian contemporaries, not being particularly pious, are unlikely to respond to a business arrangement with a thanksgiving prayer to their deity. When they formulated this point as 'contemporary gentiles do not worship idolatry', the potential was created for interesting conclusions to be drawn in subsequent generations. Rabbenu Gershom of Mainz (tenth–eleventh centuries) allowed transactions on Christian

---

7. *Vetu she'anu tserikhim latet velaset imahem mishum ḥayei nefesh.* To be sure, this point appears as the third in a series of four arguments for a permissive position. See *Ḥidushei haritva lerabenu yom tov berav avraham al-ishbili: masekhet avodah zarah,* ed. R. Moshe Goldstein (Jerusalem: Mosad Harav Kook, 1978), col. 16 (on BT AZ 6b).

holidays on the basis of a cryptic line in the Talmud affirming that 'Gentiles outside the land of Israel are not idolaters; rather, they follow the custom of their ancestors.' Here, too, the potential for a reading broader than the one intended by Rabbenu Gershom is self-evident.[8] When Tosafot permitted another sort of business arrangement on the grounds that *shituf* (lit.: association; of other powers with God, which probably applied only to an oath) is not forbidden to Noahides, the seeds were sown for the later affirmation that Judaism considers the worship of Jesus along with God entirely permissible for non-Jews.[9] In other words, when straightforward law is leavened by other considerations, it is not just the law in question that can be affected; despite what Soloveitchik once called 'halakhic federalism', a position initially intended to apply to a focused, restricted context cannot always be expected to know its place.[10] Bush v. Gore, the United States Supreme Court decision that effectively resolved the 2000 presidential election in favour of George W. Bush, is, or at least may soon become, an instructive case in point.[11]

All, or virtually all, of these mediaeval arguments for permitting problematic economic activity are perfectly plausible. The underlying question is whether, as Jacob Katz and others have taken for granted, the permissibility of such business dealings was absolutely predetermined by the economic realities that faced mediaeval Jews. Despite the instincts of historians, one cannot be utterly certain that the answer to this question is affirmative. Rabbi Yehiel of Paris told his interlocutors during the Paris disputation of 1240 that if Jews did not sincerely believe that contemporary Christians were different from ancient pagans in legally relevant ways, they would not suspend talmudic law affecting economic

---

8. A *locus classicus* presenting and evaluating these arguments is Tosafot *A Z* 2*a*, s.v. *asur*.

9. For a discussion of the various interpretations of the relevant Tosafot (*San.* 63*b* s.v. *asur*), see Appendix III of my *The Rebbe, the Messiah, and the Scandal of Orthodox Indifference* (London: Littman Library of Jewish Civilization, 2001); Heb. version, *Harebe melekh hamashiaḥ, sha'aruriyat ha'adishut, veha'iyum al emunat yisra'el* (Jerusalem: Urim, 2005).

10. I made this point in Berger, 'Jacob Katz on Jews and Christians in the Middle Ages', in Jay M. Harris (ed.), *The Pride of Jacob: Essays on Jacob Katz and his Work* (Cambridge, MA: Harvard University Press, 2002), 60–1 (repr. in Berger, *Persecution, Polemic, and Dialogue*, 72).

11. See 'Editorial Notebook', *New York Times*, 15 Aug. 2006.

matters; after all, he said, we have provided abundant evidence that we are willing to die for our faith.[12] As it happens, the grounds for suspending those laws did not require the far-reaching re-evaluation of the status of Christians that Rabbi Yehiel proffered in the disputation; moreover, the embrace of martyrdom in moments of religious ecstasy may well be more probable than the willingness of an entire community to commit slow economic suicide. Still, the observation that Jews would not provide knowingly insincere excuses for violating the Torah is surely correct. Israel Ta-Shma, the distinguished scholar who dealt with some of these issues, once told me that one's initial inclination is to assume that rabbinic decisors would conjure up any available interpretation, however flimsy, to justify a conclusion required for economic survival. Nonetheless, he added, as one reads the arguments of a figure like Rabbenu Tam in detail, an unexpected reaction begins to develop, to wit, 'This conclusion is actually correct.' While this may be a tribute to Rabbenu Tam's genius, it says something important about the subtlety and complexity of the interplay between communal need and textual analysis.

Rabbenu Tam himself famously asserted in a related context that it is a mitzvah to provide Jews with sustenance,[13] and this leads us to a key element in this discussion, namely, the overt consideration of concerns that are not part of the narrow textual discourse. I call these competing religious values, by which I mean that they compete with the legal conclusion that would follow from a simple reading of the directly relevant texts, and we shall encounter them in various guises in the course of our discussion. It is, moreover, important to note what Rabbenu Tam's formulation affirms, namely, that the recognition of economic needs is itself a religious value, so that it may legitimately be considered in choosing a plausible halakhic position over a competing one that would be more compelling in a world without real people and critical human needs.

Despite Katz's emphasis on the role of economic pressures in

---

12. *Vikuaḥ rabenu yeḥi'el miparis*, ed. Reuven Margaliyot (Lvov: 1928), 21.
13. R. Isaac b. Moses, *Or zarua*, no. 202. The passage is reproduced in Soloveitchik, *Halakhah, kalkalah, vedimui atsmi*, 136, document 21. (Note 26 on p. 66 mistakenly refers the reader to document 22.)

driving halakhic decision-making, he was not only cognizant of the role of texts but also emphasized the intuitively less-obvious impact of what he called ritual instinct. Such an instinct can sometimes overcome dire economic needs to the point where pious laypeople will not even ask their rabbis if a particular act might be permitted, given exigent circumstances. If the forbidden act has been avoided since childhood to the point where the prohibition is embedded in the deepest layers of the individual's psyche, it becomes almost unthinkable, especially if it requires an unmediated physical action.[14]

In examining this complex matrix of texts, instincts, needs, values, and convictions, let me now turn to competing religious values of two major sorts: ideological and humanitarian. These are independent categories, but they can interact in a striking fashion.

With the rise of both the Reform movement and the general estrangement from all forms of Judaism, Orthodox rabbinic authorities reacted in diverse and sometimes contradictory ways. Here, the religious value was the protection of the traditional community from deviation, a value with the potential for conflict with straightforward law. In some cases, this value extended to the need to establish a modus vivendi with a deviationist movement that could not be vanquished. To accomplish these ends, some authorities endorsed mild innovations like a vernacular sermon or a male choir. More significantly, there were rabbis in Central Europe who were prepared to classify Reform Jews under a talmudic rubric that exempted children brought up among non-Jews from the harsh sanctions applicable to heretics.[15] In the twentieth century, no less a figure than the Hazon Ish (Rabbi Avraham Yeshayahu Karelitz, 1878–1953) famously argued that because of the absence in our time of

---

14. See his summary paragraph in Jacob Katz, *The 'Shabbes Goy': A Study in Halakhic Flexibility* (Philadelphia, PA: Jewish Publication Society, 1989), 231. Haym Soloveitchik emphasizes Jewish revulsion at drinking gentile wine as a decisive factor in determining actual behaviour in mediaeval Ashkenaz. See Haym Soloveitchik, *Yeinam: saḥar beyeinam shel goyim: al gilgulah shel hahalakhah be'olam hama'aseh* (Tel Aviv: Alma, 2003), 104–21.

15. For a recent discussion, see Adam S. Ferziger, *Exclusion and Hierarchy: Orthodoxy, Nonobservance, and the Emergence of Modern Jewish Identity* (Philadelphia, PA: University of Pennsylvania Press, 2005), 99–105.

evident divine providence, the most extreme of those sanctions against heretics are no longer applicable at all.[16]

In contrast, there were simultaneously more stringent responses to Reform Judaism, which incorporated a rhetoric that went beyond the plain meaning of the controlling texts. Thus, rabbis mobilized the most extreme categories of Jewish law in prohibiting the construction of a synagogue without a platform in the centre or the recitation of public prayer in a language other than Hebrew. They did so more categorically than precedent could easily justify, and they subjected all innovation to intense suspicion and scrutiny.[17]

The imperative of retrieving Jews estranged from tradition created halakhic pressures of its own, which could also elicit either lenient or stringent approaches. Thus, Rabbi Moshe Feinstein and Rabbi Shlomo Zalman Auerbach, two of the twentieth century's most eminent decisors, took very different positions on the question of organizing events on the sabbath intended for non-observant Jews who would surely travel to the event in a manner that violates the sabbath.[18] In this instance, Rabbi Auerbach's lenient view required the daring affirmation that the objective of enhancing observance in the long run meant that the organizer of the event is not leading people to sin in the technical sense of the prohibition.

Another historical development with profound ideological freight, religious and otherwise, was the Zionist movement and the state that it produced. Here, there can be no question that the decisor's ideological position can affect his ruling. Once we recognize that a competing religious value can legitimately play a role in reaching a

---

16. R. Avraham Yeshayahu Karelitz, *Ḥazon ish,* 'Yoreh de'ah' (Benei Berak: Harav Grainiman, 1961 or 1962), 'Hilkhot sheḥitah' 2:16.

17. See, for example, Jacob Katz, *A House Divided: Orthodoxy and Schism in Nineteenth-Century Central European Jewry,* trans. Ziporah Brody (Hanover, NH: Brandeis University Press, 1998), 77ff.

18. For a brief summary, see R. David Sperling, 'Inviting Shabbat Guests Who Will Drive', www.nishmat.net/article.php?id=5&heading=0. Sperling also points to the permissive ruling of R. Moshe Sternbuch. See, too, the discussion in R. Yehuda Amital, 'Rebuking a Fellow Jew: Theory and Practice', in Jacob J. Schacter (ed.), *Jewish Tradition and the Non-Traditional Jew* (Northvale, NJ: Jason Aaronson, 1992), 127–38.

decision, much depends on whether or not the rabbi in question recognizes the legitimacy of that competing value. A striking example of this dynamic is Rabbi Avraham Yitshak Kook's letter in response to a rabbi who opposed the strategy of effecting a formal sale of the land of Israel to a non-Jew during the sabbatical year, so that Jews would be permitted to work the land:

> I must stand in the breach against those who besmirch people who come to settle the land of Israel and who, in the absence of an alternative, are forced to depend on this permissive ruling, which has already become widespread and has a basis in the positions of the Talmuds and the decisors. Such besmirching damages the *yishuv* [Jewish population of the land] both spiritually and materially. Materially, because it is impossible for all to observe the laws of the sabbatical year without annulment, since if they will not export the goods...the land will literally become desolate, God forbid.... Spiritually, because publicizing the prohibition will close the door to entry into the land of Israel...to all loyal Jews, so that only those who throw the religion behind their backs will immigrate.

He goes on to posit that even religious Jews currently living in Israel will in large measure feel unable to abide by the prohibition, in which case they will come to see themselves as sinners and will stop observing the Torah in other respects as well. Although it is true, he concedes, that from a purely spiritual perspective it would be better to maintain a stringent position, this fails to take into account a reality in which clearheaded people will understand the unacceptable consequences of doing so.[19]

While Rabbi Kook insists in this letter that the old *yishuv* and the new one are intertwined, so that the destruction of the latter entailed by a stringent ruling would also destroy the former, in another letter he explicitly connects his permissive position to his conviction that

---

19. R. Avraham Yitshak Kook, *Igerot hare'iyah*, vol. 1 (Jerusalem: Mosad Harav Kook, 1985), no. 311, pp. 346–7.

strengthening and increasing the new Jewish settlement in the land of Israel will hasten the redemption.[20] A rabbi who did not support the Zionist enterprise would have been far more likely to affirm the stringent position that Rabbi Kook himself recognizes as preferable in the abstract. Rabbinic stands on other issues of Jewish law also vary to a significant degree depending on the decisor's attitude towards Zionism and the state, though there is certainly no absolute correspondence across the board. Examples include the propriety of exempting yeshiva students from army service, returning land to Arab states or ceding it to Palestinians, and matters that should theoretically have little or nothing to do with Zionism but operate in its penumbra, such as celebrating one day of a festival rather than two when visiting Israel and accepting the rabbinate's ordinary *kashrut* supervision rather than insisting on a more stringent standard.

In addition to these ideological factors, humanitarian values can also stand in tension with the plain meaning of legal texts. Here, too, historical developments create new situations in which such concerns become acute. Since issues of personal status tend to provide the most poignant illustrations, they will be the focus of our discussion.

Several movements and crises have forced Jews to face the question of whether a significant number of individuals who wanted to contract a marriage but whose status rendered such an action problematic should be permitted to do so. In the case of Karaism, whose adherents deny the authority of the Oral Law, the procedure for marriage was essentially the same as that of Rabbanites, but the divorce document did not meet rabbinic requirements. It appeared, then, that Karaite marriages may be valid and their divorces invalid. For those rabbinic authorities who embraced this position, a terrible consequence followed, to wit, that the child of a divorced woman's second marriage would be the product of an adulterous relationship and hence essentially unmarriageable. This conclusion was captured in a morbid play on words based on the law that garments rent in mourning over one's parents may never be repaired. *Hakera'im* (with an *ayin*) *einam mitaḥim le'olam* ('Torn garments can never be repaired'). By changing the *ayin* to an *alef*,

---

20. Kook, *Mishpat kohen* (Jerusalem: Mosad Harav Kook, 1966), no. 63, p. 129.

we produce a tragic variant: *Hakara'im einam mitaḥim le'olam* – 'The Karaites can never become brothers.'[21] The most plausible argument for avoiding this unfortunate conclusion is that Karaite marriages do not take effect *ab initio* because the witnesses are invalid,[22] and we shall have occasion to examine this approach as we proceed.

In the aftermath of the mass conversion of Jews in the crucible of late-fourteenth- and fifteenth-century Iberia, the problem of marriage-ability arose in a different context, generated by the law of levirate marriage. A childless *converso* couple would leave Spain for a location where they could observe Judaism. Upon the death of the husband, the widow would ask if she could remarry without obtaining the release (called *ḥalitsah*) from her deceased husband's brother, a *converso* residing in Spain or Portugal. Any argument to permit such a marriage depended perforce on the assumption that the *converso* community is to be seen as a community of sinners, even of willing sinners. Thus, the original witnesses would be delegitimized or, in an even more extreme formulation, the levir would not be classified as a real 'brother'. In the context of the historians' debate over the beliefs and practices of this community, Yosef Hayim Yerushalmi argued, I think correctly, that one reason for questioning the historical validity of rabbinic assertions (in this context, that the *conversos* were in fact willing Christians) is that the decisors were facing a humanitarian imperative to relieve this woman's suffering. Their desire to achieve this result would incline them to accept judgements about *converso* sinfulness that they might otherwise have examined more critically.[23] This does not mean that their assessment was insincere, or even incorrect, only that we must approach it with care.

An extraordinary expression of the passions that swirled around this question, and the role of religious and human considerations that impinged upon it, appears in a remarkable outburst by Rabbi Moses

21. See R. Ben Zion Hai Uziel, *Sefer mishpetei uzi'el: mahadura tinyana*, 1st edn., part 2, vol. 1 (Tel Aviv: Jacob Levitski, 1935), 'Yoreh de'ah', no. 63, p. 218.

22. See, for example, R. David b. Solomon ibn Abi Zimra, *She'elot uteshuvot haradbaz*, vol. 1 (Jerusalem: Yerid Hasefarim, 2004), no. 73, p. 52.

23. Yosef Hayim Yerushalmi, *From Spanish Court to Italian Ghetto: Isaac Cardoso, A Study in Seventeenth-Century Marranism and Jewish Apologetics*, rev. edn. (Seattle, WA: University of Washington Press, 1981), 25–6.

Kapsali, the leading Turkish rabbi during the period of the expulsion from Spain. He permitted such women to remarry, and those who, ruling stringently, did not permit them to do so were in his view

> agents of idolatry, whose intention [!] is only to prevent these forced converts from worshipping God, may He be blessed. For if these women will believe after hearing such rulings that they will be unable to marry, they will not return to the worship of God ... and will return to their improper path. And those rabbis are close to being instigators [to idolatry], and it is almost the case that they are subject to the death penalty in accordance with the law that applies to a seducer and instigator.[24]

In contemporary times, the strategy of invalidating a marriage on the grounds that the witnesses were not observant Jews is associated most prominently with Rabbi Moshe Feinstein, who mobilized it to permit Reform Jews to remarry after a civil divorce, to permit Reform divorcees to marry – or at least to remain married to – men of priestly lineage, and to remove the taint of illegitimacy from the children of the second marriage of Reform divorcees.[25] While some prominent authorities disagreed with this position, it has largely won the day as a result of its humanitarian consequences as well as its preservation of marriageability across denominational lines, and, ironically, because the invalidating of Reform witnesses appeals to the anti-Reform ideology of traditionalist Orthodox Jews, who might otherwise have resisted such a lenient decision.

Another ruling promoting Jewish unity has also more or less prevailed in a somewhat ironic fashion. Ethiopian Jews have been declared unequivocally Jewish by Rabbi Ovadiah Yosef on the basis of a sixteenth-century responsum affirming their descent from the tribe

---

24. Quoted in R. Benjamin b. Mattityahu, *She'elot uteshuvot binyamin ze'ev* (Jerusalem: Defus Safra, 1959), no. 75. The author (no. 76) rejects R. Kapsali's position. Cited along with additional sources by Simcha Assaf, *Be'oholei ya'akov* (Jerusalem: Mosad Harav Kook, 1943), 178–9.

25. R. Moshe Feinstein, *Iggerot mosheh*, 'Even ha'ezer' (New York: Moriah, 1973), sec. 3, no. 23, pp. 445–6.

of Dan.[26] The historical evidence militates strongly against this position, but Modern Orthodox Jews, who sometimes denounce traditionalist authorities for excluding non-traditional evidence from their purview, are happy to endorse this unhistorical conclusion because it serves needs with which they identify.[27]

Finally, the spectrum of positions on proper standards of conversion also reflects concerns about unity and social cohesion. The classic prohibition against conversion in contemplation of marriage has been dismissed by many authorities as inapplicable in an age when civil marriage and even cohabitation are socially acceptable alternatives to religious marriage. But the question of recognition, before or after the fact, of a convert who did not genuinely accept the obligation to observe the Torah, as Orthodoxy understands it, remains a matter of deep contention. De jure, and to a growing extent de facto, the stringent position dominates, but the Jewish social fabric, especially in Israel, is imperilled in different ways by all the positions, and there is no question that decisors have been influenced by their varying perceptions of the imperatives of national/communal unity.

Have rabbinic decisors, then, allowed their rulings to be affected by economic and communal needs, by ideological commitments, and by humanitarian concerns? Of course they have. Have these influences operated primarily on a subconscious level? I do not think so. Rabbinic authorities generally know what they are doing, and they are well aware of the factors that they weigh in rendering a decision. Jacob Katz noted a striking interpretation by Rabbi Moses Sofer (Hatam Sofer, 1762–1839)

---

26. R. Ovadiah Yosef, *Shut yabia omer*, 'Even ha'ezer', vol. 8 (Jerusalem, 1995), no. 11, pp. 404–09. The responsum also rules leniently with respect to the question of marriageability, and in the course of the discussion, surveys opinions on the marriageability of Karaites as well.

27. I made this point in 'Identity, Ideology, and Faith: Some Personal Reflections on the Social, Cultural, and Spiritual Value of the Academic Study of Judaism', in Howard Kreisel (ed.), *Study and Knowledge in Jewish Thought* (Be'ersheva: Ben Gurion University of the Negev Press, 2006), 25–6, repr. in Berger, *Cultures in Collision and Conversation: Essays in the Intellectual History of the Jews* (Boston, MA: Academic Studies Press, 2011), 17. On the historical evidence, see Steven Kaplan, *The Beta Israel (Falasha) in Ethiopia: From Earliest Times to the Twentieth Century* (New York: New York University Press, 1992).

of a prayer that entreats God to provide us our livelihood in permissible rather than forbidden ways. This means, said the Hatam Sofer, that we ask not to be put in a position in which we have to permit something that, on a straightforward reading, would be prohibited.[28] On rare occasions, we can envision pressures so powerful that Herculean efforts would be exercised to bend the texts towards a predetermined conclusion. To take a contemporary example from the realm of technological change, we need only reflect on the challenges of sabbath observance in a world where lights go on and off as you stroll past homes, walk through the corridors of hotels, or enter the rest rooms of hospitals. In a recent article in a Torah journal about this topic, the author noted with complete candour that he was making extreme efforts to reach barely plausible conclusions in cases where avoiding problematic behaviour entailed overcoming the most daunting difficulties.[29]

The goal of maintaining fidelity to the law while striving to accommodate humane concerns is given moving expression in a responsum by Rabbi Feinstein that encapsulates the challenges faced by men of learning and integrity bearing a burden that mere observers have no way of understanding in its fullness. Rabbi Feinstein had been asked by a European rabbi about the marriageability of a pious young woman whose lineage was problematic, and he responded with a permissive ruling. But the rabbi who had sent the initial inquiry was plagued by a guilty conscience, wondering if he had formulated his question in a manner likely to skew the ruling in a direction supportive of a woman whom he so badly wanted to help. And so he sent a second letter sharing these doubts. I conclude with Rabbi Feinstein's reply:

> As to [your] concern about your effort to permit this young woman, who is a precious, wholehearted soul – on the contrary, it is appropriate, decent, and desirable in the eyes of God to exercise effort on behalf of modest and precious women, just as we have been commanded to attempt to permit the marriage of

---

28. R. Moses Sofer, *Shu"t ḥatam sofer*, no. 59, cited in Katz, *The 'Shabbes Goy'*, 190.

29. R. Ya'akov Shlomo Mozeson, 'Be'inyan halikhah beli kavanah leyad ayin elektroni vehamista'ef', *Kovets beit aharon veyisra'el*, 72 (Av-Elul, 5757 [1997]), 63–8.

agunot, provided that this effort is made in accordance with the laws of the Torah in truth.[30]

There are no magic formulas for the balancing of humanitarian and ideological concerns, on the one hand, and the straightforward meaning of texts on the other. For this task to be accomplished with integrity from the perspective of Orthodox Judaism, the decisor must genuinely believe in the authority of the Torah, in its divine origin, and in its eternal validity. In other words, what is nowadays described as 'the halakhic process' rests upon a foundation consisting of theology as well as legal analysis. It is not just that one who does not share the theological premises of Orthodox Judaism is excluded in principle as an authority. The legal arguments themselves become suspect because of the concern that they are unrestrained by the discipline of faith, that one pole of the dialectic between authoritative text and personal or communal need is deficient. Both elements of that dialectic have been essential to the dynamic of Jewish law; to undermine either of them is to distort not only halakhah, but the history of halakhah as well.

30. R. Moshe Feinstein, *Iggerot mosheh,* 'Even ha'ezer', sec. 3, no. 10, p. 432.

Chapter 13

'From Another Shore':
Moses and Korah

Avivah Gottlieb Zornberg

BRUTE APOCALYPSE

On the face of it, the Korah rebellion is a struggle over questions of power and ambition. Korah and his followers suddenly appear as a faction within the Israelite community, confronting Moses with their manifesto of resentment: 'Rav lakhem – you have gone too far! For the whole community are entirely holy, and in their midst is God. Why then do you exalt yourselves over God's congregation?' (Numbers 16:3). 'Rav lakhem – you overreach yourselves!' – these words are twice picked up by Moses in his response: 'You have gone too far, sons of Levi!' (16:7),

---

I have known Chief Rabbi Sacks for over forty years, from the time we were at Cambridge together. Already at that time his brilliance was obvious. But what most moved me was his passionate interest in Judaism and his willingness to devote his talents and energy to the cause of the Jewish people. He has always been most generous in his encouragement of my work. I wish Jonathan and Elaine a long, happy life, with lots of opportunities to enjoy the fruit of their labour – including their grandchildren!

and, in paraphrase: 'Is it not enough for you?' (16:9). The same rhetoric of *too much* and *too little* appears again in the riposte of Dathan and Aviram: 'Is it not enough?' (16:13). Implicit in this language is the issue of desire and greed, of legitimate and illegitimate ambition.

On the rebels' lips, the words are sarcastic jibes at the power-hunger of the leaders. When Moses speaks them, however, they are less rhetorical; they frame a genuine questioning of the rebels' dissatisfaction with the roles assigned them by God:

> Hear me, sons of Levi. Is it not enough for you that the God of Israel has set you apart from the community of Israel and given you access to Him, to perform the duties of God's Tabernacle and to minister to the community and serve them? Now that He has advanced you and all your fellow Levites with you, do you seek the priesthood too? Truly, it is against God that you and all your company have banded together. [16:8–11]

In this essay, I would like to discuss the relation between two attitudes to the oral, two uses of the mouth, as embodied in the relation between two men, Moses and Korah, who are first cousins and whose differences arise out of a shared history. Beyond the power struggle between them, the narrative raises profound questions about the nature of language itself. Metaphors of rising and falling, up and down, haunt the text – haunt, particularly, the language of both Moses and the rebels. At issue between them, in the end, is the world-creating, fictive character of language. We will look at the exegetical traditions that run from the *midrash* to hasidic teachings, where the central issue of *maḥloket*, of schism, turns out to hold surprising and conflicting meanings.

From the beginning of the narrative, the Korah rebellion sounds a strangely mixed note of resentment and envy, on the one hand, and, on the other, of a certain idealized beauty: 'the whole community are entirely holy, and in their midst is God.' Moses' response echoes their rhetoric but to different effect: he speaks of God's will as the source of the power hierarchies and of the rebels' ambition as a conspiracy against

God. By placing their worldly relation to God at the centre of the discussion, Moses attempts to move the discourse from the rhetorical to the pragmatic/theological plane.

At this juncture, the rebels divide into two groups. Korah and all his followers place incense in their fire-pans and gather mockingly at the entrance to the Tabernacle. God's glory appears, and God instructs Moses and Aaron to separate from this group. Moses and Aaron then move to the other site of rebellion, around the tents of the rebels. Moses tells the people to distance themselves from the rebel tents and the terrible narrative of apocalypse is played out:

> Now Dathan and Aviram had come out and they stood at the entrance of their tents, with their wives, their children, and their little ones. And Moses said, 'By this you shall know that it was God who sent me to do all these things; that they are not of my own devising [lit.: not from my heart]: if these men die as all men do, if their lot be the common fate of all mankind, it was not God who sent me. But if God brings about something unheard-of [lit.: if God creates a new creation], so that the ground opens its mouth and swallows them up with all that belongs to them, and they go down alive into Sheol, you shall know that these men have spurned God.' Scarcely had he finished speaking all these words when the ground under them burst asunder, and the earth opened its mouth and swallowed them up with their households, all Korah's people and all their possessions. They went down alive into Sheol, with all that belonged to them; the earth closed over them and they vanished from the midst of the congregation. All Israel around them fled at their shrieks, for they said, 'The earth might swallow us!' And a fire had gone forth from God and consumed the two hundred and fifty men offering the incense. [16:27–35]

Two kinds of death befall the two groups of rebels: those bearing incense pans, challenging the priestly prerogatives, are burned by divine fire, while those around the rebel tents are swallowed up in the earth.[1] The fire receives short shrift at the end of the passage; it happens at the same time as the other scene of punishment.[2] The latter scene, however, is both longer and more fraught with tension. Moses announces the showdown to come, dramatically expressing his view of the whole narrative: 'By this *you shall know* that it was *God who sent me* to do all these things, that they are *not of my own devising*: if these men die as all men do.... It was *not God who sent me*. But if God brings about something unheard-of.... *You shall know* that these men have *spurned God*' (16:28–30).

It is *knowledge* that is to be achieved, knowledge that Moses' role in 'all these things' – the whole history of the Exodus, Mount Sinai, the desert journey – is an expression of God's will. 'For it was not from my heart': here, it seems, is the crux of the matter. Moses exposes the nub of the argument: did God send him, or is the whole story a fabrication, in conscious or unconscious pursuit of power? Moses is willing to set the stakes high. The truth of his claim is to pivot on the exceptional, the prodigious nature of what is to befall the rebels. There is to be an opening of the mouth of the earth, a swallowing, a descent into the underworld – else, 'it was not God who sent me'.[3] The fact that Moses is willing to articulate such words, annihilating in retrospect his whole mission, indicates the seriousness of the moment. He is willing to risk his credibility on the event of an apocalyptic moment. In this way, the truth of the matter will be clarified for all time.

And indeed, 'The ground under them burst asunder, and the earth opened its mouth and swallowed them up.' The text insists on the grotesque oral imagery of Moses' scenario. That the ground bursts asunder and the rebels go down to the underworld is apparently not sufficient to convey the scene. The earth must become a maw yawning wide, swallowing up its victims. When does this moment of oral horror

---

1. There is some ambiguity in the narrative as to the fate of Korah and his people (v. 32). See also BT *San.* 110a).

2. *Ve'esh yatsah* is probably to be read in the pluperfect: 'A fire *had gone* forth from God' (v. 35).

3. This might be read more strongly as 'not-God sent me'. Has some demonic force been driving Moses to invent a narrative of divine calling?

arrive? With great precision, the narrative presents the timing: 'Scarcely had he finished speaking all these words…' (v. 31).

Moses finishes speaking all these words. He comes to the end of words – and the earth opens its mouth and swallows…. Implicitly, a tension is set up between speaking and eating, the two oral functions. As long as Moses speaks, the mouth of the earth remains closed. When it opens, it is not to speak but to consume.[4] The terrible alternative to spoken words is the cataclysm of final and irrefutable revelations. Moses had, as it were, *exhausted* (*kekhaloto… et kol hadevarim*) all the resources of language, so that nothing remained but the brute apocalypse. The limitation of human language, indeed, is that words can never achieve that finality, the *last word*, of the consuming earth. Moses speaks to the very last moment, in order, in a sense, to hold an option open. Strangely, he speaks of the destruction of language – the hungry earth's mouth, the site of death – as *beriah*, 'creation' (v. 30). As though in this moment of destruction, something, some world, might still be created.

The horror of the scene comes to its climax in the last detail: 'All Israel around them fled at their shrieks, for they said, "The earth might swallow us!"'. The shrieks of the doomed cause a stampede of the survivors, fleeing with words of torment on their lips. They are left with one wish: to avoid the fate of their companions. The physical terror of the survivors is matched by their imaginative repulsion from *this* death, *this* engulfing mouth.

A ZONE OF VULNERABILITY

When words come to an end, the mouth consumes. The tension between eating and speaking, two uses of the mouth, is enacted through the relation between Moses and Korah. Each comes to represent a different way of living that tension. From the beginning of the story, the two cousins manifest this difference.

The rebels' opening statement, their slogan, is 'The whole community are entirely holy and God is in their midst' (v. 3). They proclaim a totality of holiness – a world of all, of wholeness, of perfect circles,

---

4. It is striking that the other punishment is also described as 'consuming': 'a fire had gone forth from God and consumed the two hundred and fifty men' (v. 35).

with God at the centre. Malbim (Meir Leibush ben Jehiel Michel Weiser, 1809–79) reads this: 'The whole people, without exception, are holy, from the tops of their heads to the soles of their feet.' Without difference, without more or less, without excellence, without gaps, the people are *wholly holy*.[5]

Such a political platform allows for no debate – like the image that the *midrash* introduces here: the rebels appear before Moses wearing *talitot shekulan tekhelet*[6] – prayer-shawls entirely woven of blue-dyed wool. Instead of one statutory blue thread, these shawls – all 250 of them – flaunt a total blue; a sea of blue confronts Moses, as Korah provocatively demands, 'Do *these talitot* still require a single blue thread?' Clearly this theatrical moment represents in visual form the central issue of the rebellion – of holiness and sacred roles as concentrated in a particular man, or a particular family, rather than democratically shared by all. The image speaks louder than a thousand words, ridiculing and silencing Moses.

Moses responds to this demonstration with silent despair: 'And Moses heard, and he fell on his face' (v. 4). His face on the ground, his body expresses speechlessness. What can be said in reply to the theatrics of totality? As Rashi puts it: 'his hands fell limp.' But, surprisingly, in the next verse, he is speaking – at some length – to the rebels. First, he addresses Korah and his group, then Korah alone, and finally Dathan and Aviram. Transcending his despair, he attempts to engage with the rebel leaders. But Korah has no reply, so that Moses' words fall on deaf ears:

> With all these arguments, Moses tried to win Korah over, yet you do not find that the latter returned him any answer. This was because he was clever in his wickedness and thought: 'If I answer him, I know quite well that he is a very wise man and will presently overwhelm me with his arguments, so that I shall be

---

5. God's promise to dwell in their midst (Exod. 25: 8) refers to the structure of the camp arranged around the Tabernacle. This is a physical reality, as well as a mystical idea, a project of aspiration for the people. Cf. the dancing circle of the righteous as an image of transcendent bliss in the world to come (*Vayikra raba* 11: 9; BT *Ta'an.* 31a).

6. It is striking that even the words *talit shekulo tekhelet* play on the theme of totality, both explicitly and implicitly – *tekhelet* contains *kol*, 'wholeness', at its centre.

reconciled to him against my will. It is better that I should not engage with him.' When Moses saw that there was no good to be got of him he took leave of him ....

'And Moses sent to call Dathan and Aviram' [v. 12]. They too persisted in their wickedness and did not deign to answer him. 'And they said: We will not come up.' These wicked were tripped up by their own mouth; there is a covenant made with the lips, for they died and went down into the bottomless abyss, after they had 'gone down alive into the underworld' [v. 33] .... 'And Moses was very angry' [v. 15]. Why? Because when a man argues with his companion and the other answers him in argument, he has satisfaction, but if he does not answer he feels grieved.[7]

In the view of the *midrash*, Moses attempts to make peace with Korah, who is too canny to respond. Korah considers Moses' power with words to be dangerous, seductive. Perhaps it is language itself that he senses as treacherous: better to avoid any relationship in which communication is given free play. Observing that there is 'no good [lit.: no benefit] to be got of him', Moses turns to Dathan and Aviram. What had Moses hoped for in addressing Korah? At best, presumably, to win him over, convince him to abandon his rebellion. But perhaps Moses had hoped at least, simply, for dialogue, for words in reply to his words.

Compelled to abandon this project, he turns to the other rebels, where he fares just as poorly. Dathan and Aviram do, in fact, technically reply to Moses' overture, but the gist of their reply is *lo na'aleh* – 'We will not come up!' In other words, they use words to refuse dialogue, ending their scathing speech by repeating *lo na'aleh!* Their reply is a verbal sneer.

Here, the *midrash* makes a startling interpretation: 'they were tripped up by their own mouth, and there is a covenant made with the lips'. Dathan and Aviram find themselves speaking words whose sinister meaning they cannot even begin to fathom. The midrashic idiom here is a way of referring to the Freudian slip: refusing to *come up*, they will very shortly find themselves on the way *down* to the underworld. Unwittingly foretelling their own macabre fate, they speak unawares.

---

7. *Bemidbar raba* 18:8.

Perhaps indeed they are not so much foretelling as *testifying* to the course they are already set upon. Rejecting language, refusing to negotiate with Moses, they are already turned towards death. The biblical motif of 'the silence of the grave' is implicit here. 'The dead shall not praise God, nor any that go down into silence,' says the Psalmist.[8] The dead cannot speak, praise, communicate. Silence becomes, in many biblical passages, a synonym for death. In choosing not to respond to Moses' call, the rebels have refused language; they have chosen death over life. If they will not *come up*, they are already on the way down into the silent shades.

Moses' angry reaction to their repudiation becomes in the *midrash* a deep grief.[9] In the *midrash*, this is presented as a normal human reaction to being ignored by another. But, we may remember, Moses has particular reason to be pained by such an experience. In terms of his personal history, when his overtures fall on deaf ears, his worst fears are fulfilled. At the Burning Bush, at the very beginning of his mission, he had shied away from God's call with the words: 'But they will not believe me, they *will not listen to my voice*, they will say: God never appeared to you!' (Exodus 4:1). Pleading his inability to make the people listen to him, he went on to use idioms and metaphors to convey his radical rejection of God's mission: 'Please, O God, I have never been a man of words, neither yesterday nor the day before, nor now that You have spoken to Your servant; I am heavy of speech and heavy of tongue' (v. 10); 'Moses spoke to God, saying, "The Israelites would not listen to me; how then should Pharaoh listen to me, a man of uncircumcised lips!"' (6:12).

When he complains of being unable to speak, he means he is unable to make people listen to him. If the other refuses to respond, clearly communication has failed. To *speak* in the fullest sense is to make the other speak, to elicit a response.[10] It is this nexus of communication that from the outset arouses dread in Moses. Now, in his scene with the rebels, it seems that his dread is realized in the most painful way. Reach-

---

8. Ps. 115:17. See also, among many other examples, Pss. 94:17; 88: 2.
9. The biblical word *vayihar*, without the word *af*, is often translated in this way in the *midrash*, as though it refers to a generalized emotional agitation.
10. See *Sefat emet*, 'Va'era', p. 84, s.v. *uvileshon hapasuk… kabalat benei yisra'el*.

ing out to them, his gesture meeting with no response, an old wound reopens: he has failed to *speak*.

God responds in an unexpected way to Moses' complaint at the Burning Bush. Instead of reassuring him, promising him fluency, communicative power, God asks a question: 'What is that in your hand?' This is the scene that follows:

> And he replied, 'A rod.' He said, 'Cast it on the ground.' He cast it on the ground and it became a snake; and Moses fled from it. Then God said to Moses, 'Put out your hand and grasp it by the tail' – he put out his hand and seized it, and it became a rod in his hand – 'so that they may believe that God, the God of their fathers, the God of Abraham, the God of Isaac, and the God of Jacob, did appear to you.'
>
> God said to him further, 'Put your hand into your bosom.' He put his hand into his bosom; and when he took it out, his hand was encrusted with snowy scales! And He said, 'Put your hand back into your bosom.' He put his hand back into his bosom; and when he took it out of his bosom, there it was again like his own flesh. [Exodus 4:2–7]

Instead of healing Moses of his oral dread, God enacts with him the very experience, in the flesh, of his dread. The rod in his hand is no sooner named as such than it becomes a snake – 'And Moses fled from it.' An object that has just emerged from his own body, a safe, definable object, which was, in a sense, a symbolic extension of the power of his hand, now arouses in him an uncontrollable, visceral fear. In an instant, as it leaves his hand, it becomes unrecognizable, terrifying. Then, at God's command, he overcomes his fear, and grasps the snake, which re-transforms in his hand into a rod. 'This is the first sign', designed to create belief in the Israelites (v. 8); but a sign, as well, to himself, a staging of his own fear of that which emerges from his body and can no longer be mastered.

The second sign is even closer to the bone: his hand emerges from his bosom covered with snowy scales; when he puts it back in his bosom and again withdraws it, it has been restored *kivsaro* – to be part of his flesh again. Here, Moses' very flesh goes dead as it goes forth towards the world – a kind of ghastly birth; the very same movement of *in-out*, then brings his hand back to life, to be again his own flesh.

I suggest that in addition to the public role of these signs – to convince the people of the truth of Moses' claim that God indeed appeared to him – they have another purpose: Moses is being brought face-to-face with the dynamic of his own fear. Both signs re-enact the trauma of the act of speech: the movement from an interior to an exterior world, and the dread of what cannot be controlled in that movement of communication. In speaking, in meeting the other, there is sacrifice, there is transformation, even a fantasy of losing himself. Taken through a flesh-parable of fear, death, and resurrection, Moses must think of the edges of his body, his hand, his skin – and of that quintessential edge which is the mouth.[11] Here, the self touches the outer world; here, volatile changes and exchanges take place. This is the site of desire and fear, the boundary that creates longing and recoil. Between the lips rises the erotic space, the wish to transmit messages, to dissolve boundaries.

This erotic reach is the very nature of language, flouting the edges of things, enhancing meaning, inspired by an impossible desire. It begins with the first oral experience of the infant at the mother's breast.

It is striking that the Torah devotes considerable space to a description of Moses' infant nursing history. Clearly, if the baby Moses is to be saved from the fate of Israelite male infants, some provision will have to be made for feeding him. But the fact that the Torah gives prominence to this technical issue (the wet-nurse is a common resource in ancient aristocracies) signals a site of tension.

It is Miriam, Moses' sister, who volunteers to bring Moses' mother to act as a surrogate for the Egyptian princess. But several verses (Exodus 2:7–10) then recount, in slow motion, the process of her hiring and feeding of the child, as though to allow the reader to dwell on the paradox of the situation. Moses is to be nurtured by the princess's hired surrogate – who happens to be his birth mother.

Rashi quotes from the Talmud: 'The princess tried out many Egyptian wet-nurses, but he refused to nurse, because he was destined

---

11. The Hebrew word for 'two lips' – *sefatayim* – is also the word for 'two edges'.

to speak with the Shekhinah' (BT *Sotah* 12b). Here, the double sense of orality is explicit: the mouth that will engage with God cannot feed from foreign breasts. The basic oral impulse – to feed – is in this child inhibited at the earliest stage. Fraught with his future, he cannot inhabit his body, reach beyond its edges with full spontaneity. Even when he is reunited with his mother, she nurses him in a double role – as his mother, and as the princess's surrogate.[12]

Could there be a connection between this element of alienation in his infant oral experience and his later description of his relation to his people? 'Did I conceive this entire people, did I bear them, that You should say to me, "Carry them in your bosom as a wet-nurse carries an infant," to the land that You have promised on oath to their fathers?' (Numbers 11:12). The bizarre image of Moses as failed male wet-nurse suggests a deep frustration, a yearning for a simpler, more organic world of connection. Wishing and fearing to feed, to be fed, to speak, to evoke response, Moses knows the traumatic gap that makes *dibur*, the human speech function, a zone of vulnerability.

THE WORLD OF 'AS IF'

Returning now to the Korah narrative, we may appreciate the history of Moses' despair. When the rebels make their stand, with their dazzling and unanswerable assertion of total holiness, 'Moses heard, and he fell on his face' (v. 4). However, after this moment of speechlessness, he gets to his feet and attempts to speak, to Korah and to Dathan and Aviram. Both overtures are rejected, one in silence and the other in words of repudiation. But the fact that he tries again after Korah has rebuffed him becomes the source of an important talmudic teaching: 'From here we learn that one should not maintain a dispute (*maḥloket*), for Moses sought them out [lit.: courted them] in order to come to terms with them through a peaceful dialogue.'[13]

The lesson is phrased in the negative: one *should not persist* in a

---

12. The idiom, *lehanik le-* 'nursing for' is used in Miriam's proposal and in the princess's speech to Moses' mother. Interestingly, when she nurses him, the text drops the *le-* idiom – simply, 'she nursed him'.

13. BT *San.* 110a. See also Rashi on Num. 16:12.

maḥloket, in a dispute. This is learned from the fact that Moses *courts* the rebels, trying by every means to win them over. The imagery of court-ship, with its erotic implication, evokes Moses as willing to sacrifice his dignity in his desire for connection with the rebels. A tension is set up between the static hold of *maḥloket* and the dynamic, even seductive project of speech. To persist [lit.: hold on tight] in *maḥloket* is to create a rigid, unchangeable situation. Moses overcomes his own resistance to language in order to reach out to Korah, and then again to Dathan and Aviram.

The sarcastic reply of the latter raises further questions about language:

> And they said, 'We will not come up! Is it not enough that you brought us out from a land flowing with milk and honey to have us die in the wilderness, that you would also lord it over us? You have not even brought us a land flowing with milk and honey, and given us possession of fields and vineyards – will you gouge out these men's eyes? We will not come up!' [Numbers 16:12–14]

Beginning and ending their speech with refusal, Dathan and Aviram repeat, 'We will not come up!'[14] As we have noticed, the *midrash* reads this as referring ominously to their final descent into the earth. We suggested that this descent reflects the movement away from language, downwards into silence. In addition, on a conscious level, the rebels mock Moses' pretensions: he claims to be bringing them up, to life and the inheritance of the land, when the reality is that they will all die in the wilderness. *Lo na'aleh* means then, 'Your use of idioms of *aliyah* (going up) is mere propaganda. The truth behind your rhetoric is *yeridah* (loss, the final descent to death).'[15]

Obadiah Sforno (*c.*1475–1550) makes a fascinating suggestion. The problem he addresses is that 'You have not even … given us possession of fields' reads in Hebrew as though it is a positive statement [lit.: you

---

14. Rashbam (R. Shmuel ben Me'ir, *c.*1085–*c.*1158) reads this as refusing to submit to judgement.
15. See R. Hayim Ibn Atar, *Or haḥayim* on Num. 16:12.

have given us]. (The word 'not' must be carried forward from the previous phrase). He reads: 'Is it not enough that you have brought us out of a land flowing with milk and honey to this wilderness, but *you are also mocking us*: *your rhetoric pretends* that you are giving us an inheritance of fields and vineyards. Every time you speak about the commandments to be fulfilled in the land, it is *as though* the land is really to be ours, with its fields and vineyards.'

In this reading, the rebels are exposing the propaganda language of a ruler who is trying to pull the wool over their eyes – in the text, to gouge out their eyes. Unmasking his rhetoric, the rebels accuse Moses of demagoguery. Perhaps we can even say that they here express a deep distrust of language itself. Twice, Sforno uses the word, *ke'ilu* (as if), about Moses' way of using language. 'You are mocking us, playing with us,' they claim. What they cannot tolerate is the very nature of language – metaphorical to the core. 'Your words are "as if",' they say. Perhaps all significant language is 'as if', referring only partly to a demonstrable reality, but otherwise expanding the edges of plain meaning, in the effort to encompass the not-yet-known.

Rabbi Hayim Ibn Atar (1696–1743), in his commentary *Or hahayim*, for instance, notices the same phenomenon that the rebels resent and satirize (in Sforno's reading). When Moses tells the people, 'When you enter the land that I am giving you to settle in' (15:2), he seems to be projecting a future that this generation will, in a literal sense, never see. *Or hahayim* reads this as a subtle reframing of the people's hope: they are being asked to imagine their children's prosperity as their own. 'You' can mean the concrete individuals who stand before him, or it can refer to the enlarged 'you' of the self connected with others. 'You' need not be hollow rhetoric, but an expression of the fictive nature of language itself.

Dathan and Aviram are the 'unmaskers'. They will not be fooled by Moses' language. Of course, they themselves use language in order to unmask Moses, but their language, they would claim, hews to the 'plain meaning' of words. 'A land flowing with milk and honey', for instance: this simply means a fertile land, and anyone with eyes in his head can see that Egypt, and not the unachieved land of Israel, is the fertile land. This literal understanding of language, however, is a travesty of the meaning of the iconic phrase, 'a land flowing with milk and honey'. This is always used to refer to the land of Israel;[16] when the rebels use it to refer to Egypt, it is they who are dislocating meaning.

Their disenchanted sneer is itself unmasked. The world of *dibur*, of language, is a world of 'as if', which acknowledges imagination, desire, the role of *eros*. The fiction of the future, the ongoing invention of the self, and the attempt to dissolve boundaries are all part of the project of language. As Jacques Lacan puts it, *Les non-dupes errent*: 'Those who will not be duped are themselves in error.'[17] Compulsively suspicious, the rebels attack Moses' language, ignoring their own implication in the world of *dibur*. They may, in fact, be the most duped of all, since their own fantasy world remains unacknowledged.

In his struggle for integrity in language, Moses is now faced with the silence of Korah, on the one hand, and with the verbal sneer of Dathan and Aviram, on the other. Both represent a radical rejection of the world of *dibur*. Indeed, the drama of this confrontation rises partly from Moses' own history of refusal to speak. But Moses' history indicates a struggle with that refusal. Perhaps from the moment when he describes himself as 'of uncircumcised lips', there is born in him an awareness of an *impediment*, a block to be overcome.[18]

EVOCATIVE SPACES

The great sixteenth-century philosopher and commentator on the Torah, Maharal (Rabbi Judah Loew ben Bezalel), offers a striking insight into the nature of *mahloket*.[19] Usually translated 'dispute' or 'dissension', this is the vice that is associated in midrashic sources with Korah. Maharal characterizes the personality-type, *ba'alei mahloket*, 'masters of dissension', 'schismatics', as those who, in the words of the Talmud, 'set all their words upon *din* (strict law)'. The paradigm for this is the generation of the destruction of the Second Temple, whose pathology is defined in this way. Like that generation, Korah's discourse is one of total right-

---

16. Nineteen out of twenty biblical usages of the phrase have this meaning.
17. Jacques Lacan, *Seminar XXI*, November 1974.
18. See Rashi's translation of 'uncircumcised' as 'blocked', on Exod. 6:12.
19. See Maharal, *Gur aryeh* on Num. 16:27.

ness, of uncompromising and transparent righteousness. Such people bring ruin upon the world: inflexible, unyielding, they are incapable of 'going beyond the strict line of law'. This type is *kulo din* (unequivocal, all of a piece), and inevitably he brings destruction on himself and others. His proper place is Gehinnom (the underworld), where all language is silenced.

What is striking about this passage is the implication that the 'master of dissension' is precisely not one who cultivates argument: he is one who is so 'right' that there is no possibility of discussion. He knows nothing of the yearning, the inner lack, that reaches out to know, to court, to love – to the utterance that is informed by *eros* – *l'amour de loin*, as the troubadours called it. The 'master of dissension', then, suffers from a kind of manic rationality. His words avoid metaphor, questions, any indication of the incompleteness that inspires language. In this sense, he represents a *resistance* to language, to *dibur*.

One might say that such a person refuses to mourn, to acknowledge the gaps, the differences that beset human experience. Perhaps harking back to a lost paradise of oceanic wholeness, but unwilling to admit the loss, he is aware neither of his own edges nor of his desire to transcend them.

This is Korah: compulsively sane, he knows nothing of the dynamic inner void, the question that lives at the heart of creative language. The French philosopher Maurice Blanchot writes:

> The question is movement... there is the request for something else; incomplete, the word that questions recognizes that it is only a part. Thus the question is essentially partial; is the setting where speech offers itself as ever incomplete.... The question puts the sufficient assertion back into the void; it enriches it with this pre-existing void.[20]

Speech of this kind is a form of desire: declaring itself incomplete, it achieves itself. Paradoxically, it is the sense of the void that moves language to its erotic quest.

---

20. Maurice Blanchot, *L'Entretien infini* (Paris: Gallimard, 1969), 13–14.

Maharal's reading of Korah brings to mind G.K. Chesterton's provocative statement: 'The madman is not the man who has lost his reason. The madman is the man who has lost everything except his reason...his mind moves in a perfect but narrow circle.'[21] The perfect circle of the mad mind may take the form of a world of wholly holy people, undifferentiated from one another and from themselves, defined by their rightness.

The paradox, of course, is that this mentality is described by Maharal as the *maḥloket* mind, while, in a sense, it is precisely argument, discourse, that this mind avoids. There are two kinds of *maḥloket*, then: one expressing itself in open and passionate discourse, the other closed within its own perfect but narrow circle. The positive model is the subject of one of the most important teachings of Rabbi Nahman of Bratslav: 'Know, too, that *maḥloket*, dispute, is a feature of Creation.'[22]

Basing himself on the cosmological model of Lurianic kabbalah, Rabbi Nahman focuses on the moment of creation. Before that moment, God, the Infinite One, encompassed all reality. Desiring the existence of a world, He retracted His light, drawing it in so as to leave a *ḥalal panui*, a vacated space, in which, through language, to project a world: such a world as ours, with boundaries, separations, objects, space, and time. In the same way, suggests Rabbi Nahman, if all thinkers thought alike, there would be no place, no *space*, for the creation of worlds. Drawing in their own light, scholars allow that space between themselves where language can create something else. The very purpose of the discourse of scholars, of their mode of debate, is, in *imitatio Dei*, to create the world.

The creative discourse of scholars is based on the separations, the edges that characterize difference, and that lend movement and passion to communication. What is *between* the scholars, that evocative space, makes it possible for new scholars and new scholarship to come to the world. Between any two who speak or argue, it is the void allowed by each, the willingness to suspend prejudices, that opens to unpredictable insight.

Walter Benjamin writes: 'Friendship does not abolish the dis-

---

21. G.K. Chesterton, *Orthodoxy* (New York: Doubleday, 1959), 19–20.
22. R. Nahman of Bratslav, *Likutei moharan*, i, 64:4.

tance between human beings, but brings that distance to life.'[23] This, too, for Rabbi Nahman, is the role of *maḥloket*: to bring to life worlds not yet seen. This gestation requires a space – the irreducible distance between human beings.

Similarly, D.W. Winnicott writes of the 'potential space' that is the young child's first experience of separation from the mother. The child moves from an imagined omnipotence, a magical control of the world, into an intermediate area which belongs to both inner and outer reality. Here, she is lost in play, objects are caught up in a private game with the materials of the world. Winnicott calls these 'transitional objects', and the play space, 'transitional space'. This will become the location for cultural experience, the space in which worlds of philosophy and religion, art and music and poetry may emerge – all versions of *dibur*, in which human beings struggle to use the materials of external reality in their quest to give form to their inner reality.

Korah, averse to spaces, suspicious of speech, is declared in the Zohar to have 'repudiated the creation of the world'.[24] This mystifying statement may be related to Rabbi Nahman's description of world-making,[25] which is itself based on kabbalistic thought. If the creation of the world involves the acceptance, or even the creation of a containing space, then Korah is seen as allergic to such spaces from which *something else* may emerge. Intelligent, sane, like Chesterton's madman, he is all *din*, incapable of the movement of desire.

FANTASIES OF WHOLENESS

A similar reading of Korah is to be found in *Mei hashilo'aḥ*, by Rabbi Mordechai Joseph Leiner (the Ishbitser Rebbe, 1801–54). He characterizes Korah as apparently impeccable. What is missing in him is precisely any sense of his *incompleteness* (*ḥisaron*). He lacks all awareness of his own lack, of the void within him. Most pitiable of all human beings, he cannot access his own void. Engulfed in an illusion of self-possession, he is entirely 'lost'. (The word *oved*, 'lost', is the one used to describe

---

23. Walter Benjamin, *Understanding Brecht* (Brooklyn, NY: Verso Books, 1977), 73.
24. Zohar, i. 17a.
25. Cf. Nelson Goodman, *Ways of World Making* (Indianapolis, IN: Hackett, 1978).

the disappearance of the rebels into the earth: '*vayovdu* – they vanished from the midst of the community', Numbers 16:33.) Korah emerges as a non-person even in his life: the apparently successful man with an internal void that is unrecognized by himself. This hollowness is a constitutive part of being human; ignorant of this, Korah has no access to his life's spiritual project, which relates precisely to that potential space.[26]

The Korah syndrome, then, consists both of a blindness to difference, to gaps, between people, and of a similar blindness to internal gaps, places of difference with one's conscious self. These inner blind spots make growth impossible. Jacques Maritain, writing of Dante, speaks of 'some abiding despair in every great poet, a certain wound in him that has set free the creativeness'.[27] Korah, averse to gaps, wounds, spaces, cannot struggle with his limitations; by the same measure, he cannot access his subjective creativeness. Yet here the author of *Mei hashilo'ah* reverses himself, imagining possible reversal for Korah. In the future, he writes, God will reveal to him the truth of his inner world and in one instant he will become conscious of his own *ḥisaron* and move from darkness to light.

He bases his redemptive narrative on Isaiah 27:13: 'And it shall be on that day that there shall be a blast of the great shofar and the *ovdim*, those lost in the land of Assyria and those dispersed in the land of Egypt, shall come and bow down to God on the holy mountain in Jerusalem.' On the one hand, before the moment of revelation, Korah is a lost soul, his true self not yet born to consciousness; on the other, after the moment of revelation, he is transformed by a critical new awareness – of the *ḥisaron*, the incompleteness in himself. Till then, Korah is seen as living an almost-life, essentially disabled by a blindness.

This blindness is finally described thus: he cannot experience 'the difference between himself and Moses'. *Mei hashilo'ah* is clearly referring to Korah's original slogan: 'The whole community are entirely holy'. Envious of Moses' claims to difference, to privileged status, Korah is blind to a significant otherness in Moses. But perhaps *Mei hashilo'ah*

---

26. *Mei hashilo'ah*, vol. 2, 'Korah', s.v. *ketiv*.
27. See Marion Milner, *The Suppressed Madness of Sane Men* (London: Routledge, 1988), 208.

also means to imply that Moses' difference lies precisely in the fact that he is aware of his own *ḥisaron*.

Korah and Moses are, after all, first cousins. The question of sameness and difference is particularly significant to their relationship and to the struggle between them. Perhaps similar in talent and ability, they are differentiated in their attitude to language. For Moses, too, the world of language is fraught with tension. The desire for totality, the oceanic sensibility, impeded his creation of the necessary internal space through which language might emerge. But acknowledging himself as *aral sefatayim* (of uncircumcised lips/edges) (Exodus 6:12) – he recognizes the 'foreskin', the impediment that needs to be removed. When he becomes aware of this as an impediment, a project is born: the opening of his body and mind to a sense of its own incompleteness – a circumcision of sorts.

With this movement comes a sense of his difference *from himself*. No longer all of a piece with himself or with the world, aware of his edges, internal and external, Moses is reborn as a *speaking* being capable of symbolic thinking and, therefore, of creating his own specific world. A fantasy of wholeness is relinquished. This consciousness is what distinguishes him from his cousin Korah. For Korah to understand this would be for him to understand his own difference from himself.

UNATTAINED BUT ATTAINABLE SELF

Ralph Waldo Emerson noted that:

> In every work of genius we recognize our own rejected thoughts; they come back to us with a certain alienated majesty.[28]

Emerson describes the bittersweet experience of finding one's own repressed thoughts expressed in the words of another. It is, in a sense, one's own unrealized self whose ghostly shadow one encounters.[29] One's own potential but ignored majesty comes to remind and reproach.

---

28. Ralph Waldo Emerson, *Selected Essays*, ed. Larzer Ziff (Harmondsworth: Penguin, 1982), 176.

29. 'Alienated' holds the meaning of ghostly presences.

The philosopher Stanley Cavell responds to this passage by wondering about the value of reading the work of others:

> Think of it this way: If the thoughts of a text such as Emerson's (say the brief text on rejected thoughts) are yours, then you do not need them. If its thoughts are *not* yours, they will not do you any good. The problem is that the text's thoughts are neither exactly mine nor not mine. In their sublimity as my rejected – say repressed – thoughts, they represent my *further, next, unattained but attainable, self* [emphasis added]. To think otherwise, to attribute the origin of my thoughts simply to the other, thoughts which are then, as it were, implanted in me – some would say caused – by let us say some Emerson, is idolatry.[30]

Cavell sharpens the implications of Emerson's remark. To read the work of another is to encounter not merely oneself nor merely the other; the alchemy created in the encounter acts to make more real one's own not-yet realized self. To commit idolatry, then, would be to discount the always-present activity of the mind and imagination in reading – or in any moment of encounter. Texts do not implant the thoughts of the other in my mind; these thoughts live in the potential space of interpretation, of loss and yearning and desire. 'They represent my further, next, unattained but attainable, self.' The self is not hewed in stone, it is not all of a piece. One reads, or talks, in order to arouse potential selves, pregnant voids.

For Korah, redemption might mean to become aware of the difference between himself and Moses, between himself and himself. Such awareness would mean a desire to *further* himself, a new sense of a *beyond*. In a sense, it would mean allowing the world of fantasy to open in his mind, as well as allowing for it *as* fantasy. It would no longer be possible to proclaim: 'The whole community are totally holy and in their midst is God,' as a realistic statement in the political world.

On the other hand, these same words might well become a

---

30. Stanley Cavell, *Conditions Handsome and Unhandsome* (Chicago, IL: University of Chicago Press, 1990), 57.

poetic affirmation of a fantasy image, expressing an aspiration. In fact, in another passage, *Mei hashilo'ah* credits Korah with great sincerity in speaking these words.[31] Korah sees his people in the mythic light of a dynamic centring structure, without gradations or hierarchies.[32] This present world, however, is marked by differences, separations, gaps – between fantasy and reality. In order to construct such a world, the mind requires symbolic procedures, essential discriminations that include a fine awareness of the human *hisaron*, the hairline crack of imperfection that divides the real and the ideal.

Korah's fantasy of omnipotence leads him down to silence, to the destruction of the world. And yet, *Mei hashilo'ah* suggests, Korah's blindness may be of a different order from that of popular imagination. Possibly, he is not, after all, a figure of gross ambition, but rather a worthy counterpart to Moses; their struggle may convey a sense of the complexity of the self and the subtlety of its movements and refusals: its spectrum of unattained but attainable potential selves.

'FROM ANOTHER SHORE'

These issues of language and otherness, of totality and infinity, are closely related, then, to the question of *mahloket*. If, as Rabbi Nahman will have it, *mahloket* is the exchange that maintains the vital gap between two who speak to one another, then the refusal to speak holds large implications.

This vital gap, writes Emmanuel Levinas, involves a basic 'calling into question of the I', in the presence of the Other: 'This voice coming from another shore teaches transcendence itself.'[33] There is an irreducible distance between self and other which is of the very nature of relationship: it introduces the experience of transcendence into the basic fabric of human life.

In a similar vein, Maurice Blanchot writes: 'The relationship with the other … is a transcendent relationship, which means that there is an … insurmountable distance between me and the other who belongs to the

---

31. *Mei hashilo'ah*, vol. 2, 'Korah', pp. 62–3, s.v. *ki kol ha'edah*.
32. See above, n. 5.
33. Emmanuel Levinas, *Totality and Infinity* (Pittsburgh, PA: Duquesne University Press, 1969), 171.

other shore.'[34] This gap between two people who talk to one another has the effect of suspending easy assumptions about the other.

For Levinas, this gap is also the site of revelation, which enters through the 'fracture' that opens up in a narcissistic view of the world. Indeed, God can reveal Himself to human beings only because of this human ability to allow the shock of otherness in the encounter with another human being. The face of the other creates a 'traumatic upheaval in experience', which ruptures the complacencies of one's own prejudices. The human *face-to-face* relation is thus the theatre in which revelation may be realized.

This is the vital rupture which makes it possible to experience revelation or inspiration. Ever conscious of the traumatic dimension of such encounters, Levinas disarmingly speaks of the *worry*, the uncontainable impact of God's Infinity, which in itself makes man human. When one welcomes one's neighbour, when one greets him with *hineni* – Here I am – one opens oneself to this divine worry which is divine inspiration.[35]

In this model of relationship, Korah's downfall is created by his refusal of the divine *worry* of uncontainable otherness; he closes himself against that human fracture that allows man to welcome his neighbour and to open himself to the inspiration of God's Infinity. One effect of his refusal is his repudiation of Moses' transcendent experience of revelation.

For Levinas, revelation, then, is an awakening from a stultifying self-possession: 'Are there not grounds,' he hauntingly asks, 'for imagining a relation with an Other that would be "better" than self-possession?'[36]

The figure of Moses, moreover, is for Levinas necessarily one who is 'not a man of words': 'The language of the Old Testament is so suspicious of any rhetoric which never stammers that it has as its chief prophet a man "slow of speech and of tongue."'[37] Revelation creates a rupture in him, interrupting his repose, creating the 'worry', the inspi-

---

34. Blanchot, *L'Entretien infini*, 74.
35. Levinas, 'Revelation in the Jewish Tradition', in Seán Hand (ed.), *The Levinas Reader* (Oxford: Blackwell, 1989), 207.
36. Ibid., 209.
37. Ibid., 197.

ration of response. His is to be language that never forgets its stammer, the difference between inner and outer worlds, between self and other.

THE CRACK IN THE VESSEL

The relation between Moses and Korah, then, can be read as a confrontation between two attitudes to language: response and repose. In the cluster of midrashic and hasidic sources that we have cited, we can detect a kinship with the work of Levinas and Blanchot on otherness.

At this point, I would like to introduce into the conversation a passage from *Sefat emet* (by Rabbi Judah Aryeh Leib Alter, 1847–1905) which weaves together some of the strands we have been tracing.[38] He 'creates a world' in language, a metaphysical world in which there is creation and repose, turbulence and rest, rupture and wholeness. Quoting the *midrash*,[39] he declares that the world cannot exist on *din* alone: that is why God created it ultimately through two projections of his Being, two different divine Names, *ḥesed* and *din*, signifying grace and law. But *Sefat emet* takes this in a different direction: total rightness (*din*) is unworkable in this world because of the essential *incompleteness* of this world. In the language of Levinas, we might say that there is a rupture, a crack in the cup, which does not allow for total self-possession. In human experience, there is a great *ḥisaron*, an unappeased yearning for wholeness.

Since this world is not a closed system, this yearning will always build towards a transcendent source of grace (*ḥesed*) – such as the sabbath. Quoting from the Zohar, *Sefat emet* remarks on the last-minute creations of the twilight moment 'between the suns' – the *mazikin* (the demons of chaos). These demons are a kind of inevitable explosion of the forces of *ḥisaron*, of lack, which are endemic to this world. At the very moment when God has completed His creation, these demons threaten to overwhelm the apparently ordered world, exposing its inherent turbulence. And at that moment, the sabbath comes to close the fissure, to lay the demons to rest. The world is for the instant of the sabbath reconnected with a primal wholeness.

That liminal hour, between the apparent order of the world and

---

38. R. Judah Aryeh Leib Alter, *Sefat emet*, 'Bemidbar', 113.
39. *Bereshit raba* 12:15.

the transcendent peace of sabbath, draws out an essential rest-lessness and raises it to fever-pitch. Only in the full experience of the yearning for wholeness – that is, in the experience of its lack – can the sabbath flow in and transfigure reality. At this moment, 'between the suns', the crack, the fracture in self-possession becomes a radical opening to the light of infinity.[40] The broken vessel becomes whole, containing blessing. Or, in a different register, as the Kotzker Rebbe put it: 'There is nothing as whole as a broken heart.'

At this point, *Sefat emet* turns to the Korah narrative. The 'mouth of the earth', the gap in the surface into which the rebels vanish – it too was created in that primal twilight. Like the demons, the hungry mouth represents the fracture in the nature of this world, which Korah sets himself to deny. In its place, he holds to a world of unyielding *din*, of total coherence. Manically rational, he is precipitated into the madness that he has denied: 'there leaps upon him the fury of the underworld'. The demonic forces take their revenge and engulf him. The *ḥesed* that he has repudiated encompasses the dynamic of longing, the erotic reach that informs language. Rigid with selfhood, Korah has lost the sense of the gaps and edges of human experience; and with it the ability to be permeated by infinity. Like a stone, he sinks into silence.

REOPENINGS

In the biblical narrative, this is the conclusive end of the Korah narrative. And yet, in the Talmud (the *Oral* Torah), a question is raised which comes to disturb the dark repose of the ending: are the Korah conspirators destined to re-ascend from the underworld?[41] Rabbi Eliezer declares

---

40. Cf. Leonard Cohen's 'Anthem':
    Ring the bells that still can ring
    Forget your perfect offering
    There is a crack, a crack in everything
    That's how the light gets in.
    See also W.B. Yeats, 'Crazy Jane Talks with the Bishop':
    For nothing can be sole or whole
    That has not been rent.
41. See BT *San.* 108a.

that they will be redeemed; other sages declare that Moses and Hannah will pray for them.[42]

In the biblical text, the reopening of the question is focused on Numbers 26:11; in the course of a census of the people, the Korah story is retold and a full verse is devoted to the statement, 'And the children of Korah did not die.'[43] This seems to be in contradiction with our narrative: 'And the ground under them burst asunder, and the earth opened its mouth and swallowed them up with their households, *all Korah's people*' (v. 32) – which seems to indicate that his sons did die. On the other hand, his children could not have died, since they later are recorded as the singers in the Temple; several of the psalms are attributed to the sons of Korah.[44] Yet the Torah creates a sense of tension around the apparently unequivocal moment of engulfment. Is it possible that they are swallowed up, but they do not die?

One resolution is offered in the Talmud: 'A place was reserved for them in the underworld and they sat there and sang.'[45] That is, they go down with all the other conspirators, but at the last moment they repent; or, more precisely, they experience pangs (*hirhurim*) of repentance – qualms, pangs of *worry*. Some revelation comes to them, brings them, at the last moment, their humanity. In a time out of time, those who were sealed in their stupor are cracked open, disrupted, and their mouths finally open – in song?

What the Talmud may be suggesting is that at this place at the edge of up-and-down, of life and death, an uncontainable awareness comes to them, and they burst forth in the song which their descendants will sing in the Temple.

Here is part of one of the psalms later attributed to them (Psalm 88:2–7, 12, emphasis added):

---

42. See BT *San.* 109*b*; cf. JT *San.* 10:4, 53*a–b*.

43. This is, in fact, an interrupted verse – a half-verse, as it were. Perhaps the very form of the verse enacts its meaning: it serves to disrupt the smooth flow of names and numbers of the national census, creating a suspension in the midst of the chronicle. Perhaps closure is not, after all, complete?

44. See Pss. 84, 85, 87, 88, etc.

45. See BT *San.* 110*a*.

A song, a psalm of the sons of Korah....
O Lord, God of my salvation,
By day I cried, in the night before You.
Let my prayer come before You,
Incline your ear to my cry.
For my soul is sated with troubles,
And my life comes close to the grave.
I am counted with those that go down into the pit;
I have become as a man that has no help;
Set apart among the dead,
Like the slain that lie in the grave,
Whom You remember no more;
And they are cut off from Your hand.
You have laid me in the nethermost pit,
In dark places, in the deeps....
Shall Your mercy be declared in the grave?
Or Your faithfulness in destruction?

The whole psalm is imaginable as the explosion of a spirit threatened with extinction. If this is the song of Korah's sons, it comes to teach, in the most rigorous way, the truth of Levinas's perception: 'The "less" is forever bursting open, unable to contain the "more" that it contains.'[46] Even the conclusive ending of the Korah story, which Moses has invoked to prove the truth of his narrative, even the resealed face of the earth cannot fully absorb the otherness of those who have been swallowed. As long as there is life, there is always a mouth that will open; language will make a crack in things – worry, questioning, seeking, desire – intimations of a relation with an Other.

This is the talmudic scenario of repentance and of song as forces that may reopen the most closed of narratives. One more way of telling the story is hinted at in a beautiful teaching of *Sefat emet.* Here, the issue is: what happens, in this world of *dibur,* where gaps and differences and shortfalls must be confronted, to that other world of fantasy that can never be fully spoken? In the world to come, the righteous may wheel

46. Levinas, 'Revelation', 209.

endlessly around God, all equal, dancing their praise. But in this world, does the heart's desire survive its representation in words, or steps, or strings plucked? Does the fantasy of wholeness and holiness, the vision of the lover, of the new parent, of the composer whose melody lives its primal life within her – are these fantasy worlds entirely subsumed in the forms and structures of reality?

Contemplating another song, *Sefat emet* quotes the beginning of Moses' Song of the Sea: '*Az yashir Moshe* – Then Moses sang/would sing'. Rashi reads the unusual future-tense narrative form: 'Then there came up in his mind the intention to sing a song.' He also quotes the midrashic reading: 'This is a biblical indication of the resurrection of the dead.' What Moses actually sings is that part of his internal song that lends itself to the words of this world. But an ineffable residue remains within, the fantasy of praise that cannot pass the barrier of consciousness. This unconscious life is what the *midrash* refers to, when it says that the text hints at the resurrection of the dead. *Then*, in that unspeakable time, the heart's song will be consummated in a shared space.[47] The infinite desire of a human being, which he or she struggles to express in fragmentary ways in this world, will have its future.[48] It is vindicated, then, also in its unknowable presence.

Perhaps the talmudic notion of the song that Korah's sons sing at the very verge of the underworld also suggests that the fantasy world of Korah does after all receive some recognition. What is revealed to his sons is a space between the ideal and the real, which is the world of song, with its infinite desire and its formal expressions of that desire, as well as its residue held over for another time and place.

In this hasidic teaching, nothing is wasted, even the untimely and destructive fantasy of Korah's band. From the edge of the pit, living voices find their true desire. Somehow, from that liminal space, live children emerge, whose choirs fill the Temple with song.

---

47. My thanks to Sara Friedland, who drew my attention to this teaching.
48. *Sefat emet*, Vayikra on Pesah, 79.

Afterword

A New Musar?

Tamra Wright

In tribute to the intellectual contributions of Jonathan Sacks, this Festschrift has brought together essays on ethics, justice, religion, and leadership by some of the leading experts in these fields, with complementary essays on similar themes by prominent Jewish studies scholars whose work the Chief Rabbi admires. Each section of the book reflects the value of bringing Jewish teachings and secular wisdom into dialogue with one another. Before concluding, we would like to explore briefly a specific new direction for further creative intellectual work inspired by Rabbi Sacks's teaching.

Over the years, Rabbi Sacks has sometimes mentioned specific areas of secular wisdom which could fruitfully be studied together with Torah to generate new insights into both domains. One intriguing suggestion is that contemporary approaches to psychology, particularly cognitive behaviour therapy and positive psychology, could be combined with Torah to create a 'new *musar* movement'. In *Future Tense*, Rabbi Sacks notes that these approaches to psychology are more in keeping with the spirit of Judaism than Freudian psychoanalysis, which is based on the Greek myth of Oedipus, and presents an essentially tragic conception of human existence.[1] The leitmotif of Judaism, by contrast, according to Rabbi Sacks, is hope; indeed, the Jewish task in the contemporary world is 'to be the voice of hope in an age of fear; the countervoice in the conversation of mankind'.[2] Hope, however, must be distinguished from naïve optimism:

> One of the most important distinctions I have learned in the course of reflection on Jewish history is the difference between optimism and hope. Optimism is the belief that things will get better. Hope is the faith that, together, we can make things better. Optimism is a passive virtue, hope an active one. It takes no courage to be an optimist, but it takes a great deal of courage to have hope. Knowing what we do of our past, no Jew can be an optimist. But Jews have never – despite a history of sometimes awesome suffering – given up hope.[3]

What might a 'new *musar* movement' or a contemporary 'Jewish' psychology, rooted in hope, look like? After a brief introduction to traditional *musar*, cognitive behaviour therapy, and positive psychology, we will suggest ways in which such a movement could draw on Jewish thought and practice together with these approaches to psychology.

Musar is a Hebrew word meaning 'instruction', 'discipline', or 'conduct'. The movement, which originated among non-hasidic Orthodox Jews in Lithuania in the nineteenth century, was noted for its focus on the individual's development of virtues or good *midot* (personal qualities), and, in particular, for emphasizing the relationship between human beings at least as much as that between the individual and God. Many stories are told that highlight the ethical sensibilities of Rabbi Israel Salanter and the other *ba'alei musar* (*musar* teachers). For example, Rabbi Salanter was once observed using only the bare minimum amount

---

1. Jonathan Sacks, *Future Tense* (London: Hodder & Stoughton, 2009), 229.
2. Ibid., 263.
3. Jonathan Sacks, *The Dignity of Difference* (London: Continuum, 2002), 206.

of water to wash his hands in the ritual fashion. When a surprised student asked whether it wasn't religiously preferable to wash more thoroughly, he replied, 'Not at the expense of the water carrier', who would then have a heavier burden to carry. This focus on responsibility for the material well-being of other people as a central religious value is one of the hallmarks of Rabbi Salanter's teaching, and has been translated into a contemporary philosophical idiom by Emmanuel Levinas as 'the other's material needs are my spiritual needs'.[4]

Although *musar* still forms part of the curriculum in some Orthodox yeshivas, and is undergoing a modest revival amongst progressive Jews as well, there is no doubt that its heyday has long since passed. The 'new *musar*' would not necessarily use any of the same techniques as the old, but it would address some of the same questions: how can we best help ourselves and each other to change negative behaviours and to develop the *midot* the Torah demands of us? In addition, as the Chief Rabbi has pointed out, the contemporary era necessitates an increased emphasis on interpersonal skills, particularly 'listening, respecting, praising, mediating and finding lateral solutions offering a way beyond the zero-sum game of conflict', and the new *musar* would need to help people develop these interpersonal virtues.[5] Finally, in the spirit of Jonathan Sacks's writings, the new *musar* would aspire to be of relevance to both Jews and non-Jews, regardless of their level of religious observance.

Before looking at the specifically Jewish contributions that would form part of the new *musar*, it will be helpful to consider which secular disciplines would need to be deployed to meet the aims the Chief Rabbi has identified. To begin with, if the new *musar* aims to help people replace conflict with co-operation, it will need to draw on the findings of leadership studies, including, for example, the important distinction between technical and adaptive challenges discussed by Ronald Heifetz in his contribution to this volume. Theoretical and practical insights into

---

4. Emmanuel Levinas, *Nine Talmudic Readings*, trans. Annette Aronowicz (Bloomington, IN: Indiana University Press, 1990), 99.

5. Jonathan Sacks, 'Foreword' to Michael Roness (ed.), *Conflict and Conflict Management in Jewish Sources*, Program on Conflict Management and Negotiation (Ramat Gan: Bar-Ilan University, 2008); online publication http://www.biu.ac.il/interdis/pconfl/doc/conflict_handbook.pdf.

negotiation and mediation can be drawn from a number of disciplines, including law, history, international relations, war studies, and family therapy, to name but a few.

Turning to psychology, what aspects of cognitive behaviour therapy and positive psychology might make these approaches particularly fruitful for creating a new *musar*? Rabbi Sacks sees these approaches as compatible with Judaism primarily because of their essentially hopeful stance – the theoretical framework underpinning each of these approaches rests on the assumption that with the right guidance people can successfully make changes in their outlook and behaviour; these approaches also emphasize the autonomy and responsibility of the individual.[6] For Rabbi Sacks, such an outlook is characteristically, but certainly not exclusively, Jewish:

> Hope does not exist in a conceptual vacuum, nor is it available to all configurations of culture. It is born in the belief that the sources of action lie within ourselves. We are not unwitting products of blind causes: the selfish gene, the Darwinian struggle for survival, the Hegelian dialectic of history, the Marxist war of classes, the Nietzschean clash of wills, a Durkheimian set of sociological trends, or a Freudian complex of psychological drives of which we are only dimly aware.[7]

Cognitive behaviour therapy (CBT), as the name suggests, combines behavioural and cognitive approaches to therapy. The behavioural part is based on approaches and techniques developed in the 1950s and 1960s as alternatives to psychoanalytic and psychodynamic therapies. Although the umbrella of 'behaviour therapy' includes a range of techniques, they share two basic features: first, their aim is to remove symptoms by dealing not with underlying causes but with the symptoms themselves; second, the techniques were designed to be empiri-

---

6. The importance of autonomy and the responsibility of the individual within Judaism are emphasized by Jacob J. Schacter and Binyamin Lau in their contributions to this volume.

7. Sacks, *Dignity of Difference*, 206–7.

cally testable.[8] The cognitive aspect is based on a model first proposed by Aaron T. Beck in 1976. His model illustrated 'how emotional problems could be driven by patterns of negative thinking, and proposed that problems could be alleviated by changing the thinking processes.'[9] The model has been further developed by other researchers over the past several decades, and the CBT approach has expanded to include a number of other elements.

According to the CBT model, 'situations in themselves do not cause psychological distress'; instead, it is people's interpretations of and reactions to situations that cause the problems.[10] The interrelationships among thoughts, feelings (both emotions and physical sensations), and behaviours are such that making a change in one can produce change in any of the others. To take a simple and common example, someone who is nervous about making presentations might have negative thoughts about the task or his or her abilities ('I am very bad at public speaking'); experience anxiety and the accompanying physical sensations (shallow rapid breathing, sweaty palms, etc.); and exhibit unhelpful behaviours (perhaps speaking too quickly or avoiding eye contact). A CBT intervention could address any of the three elements. A cognitive intervention could, for example, help the person reframe the situation ('This is a good opportunity to practise public speaking in front of a small audience; I can learn from this experience'); a behavioural intervention might include rehearsing speaking slowly; breathing exercises or visualizations might help the client to address the emotions and physiological sensations. Any of these three types of interventions might, according to this model, lead to positive changes in the other elements.

Much of Beck's pioneering work in cognitive therapy focused on helping clients to overcome depression. Unlike earlier therapists who focused on the affective aspects of depression, Beck realized that patients who suffer from depression characteristically exhibit distorted

---

8. Peter Cooper, 'Introduction' to Gillian Butler, *Overcoming Social Anxiety and Shyness* (London: Robinson, 1999), p. x.

9. Jane Simmonds and Rachel Griffiths, *CBT for Beginners* (London: SAGE Publications, 2009), 20.

10. Ibid., 22.

thinking: they construe their experience in a negative way, have a negative view of themselves, and have negative expectations of the future. The pattern of distorted thinking in depressive patients is different from that of patients with other psychological illnesses; for example, a paranoid patient will also construe her experience in a negative way and have negative expectations of the future, but she will blame others rather than herself, whereas the depressed patient will blame himself. Beck found that when he was able to help patients change their thoughts about themselves, their experience or the future, the patients also experienced positive changes in mood.[11]

Over time, Beck and other researchers further refined the cognitive model. CBT practitioners now help their patients to identify different levels of cognitions: automatic thoughts, assumptions, and core beliefs. Automatic thoughts are the easiest to identify: in a therapy session or by writing in a journal, clients can be asked to reflect on a situation in which they felt a strong negative emotion and then to try to identify the thought that occurred to them immediately before experiencing that emotion. Assumptions are not as easy to access. Unlike automatic thoughts, they are not localized but are general rules. When the client becomes conscious of them, they can usually be articulated in the form of 'if…then' statements or 'should' statements: for example, 'If I don't pass an exam, then I am stupid' or 'I should always succeed'. Assumptions are closely connected with the third type of cognitions, core beliefs, which operate at the deepest cognitive level. They are global and absolute beliefs such as 'I am a bad person' or 'I am worthless'. According to CBT theory, people develop assumptions in order to protect themselves from the emotions associated with their negative core beliefs.[12] Cognitive behaviour therapy helps people to identify, challenge, and modify or replace their negative thoughts and is most effective when it is able to reach negative core beliefs and replace them with more empowering beliefs.

A new *musar* could draw on CBT theory and techniques to help people mould their behaviour and character in accordance with Jewish

---

11. Aaron T. Beck, *Depression: Causes and Treatment* (Philadelphia, PA: University of Pennsylvania Press, 1970), 252–68.

12. Simmons and Griffiths, *CBT for Beginners*, 27.

values; for example, people who habitually lose their temper could learn CBT anger management techniques. In addition, Jewish theology could be drawn upon to establish not only the desired outcome (such as becoming more patient and compassionate), but also to provide empowering core beliefs such as 'I was created in the image of God' to replace negative beliefs like 'I am worthless'.

Like CBT, positive psychology theory is based on an understanding of the interactions between thoughts, feelings, and behaviour, which rejects the psychoanalytic search for underlying, historic causes of symptoms or behaviours; and like CBT, its techniques are designed to be tested empirically. Indeed, the positive psychology movement was founded in the late 1990s and has been able to take advantage of technological advances to test its techniques on thousands of people via online questionnaires and so forth.[13]

Unlike CBT, however, it is not primarily concerned with studying and curing psychological disorders but with understanding human flourishing. According to one definition, it is 'the scientific study of optimal human functioning and what makes life worth living'.[14] The second half of this definition seems to suggest that positive psychologists have moved into a field more traditionally seen as the domain of theologians and philosophers, and, indeed, some of the debates between positive psychology theorists echo those of philosophers through the ages.

Positive psychologists study 'happiness' or 'well-being'. They commonly distinguish between 'hedonic' and 'eudaimonic' well-being. The former refers to subjective feelings of pleasure, whereas the latter is a broad term used to 'refer to the happiness we gain from having meaning and purpose in our lives, fulfilling our potential and feeling that we are part of something bigger than ourselves'.[15] Some positive psychologists reject the prescriptive overtones of emphasis on eudaimonic well-being; others are more troubled by the methodological problems of combining

---

13. Millions of people have completed questionnaires and used noted psychologist Martin Seligman's exercises via his website www.authentichappiness.org (see below).
14. Bridget Glenville-Cleave, *Introducing Positive Psychology: A Practical Guide* (London: Icon, 2012), 1.
15. Ibid., 9.

both hedonic and eudaimonic well-being in one theory, particularly since the pursuit of meaning and purpose can actually have a negative effect on one's hedonic well-being.[16]

Martin Seligman, professor of applied psychology at Pennsylvania State University and past president of the American Psychological Association, is the founder of the positive psychology movement. A brief comparison of two of his most popular books on positive psychology will provide a sense of the trajectory of his academic research. In very general terms, Seligman's early work on positive psychology emphasizes hedonic aspects of happiness, whereas the later work emphasizes eudaimonic well-being. In *Authentic Happiness*, published in 2002,[17] Seligman argued that happiness (which he defined as 'that which we choose for its own sake') could be analysed into three elements: positive emotion, engagement, and meaning. His goal for positive psychology at this stage was to help people increase their life satisfaction through exercises and activities that make one's life more pleasurable (*positive emotion*); challenging and rewarding (*engagement*: 'flow' or 'concentrated attention'); and purposeful (*meaning*: 'belonging to and serving something bigger than yourself'). The measure of life satisfaction was simply a self-reported response to the question 'How satisfied are you with your life?', using a one-to-ten scale.[18]

Although the exercises incorporated elements of cognitive therapy, the approach went far beyond the cognitive. For example, Seligman encouraged readers to 'savour' physical pleasures, by eating favourite foods very slowly and consciously, or luxuriating in a warm bath. Other exercises focused on the cultivation of gratitude. Students in Seligman's positive psychology classes at the university were instructed to write a thank-you letter to someone who had helped them in a significant way but had never been properly thanked. They were not to post the letter but instead were asked to arrange to visit the recipient and read the letter out loud to him or her. Another gratitude exercise involves keeping

---

16. Ibid., 9–10.
17. (New York: The Free Press).
18. Seligman, *Flourish: A New Understanding of Happiness and Well-being – and How to Achieve Them* (London: Nicholas Brearley, 2011), 11–12.

a journal and recording 'what went well' every evening. According to Seligman's research, the gratitude exercises lead to a significant and sustained increase in life satisfaction scores.

What do the life satisfaction scores really measure? In his more recent book, *Flourish* (2011), Seligman notes that subsequent research has shown that the subject's mood at the time he or she answers the question has a much stronger influence on the answer than previously expected. He reports that on average, mood determines more than 70 per cent of the score, whereas dispassionate judgement of how one's life is going determines less than 30 per cent.[19] This is obviously a significant flaw in the 2002 version of positive psychology theory.

Another flaw also relates to mood – the popular understanding of 'happiness' is too closely linked to positive emotion (which comprises only one of three parts of the original theory) and neglects the elements of engagement and meaning. In addition, even the more philosophical definition of happiness as 'that which we choose for its own sake' was not well-served by the 2002 theory, since that theory left out accomplishment, which is something that people do sometimes pursue for its own sake rather than for the sake of any further goal. Seligman also notes that the importance of positive relationships was not covered in the 2002 theory. The 2011 theory, by contrast, presents itself as concerned with 'well-being' rather than 'happiness'. (Seligman uses the term 'well-being' in the later work to denote the same thing as 'happiness' in the earlier work – that which we pursue for its own sake.) His positive psychology theory no longer takes 'life satisfaction' as its goal and key measure, but instead aims to increase 'flourishing' by increasing positive emotion, engagement, positive relationships, meaning, and accomplishment.

Although Seligman's work on positive psychology, particularly the 2011 theory, can provide a valuable foundation for the development of a new *musar*, there are clearly tensions between this approach and Jewish values. Seligman's positive psychology is highly individualistic and, as befits a theory that aspires to scientific objectivity, non-prescriptive. Nevertheless, if positive psychology is to provide much of the theoretical framework and specific techniques for the new *musar*, we must explore

---

19. Seligman, *Flourish*, 13.

the tensions between its individualistic amorality and the inherently prescriptive and ethical character of Judaism in general and *musar* in particular. Moreover, as Barbara Ehrenreich and other critics of positive psychology have emphasized, we need to consider the political implications of the approach, particularly as its influence on governments and businesses continues to spread.[20] Ehrenreich maintains that positive psychology is an inherently conservative movement, since it focuses almost exclusively on changes the individual makes for him- or herself rather than changes that could be made at the social level (for example, 'more democratically organized workplaces'), and since its key metric, the 'life satisfaction' surveys, favours those who benefit most from the status quo.[21] Although Ehrenreich's critique was published before Seligman's *Flourish*, some of the concerns she raises are still pertinent. Indeed, Seligman's preface to *Flourish* sounds some disturbing notes:

> I have spent most of my life working on psychology's venerable goal of relieving misery and uprooting the disabling conditions of life. Truth to be told, this can be a drag. Taking the psychology of misery to heart – as you must when you work on depression, alcoholism, schizophrenia, trauma, and the panoply of suffering that makes up psychology-as-usual's primary material – can be a vexation of the soul. While we do more than our bit to increase the well-being of our clients, psychology-as-usual typically does not do much for the well-being of its practitioners. If anything changes in the practitioner, it is a personality shift toward depression....

20. The work of positive psychologists has major ramifications beyond academic circles and the loyal readership of personal development literature. Governments have begun to seek out metrics other than Gross Domestic Product (GDP) to help guide public policy. For example, in 2010, British Prime Minister David Cameron instructed the Office of National Statistics to begin measuring the nation's happiness.
21. Barbara Ehrenreich, *Smile or Die: How Positive Thinking Fooled America and the World* (London: Granta, 2009), 180. Although in his later work, Seligman abandons 'life satisfaction' as the key measure, it is still advocated by many positive psychologists and by influential thinkers, including Richard Layard, the eminent British economist who has led the development of 'happiness economics'.

> Teaching positive psychology, researching positive psychology, using positive psychology in practice as a coach or therapist … and just reading about positive psychology *all make people happier*. The people who work in positive psychology are the people with the highest well-being I have ever known.[22]

In fairness to Seligman, positive psychology has not completely turned its back on people suffering from the disorders that he used to find such a 'drag' and 'vexation of the soul' to treat. Later in the book, he argues that in seeking to cure psychological disorders, therapists need to use 'the entire arsenal for minimizing misery – drugs and psychotherapy' to help these people out of their suffering. The role of positive psychology, he adds, is to help such patients move on from not suffering to achieving well-being.[23] Nevertheless, the above quotation from Seligman is a salient reminder that positive psychology, to use Rabbi Sacks's terminology, is very clearly *ḥokhmah* and not Torah.

The new *musar* would take the *ḥokhmah* of Beck, Seligman, and their fellow researchers as one of the means by which to achieve Torah-inspired ends of personal, interpersonal, and social improvement. It would need to be grounded in a philosophically rigorous articulation of a Jewish conception of the 'good life' for individuals, communities, and the wider society, together with halakhic analysis that presents the Jewish legal and supererogatory obligations of the individual towards themselves, others, and the wider world. Through his writings and teaching, Lord Sacks has contributed greatly to the philosophical work of articulating the general vision. In addition, some of the essays in this volume, particularly David Shatz's exploration of altruism and Moshe Halbertal's detailed study of the role of subjective needs in determining the level of *tsedakah* (charity) to be provided by an individual or the community, are excellent examples of the type of work that needs to be done to elucidate the relevant halakhic obligations. Scholars like Shatz and Halbertal, whose academic approach draws on Jewish and general philosophy as well as halakhic texts and reasoning, will be able both to

---

22. Seligman, *Flourish*, 1–2; emphasis in original.
23. Ibid., 54.

clarify the halakhic obligations of Jews and to articulate the universal values and principles that underpin them.

Once the philosophical and legal framework of the new *musar* has been established, Torah scholars could evaluate the appropriateness of different aspects of positive psychology theory for Judaism. Taking Seligman's 2011 theory as a starting point, for example, scholars would explore each of the five elements in turn. How important are positive emotion, engagement, meaning, positive relationships, and accomplishment in Judaism? Are some of them valued merely as means or are they all seen as ends in themselves?

Positive psychologists could then work with Torah scholars and educators to identify the exercises and techniques that might best enhance the development of these five aspects of well-being and of the personal virtues that support them in a Jewish context. Part of this work would involve clarifying to what extent the behaviours and *midot* encouraged by Torah can be appropriately translated into secular terms. For example, positive psychologists have found that cultivating gratitude increases life satisfaction. Torah scholars would need to consider whether 'gratitude' as the positive psychologists understand it encompasses the full meaning of the Hebrew phrase *hakarat hatov*. Similarly, as Michael Walzer's essay in this volume makes clear, the meaning of the Hebrew word *tsedakah* is not adequately conveyed by the English term 'charity'. New exercises, inspired by the existing positive psychology ones, might need to be created to cultivate the values and behaviours connected with the Hebrew terms.

Traditional *musar*, of course, was not exclusively concerned with the ethical mitzvot and interpersonal relationships, but also with the cultivation of a genuinely religious personality. Positive psychology exercises and techniques for objectively measuring changes in behaviour and well-being could be adapted to help people cultivate religious behaviours that do not precisely figure in the secular positive psychology literature. For example, one might wish to develop exercises (as the original *musar* teachers did) to help cultivate *kavanah* in prayer (an attitude of focused concentration combined with the religiously correct intention). Given that expressions of gratitude form one of the three essential aspects of Jewish prayer (the others are praise of God and requests for divine assistance), the gratitude letter and other positive psychology exercises devised to help cultivate an 'attitude of gratitude' might also assist with *kavanah*. If empirical research showed that there was no correlation, other exercises might be devised and tested. The five different aspects of well-being could also be investigated to see which, if any, display a strong correlation with high levels of *kavanah*.

Another fruitful area of study would be to look at psychological studies of resilience and consider the relationship between psychological resilience and religious faith. The goal would not be simply to ascertain whether a strong faith correlates with high levels of psychological resilience, but to consider the relationship between the two in a more dynamic way. Would improved resilience help religious Jews to maintain their faith in the face of challenging life circumstances such as illness and bereavement? It would also be useful to explore whether the resilience-training programmes devised by Seligman and his colleagues could be adapted for Jewish schools, youth movements, and so forth.[24]

Although most of the suggestions above focus on the potential of a new *musar* to reinvigorate the practice of traditional Judaism, we anticipate that the exercise of bringing cognitive behaviour therapy and positive psychology into dialogue with Judaism would also lead to insights and conclusions of more general relevance. In addition, the successful creation of a twenty-first century *musar* movement could provide a model for other faith communities to follow. It is also likely that such a movement, inspired and guided by the thought of Rabbi Sacks, and drawing on both traditional Jewish teachings and secular wisdom, would be of interest to non-Jewish readers seeking more spiritual and moral nourishment than positive psychology alone can provide. This brief discussion of the potential for creating a new *musar* movement is one of many possible examples of the scope for creative dialogue between Judaism and secular wisdom, inspired by the writings of Rabbi Sacks.

---

24. Seligman's research team has tested two different positive psychology programmes for schools: the Penn Resiliency Programme and the Strathaven Positive Psychology Curriculum. They also developed resiliency training programmes for the US military. See Seligman, *Flourish*, 81–5 and 126–81.

Jonathan Sacks has identified the current alienation between 'traditional Jewish learning and academic scholarship' as a severe ailment of contemporary Jewish society, analogous to a 'cerebral lesion in which the right and left hemispheres of the brain are both intact, but the connection between them is broken'. The result of such a lesion is a 'dysfunction of the personality, a failure of mental integration'.[25] Mending this lesion has been one of the primary effects of Rabbi Sacks's writings, and this Festschrift is presented in the hope of inspiring others to continue that effort.

---

25. Sacks, *Future Tense*, 210.

Contributors

David Berger is Ruth and I. Lewis Gordon Professor of Jewish History and Dean at the Bernard Revel Graduate School of Yeshiva University. His books include *The Jewish-Christian Debate in the High Middle Ages*, the co-authored *Judaism's Encounter with Other Cultures: Rejection or Integration* (ed. Jacob J. Schacter), and *The Rebbe, the Messiah, and the Scandal of Orthodox Indifference*, as well as two volumes of collected essays on Jewish-Christian relations and intellectual history.

Joshua Berman is a Senior Lecturer in the Department of Bible at Bar-Ilan University and a fellow at the Shalem Center in Jerusalem. He is the author of *The Temple: Its Symbolism and Meaning Then and Now* (Jason Aronson, 1995) and, most recently, *Created Equal: How the Bible Broke with Ancient Political Thought* (Oxford, 2008).

Michael J. Broyde is a Professor of Law at Emory University, was the founding rabbi of the Young Israel in Atlanta, and is a *dayan* in the Beth Din of America.

Moshe Halbertal is the Gruss Professor at NYU Law School and a Professor of Jewish Thought and Philosophy at the Hebrew University. He is the author of *Idolatry* (co-authored with Avishai Margalit) and *People* *of the Book,* both published by Harvard University Press. His latest book, *Concealment and Revelation,* was published by Princeton University Press in 2007. He is a member of Israel's National Academy for Sciences and the Humanities.

Michael J. Harris is rabbi of the Hampstead Synagogue, London; Research Fellow at the London School of Jewish Studies; and Affiliated Lecturer in the Faculty of Divinity, University of Cambridge. He holds a PhD in philosophy from the School of Oriental and African Studies, University of London. He is the author of *Divine Command Ethics: Jewish and Christian Perspectives* (RoutledgeCurzon, 2003).

Ronald Heifetz is the King Hussein bin Talal Senior Lecturer in Public Leadership and founder of the Center for Public Leadership at the Kennedy School of Government, Harvard University. His first book, *Leadership without Easy Answers,* has been reprinted and translated many times. He is also co-author of *Leadership on the Line: Staying Alive Through the Dangers of Leading* and *The Practice of Adaptive Leadership: Tools and Tactics for Changing Your Organization and the World.*

Menachem Kellner is Professor of Jewish Thought at the University of Haifa and a Senior Fellow at the Shalem Center, Jerusalem. He has published twenty books and over one hundred articles in the areas of mediaeval Jewish philosophy and modern Jewish thought. Two of his recent books, *Must a Jew Believe Anything?* and *Maimonides' Confrontation With Mysticism,* were published by the Littman Library of Jewish Civilization (Oxford).

Binyamin Lau is spiritual leader of the Ramban Synagogue in southern Jerusalem and a community leader and social activist. He also lectures at Beit Morasha in Jerusalem. He is the author of many books and articles, including the series *The Sages* (available from Maggid Books).

Alasdair MacIntyre is a Research Fellow in the Centre for Contemporary Aristotelian Studies in Ethics and Politics at London Metropolitan

University and Professor of Philosophy Emeritus at the University of Notre Dame.

Daniel Rynhold is Associate Professor of Modern Jewish Philosophy at the Bernard Revel Graduate School of Jewish Studies, Yeshiva University. He has published on various topics in Jewish philosophy, including the problem of evil, Nietzsche and Jewish philosophy, and the thought of Moses Maimonides and Joseph Soloveitchik. He is the author of *Two Models of Jewish Philosophy: Justifying One's Practices* (Oxford University Press, 2005) and *An Introduction to Medieval Jewish Philosophy* (I.B. Tauris, 2009).

Jacob J. Schacter is University Professor of Jewish History and Jewish Thought and Senior Scholar, Center for the Jewish Future, Yeshiva University.

David Shatz is Professor of Philosophy at Yeshiva University, editor of the *Torah u-Madda Journal*, and editor of the series *MeOtzar HoRav: Selected Writings of Rabbi Joseph B. Soloveitchik*. He has edited, co-edited, or authored fifteen books (including a volume of his collected essays), and has published nearly seventy articles and reviews dealing with both general and Jewish philosophy. In recognition of his scholarly and pedagogic achievements, he was awarded the Presidential Medallion at Yeshiva University.

Charles Taylor is Emeritus Professor of Philosophy at McGill University. His recent books include *A Secular Age* and *Dilemmas and Connections*.

Michael Walzer is Professor Emeritus at the Institute of Advanced Study in Princeton. He has addressed a wide variety of topics in political theory and moral philosophy: political obligation, just war, and economic justice. His books, *Just and Unjust Wars* and *Spheres of Justice*, have played a part in the revival of practical ethics and in the development of a pluralist approach to political life. He is a co-editor of *Dissent* and is currently working on Volume 3 of the *Jewish Political Tradition*.

Tamra Wright is Director of Academic Studies and Educator Development at the London School of Jewish Studies and a Visiting Lecturer at King's College London. A specialist in contemporary Jewish thought, she has published articles on Buber, Levinas, and post-Holocaust philosophy, and is the author of *The Twilight of Jewish Philosophy: Emmanuel Levinas's Ethical Hermeneutics.*

Avivah Gottlieb Zornberg is the author of three critically acclaimed books: *Genesis: The Beginning of Desire; The Particulars of Rapture: Reflections on Exodus;* and *The Murmuring Deep: Reflections on the Biblical Unconscious.* She lives in Jerusalem, where she has been lecturing on Bible since 1980. She also lectures throughout the world at synagogues, JCCs, and psychoanalytic institutes, as well as at Hillel houses at prominent universities. Dr Zornberg holds a Visiting Lectureship at the London School of Jewish Studies.

About Jonathan Sacks

Jonathan Sacks became the sixth Chief Rabbi of the United Hebrew Congregations of the Commonwealth in 1991, having previously been Principal of Jews' College, as well as rabbi of the Golders Green and Marble Arch synagogues. After achieving first class honours in Philosophy at Gonville and Caius College, Cambridge, he pursued postgraduate studies in Oxford and London, gaining his doctorate in 1981, and receiving rabbinic ordination from Jews' College and Yeshivat Etz Chaim. He is currently Visiting Professor of Theology at King's College London. He holds 14 honorary degrees, including a Doctor of Divinity conferred to mark his first ten years in office by the Archbishop of Canterbury, Lord Carey.

Rabbi Sacks has received numerous prizes, including the Jerusalem Prize in 1995 for his contribution to diaspora Jewish life, and regularly contributes to the national media, delivering BBC Radio's 'Thought for the Day' and writing for the 'Credo' column in *The Times*. He has written more than two dozen books, several of which have won awards, including the Grawemeyer Prize for Religion for *The Dignity of Difference*, and a National Jewish Book Award for *A Letter in the Scroll*.

Rabbi Sacks was knighted by Her Majesty the Queen in 2005 and made a Life Peer, taking his seat in the House of Lords in October 2009 as Baron Sacks of Aldgate in the City of London.

Born in 1948 in London, he has been married to Elaine since 1970. They have three children and six grandchildren.

The fonts used in this book are from the Arno family